THE THRESHOLD OF FOREVER

THE THRESHOLD OF FOREVER

ESSAYS AND REVIEWS

DARRELL SCHWEITZER

WILDSIDE PRESS

Copyright © 2017 by Darrell Schweitzer.

Please see the acknowledgments page at the end of this volume for original publication information of individual works.

Published by Wildside Press LLC.
www.wildsidebooks.com

CONTENTS

Embracing Yesterday's Tomorrows, or, Why We Still Read
   "Obsolete" Science Fiction 7

Drilling a Core Sample: Thrilling Wonder Stories, Summer 1945 . . . 16

Robert Bloch and the Death of Science Fiction—1951 26

Rusty's Spaceship Flies Again. 32

Dying in an Ecstasy of Blood: The Half-Remembered
   Perversities of David H. Keller's "The Revolt of the
   Pedestrians" (1928) 36

Randall Garrett's "The Queen Bee": The Most Sexist Science
   Fiction Story Ever Published?. 44

Note, June 6, 2012: 53

Hooray Bradbury 54

Why Stanley G. Weinbaum Still Matters 58

Blobfest!. 69

Excavating Ourselves: A Short History of Archeology-of-the-
   Present Books. 74

The Whole Wide Lovecraft: an HPL Biopic? 82

John W. Campbell's Lovecraftian Tale 88

H.P. Lovecraft and the American Stonehenge: Hokum, Pseudo-
   archaeology, and the Imagination 100

Why Lovecraft is Funny 104

William Beckford, Caliph of Fonthill Abbey 109

Some Ancestors of Vathek. 115

M.R. James and His Pleasing Terrors 125

Peter Schlemihl and Other Classics That Nobody Reads	131
Discovering James Hogg	137
Half-Way between Lucian of Samosata and Larry Niven: Early 19th Century Science Fiction Comedies	149
The Lighter Side of Death: Robert Bloch as a Humorist	156
Reading the World's Oldest Novel: Some Further Thoughts about Genre	168
Texts, Authors, and the Enduring Mystery of Edgar Allan Poe	174
People: It's What's for Dinner (All About Sawney Bean)	179
The Complete Poetry and Translations of Clark Ashton Smith	184
All the Wonders We Seek	191
What Can Be Saved From the Wreckage? James Branch Cabell in the Twenty-First Century	194
The Word of God, by Thomas M. Disch	197
On SF, by Thomas M. Disch	200
The Discovery of Sarban	206
Atomic Mutant Hillbillies	210
Weird Tales Past: December 1936	215
About the Author	218
Acknowledgments	219

EMBRACING YESTERDAY'S TOMORROWS, OR, WHY WE STILL READ "OBSOLETE" SCIENCE FICTION

I remember the future. It started in 1970. No, really. There was a time when the common date authors picked for just around the bend, the day after tomorrow, was indeed 1970. They never quite fixated on it the way they did on *The Year Two Thousand*, but 1970 was once a kind of tripwire between the present and the pretend-futures of science fiction.

Of course that's all dated now, you say. Who wants to read something that's dated?

To which I reply, if science fiction really depended on topicality, on being as current as today's newspaper, then it would be discarded as readily as yesterday's newspaper. But it isn't. We still read *The War of the Worlds* even though the Martians did not invade England in 1898. And we still read stories set in 1970.

So what is going on here?

Science fiction dates, but it does not become *obsolete* that way, at least not if it's any good. There is a difference.

Perhaps the most myopic editorial rejection in the field's history was inflicted, so the story goes (see Sam Moskowitz's *Seekers of Tomorrow* on this) by the doddering and singularly unimaginative T. O'Conor Sloane on a young Clifford Simak, who submitted his very first story, "The Cubes of Ganymede," to Sloane at *Amazing Stories* in 1931. Two years of silence followed. In 1933, Simak learned via a fanzine article that the story was among those listed by Sloane as accepted for *Amazing*. In 1935, Sloane returned the story, remarking that it seemed a bit too dated to publish. Somehow I doubt that Sloane meant that the lofty literary standards of *Amazing Stories* had become so much loftier by 1935 that the story no longer measured up. Never mind any consideration that he owed it to Simak to publish the story after having squatted on it for four years. My point is that if it was a good *story* in 1931, it still should have been one in 1935. As for the lofty literary levels of the Sloane *Amazing*, Damon Knight once reported that in the opinion of the fans of the time, both the magazine and the editor seemed to be increasingly covered with a fine, gray mold. The middle 1930s was not a good period for *Amazing*. Maybe the reason Sloane finally declined to publish the story was that he was afraid it would wake somebody up and they'd notice how dull the rest of the magazine was by then.

Here's a homework assignment for you. Trust me; you will thank me for this, if it's something new to you. Go read *Who?* by Algis Budrys. This is a novel that grew out of a short story of the same name (*Fantastic Universe*, April 1955) and was first published in book form by Pyramid in 1958. It's a very finely constructed, moving character study about a man who may not be who he is supposed to be. The setting is the Cold War, but if we work out the chronology from the protagonist's given age and date of birth, the time is the future, maybe the late 1980s. Within the novel, there are flashbacks to what must be about 1968. A top American scientist, very close to a breakthrough on what must be a super-weapon of some sort or the means to achieving one, is nearly killed in a laboratory explosion. As this laboratory is in Europe, near the East/West border, a rescue team from the Soviet side gets to him first. He is kept behind the Iron Curtain for four months, and when he is returned, everybody is in for a shock, because he was apparently injured far worse than anybody thought, but has been worked on by a brilliant Chinese surgeon, and now has a completely mechanical arm—and a mechanical head, a device so technically advanced that the instrumentation available to our side cannot penetrate it. The question immediately and pressingly arises: who is this? Yes, he still has one natural hand and therefore fingerprints, and they could have checked his DNA if anyone knew about DNA testing when Budrys was writing this, but that's not good enough. *Whose brain* is inside that mechanical head? Is it Lucas Martino, the American physicist, or a really dedicated Soviet spy? If his identity cannot be established, what is to be done with him? Does he still count as human, or is he a *thing*? He becomes, rather like the Frankenstein monster, both a frightening and a pitiable figure.

The most superficial sort of reader would say, "Oh, that's dated. The Cold War's over. Why should I read *that?*"

The only reply I can make is that the kind of reader who dismisses this book as "dated" and uses that as synonym for "worthless" isn't likely to have understood it in the first place. *Who?* is a book about serious things: identity, self, and the limits of reason. It's not too much of a spoiler for me to reveal here that by the time it's all over, even Lucas Martino isn't sure who he is. What happens when *I think, therefore I am* breaks down and you can't even trust your own memory? Budrys was getting into Philip K. Dick territory here, a few years before Dick had firmly staked it out for himself. The modern reader is reminded of nothing so much as the futile but heroic struggle with insoluble mysteries of self that occurs in such later Dick novels as *Valis*.

Of course *Who?* is "dated" in the sense that its future setting is no longer our own. From the perspective of this novel, the Cold War seems to have gone on unabated for forty years. There was no 1960s as you and I remember them, no counter-culture, no flower children, and apparently no Vietnam War. Western Europe may have a unified government of some sort. We read of an Allied Nations Government. On the other side of the Central European Frontier District, the Soviet Union is by no means tottering toward its end.

Does this matter? What does it do to the perception of the reader who can no longer read *Who?* as a projection of a possible future?

Budrys, in an interview I did with him in 1981 (published in *Amazing*, November of that year), describes how in a recent edition of *Who?* he made changes in the text, to try to keep it up to date:

> I had to introduce a brief Russo-Chinese war that nobody in the West understood the outcome of. The purpose of that was to reintroduce the credibility of having Asiatics in contact with my protagonists. I had to find some way to get the Chinese back into the story even though the Chinese and Russians had split since the book was written. As far as missing the Vietnam War, there are a lot of references to civil unrest, and a lot of military unrest.... One thing that's not dating but will date is that in a book written in 1954 I predicted 75-cent packs of cigarettes, 50-cent bus fares, all these things that when the book came out would catch the reader's eye and keep reminding him that the book was set twenty years in the future. (p 10)

I'm hardly unique in the opinion that such exercises are not merely unnecessary, but often a bad idea. Stephen King did not help *The Stand* one bit by "updating" it in the expanded edition, with badly digested lumps of 1990 mixed into the 1975 narrative. Aren't we all glad that H.G. Wells didn't go on "updating" *The War of the Worlds* every few years, changing the price of bus tokens or whatever, until his death in 1946? Wells did update *When the Sleeper Wakes* (1899; 1925 as *The Sleeper Wakes*) without improving it. It's just as well that I read *Who?* in the Gregg Press edition of 1979, which is a facsimile of the 1958 paperback.

Budrys himself invoked Wells when he admitted at least the ultimate futility of the effort:

> ...unless I can make the transition into being H.G. Wells, where it doesn't matter that the story of *The Invisible Man* is set in the 19th Century, the book's going to date out from under me.
> (p. 10)

What I've concluded in the wisdom of my additional years (I was 28 when I did that interview; I am a few days short of 58 as I write this) is that Budrys was wrong and shouldn't have bothered. A novel has its *time*. Its meaning pivots from the year in which it was first published. In ninety-nine instances out of a hundred, the text is better off left alone.

A book will inevitably "date," but it won't date "out from under" you, in the sense of becoming useless, unless it was useless to start with. There is more going on than the details. What I'd like to suggest is that a science fiction novel doesn't depend so much on the price of cigarettes or bus tokens in the future, but the sense that the story's imaginary future is a reasoned departure from baseline reality, that it is *constructed*, not merely reported the way mainstream fiction is. The aesthetic effect remains the same, unchanging, whether the real world overtakes the ostensible year of the action or not. *Who?* now takes place in a kind of alternate *past*, but in a past which *looks forward into the future,* and that is what matters.

But to return to that celebrated future year, 1970:

Robert A. Heinlein's *The Door into Summer* (serialized, 1956; book form, 1957) begins in the near future, that magical year, 1970, and then resorts to suspended animation and time-travel to reach and return from the much farther threshold of wondrous futurity, A.D. 2000. When I first read this novel, 1970 hadn't arrived yet. I was reading the Signet paperback, which, as collectors may recall, features a man on the cover in a futuristic costume like something out of *Things to Come*—a famous film of yesterday's tomorrow which determined the look of futuristic fashions for decades. The edition you read a book in no doubt subtly influences your reading experience. To read the paperback in the 1960s gave a sense of a very current, slightly lightweight, but intelligent entertainment. I read the book again recently in the Gregg Press edition, which makes it a Classic.

Certainly the novel shows Heinlein at the top of his form, before the rot of his later career set in. The narrative is brisk and assured. There is brilliant use of detail. The pacing is excellent, probably saved by the need to get the story into the artificial lengths demanded by the three-part magazine serial and the 1950s idea of a genre hardcover. SF novels in those days were largely marketed to libraries as Young Adult books. (Remember the rocketships and atomic symbols on the spines, in your local library?) They couldn't be much more than 60,000 words long. As was painfully evident a few years later, Heinlein needed this kind of discipline; he may not have so much been a great novelist as a talented but sloppy novelist shoehorned into greatness by editorial pressure and market considerations. When the restraints were off, we got *I Will Fear*

No Evil and *The Number of the Beast*. But *The Door into Summer* is a product of the good old days.

It is also a product of its time, of the same Cold War era which produced Budrys's *Who?* It opens with a casual reference to the Six Weeks War, a nuclear exchange which seems to have occurred in the 1960s. The Soviet Union was wiped out. The United States, though it lost a few cities, seems to have recovered nicely. This was a common assumption in a lot of SF of the period: that a nuclear war was coming, like a painful tooth-pulling that we'd just have to get through, and beyond that, the Future promised by the rest of science fiction would open up. The modern reader might note that in *The Door into Summer*, for all millions were killed in the war, and everybody doubtless knew somebody who died, no one in the cast seems to have suffered much grief. L. Sprague de Camp's Viagens Interplanetarias series [1948 and on] took a perhaps more realistic view. The nuclear war happens. The USSR is destroyed, but the USA never recovers. As a result, Brazil becomes the dominant world power, and in all those novels set on the planet Krishna, Portuguese is the language of the spaceways.

After this unpleasant bump, Heinlein delivers us into the Future. His 1970 is not the one you and I remember, if you, Reader, are even able to remember 1970. It's a bit more automated. There are robots in the household. There are autopiloted cars of the sort that Philip K. Dick characters would have arguments with. Idiom has changed in subtle ways. An apparently completely automated parking meter is referred to as a "parking attendant." Heinlein is indeed very much aware of how time and technological change can alter the meanings of words. There's only one unfortunate lapse when on page 29 some dirt being cleaned from a bathtub goes *spung!*—inescapably reminiscent of some infamous nipples in *The Number of the Beast* years later. Our hero, an engineer and inventor, works on a drafting machine that sounds a little bit like a desktop computer. Once he is cheated by his business partner, betrayed by his girlfriend, and shoved into "Cold Sleep"—suspended animation -- and wakes up in 2000, things are even less familiar. Idioms have again changed, although people understand that reawakened sleepers may be out of touch and make social errors. It seems that suspended animation has been available commercially since the late 1960s, and in fact the US won the Six Weeks War by keeping a spare army on ice in the Arctic, with which to surprise and overwhelm the Commies. The year 2000 proves to be a time of radioactive checkbooks and plastic coins, although there are still phone booths down the hall. (Of course there are no personal computers and no internet.) One detail I remembered from my reading this book as a kid was that in 2000 you could still get a decent meal for three dollars as long as you didn't insist on real meat. Fashions are strange at the turn of the millennium. Our hero remarks that he's never worn bellbottoms before, but they are apparently standard men's fashion in 2000. Zippers seem to have become obsolete, there being a new sticky substance a little like Velcro in use instead—although it is possible to stick this stuff directly to the skin, which has caused some women to do eye-poppingly minimalist things with it. If you go to a dentist in 2000, he regenerates your teeth, rather than filling them, a detail which our hero has difficulty explaining when he's back in 1970, has a toothache, and must visit a dentist of that time. Of course this far future of 2000 is just filled with robots, many of which are direct descendants of the designs the hero was cheated out of in 1970.

And so on. The plot turns on time-travel and justified revenge. If, as is often the case with Heinlein, coincidences pile up as the narrative moves relentlessly toward a happy ending, but it's not as overt as the "Wasn't that *incredibly* lucky?" ending of *Orphans of the Sky* and so it feels right. The pieces of the time-travel plot fall into place with extreme precision. This was the Heinlein who would write "All You Zombies" a couple of years later. *The Door into Summer* is still an immensely readable, very entertaining book, with some very sharp and adult characterizations (I am sure there was much I simply did not understand when I first read this at 14 or so), not to mention quite a bit about cats. Heinlein was always a cat person. The title refers to a cat which, in the winter, would go to each door in the house, demanding that it be opened on the hope that one of them would lead to an outside that wasn't cold. This sort of optimism is what drives the book.

But isn't this hopelessly "dated" because it begins in one past era that didn't happen (1970) and proceeds to another (2000) that likewise didn't happen? Is it still speculative fiction if we *know*, from our present perspective, regardless of how things seemed at the time, that what goes on in the story *couldn't* take place?

Yes, it is still speculative fiction. It is worth examining precisely *why* the "datedness" of it doesn't matter. This is what Budrys was talking about when he spoke about "becoming H.G. Wells," citing the example of *The Invisible Man*. Both *Who?* and *The Door into Summer* have this same quality. It's a lot commoner than you might think.

Admittedly, if something like that were written today, it would have an effect more like Steampunk, a story set in a kind of alternate-historical past. If somebody in 2010 wrote *The Door into Summer* word-for-word the same, it would be a very peculiar achievement indeed. Think of that Borges story ("Pierre Menard, Author of the Quixote) about the writer who duplicated *Don Quixote* word-for-word, but with every word composed from a very different perspective than that of Cervantes. Well, Heinlein didn't go there, and neither did Budrys in *Who?* so we are left to consider *what has time done to the text?* What does the "dated" aspect of old science fiction actually mean?

For one thing, both examples are still good stories, on a human level. They're about characters that are interesting and emotionally convincing. The Budrys book is considerably deeper than the Heinlein, a meditation on fundamental issues of existence where the Heinlein is sort of a caper story. But what about, specifically, the science-fictional aspects, without which, because both of these are genuine science fiction novels, the story could not have taken place at all?

I think the key to it is that science fiction is a process, not a result. Or a *method,* if you will. In a realistic novel, the reader is given the world as the writer has observed it, or at least imagined it on the basis of other people's observations. If Stephen Crane in *The Red Badge of* Courage wrote about Civil War combat without ever having been in battle, that was an imaginative feat, but he was still trying to make it as true-to-life as possible. There were no deliberate departures from consensus reality. But the essence of science fiction *is* a deliberate departure. It's a contract between the writer and the reader to the effect of, "I will now create a consistent, alternate world extrapolated logically from my premise." If robots and suspended-animation existed the way Heinlein said they did, the result would be *The Door into Summer.* His is an artificial setting, as unreal when compared to the reader's lived-in world as Middle Earth, although it was arrived at by a very different method than what brought Tolkien into the Shire. The *science fictional method* is less of a myth or a vivid dream and more of a really clever tinker-toy construct. But in both cases there is still that conscious distance. The reader *knows* that the setting is made up. That is what science fiction and fantasy have in common.

Where they differ is that science fiction delves much more into how things work, and how the world got that way, using the techniques of reason and science. Magic-as-alternative-science stories inevitably fail to satisfy the fantasy reader as well as a really resonant myth precisely because the story's "how" is (to use a technical term) *bullshit* and we all know it. You *don't* fly through the air by anointing yourself with magic oil and then rubbing a broomstick with feathers. The fantasy reader is not looking for bullshit, but some deep, metaphorical truth. *A Wizard of Earthsea* would not have been improved one bit by some pseudo-physical explanation of how the magic works. When one of the later Star Wars movies tried to explain the Force in terms of subatomic particles or some such foolishness, I nearly barfed (another technical term).

But much of the aesthetic pleasure of *The Door into Summer* comes from Heinlein's immersion of the reader into a world that could be, in its own terms. The details matter, even if, in terms of historical accuracy, they are "wrong." 1970 was not like that. 2000 was not like that. But here is a whole world that blossoms from the story's central premise like crystals in a super-saturated solution. We're in the "future" by the time we reach Heinlein's 1970. It is not our world. The characters may remember some things in common with us, e.g. World War II or the Great Depression, but otherwise their memories, perceptions, and assumptions are *not* our own. The whole idea of science fiction is to insert the reader into such a "future," and because it is done well, *The Door into Summer*, with its action opening in 1970, still has in 2010 what editors call "future feel." More daringly than most SF writers, Heinlein has actually created *two* futures, 1970 and 2000, and both of them, when the book is read in 2010, are just as satisfyingly futuristic as ever. Science fiction, particularly of such an optimistic and technophilic sort, flatters its readers with the sense that in such a future we can see all the strings and wires that make this construct work and that we can understand them, which in turn gives us some sense that we can understand the world we actually live in as well. It's like that PBS science program, *Connections,* on a very large scale.

The Budrys novel is darker in tone than Heinlein's, but it works the same way. Its theme, if summed up as *I think, therefore I am not sure I am*, requires an alternate-reality stage on which this drama can be played out, one in which a bomb-blast victim *could* have an artificial head with *somebody's* brain inside it. Yes, a novelist could write something like that today, setting it perhaps a little less plausibly in the actual present, here, now, 2010, not in a Cold War setting, but maybe with the injured scientist being returned from Iran and suspected of being a terrorist. If the novel is any good, it will still be just as compelling in 2050, when these specific circumstances have all passed into history.

The reason is, as so many others have observed, sometimes to the bafflement of non-SF types, is that science fiction is *not* prophecy, but a kind of intellectual and aesthetic exercise which is about the *process* by which the future is created. Or I should say *a* future, as opposed to *the* future. We *know* when we read a novel set in the near future, that what is described is *not* what we or our children are going to live to see. It's going to be, inevitably, "wrong," but that really *doesn't* matter. That's why an old-time future, like Heinlein's or Budrys's still satisfies. It is why these books, like the best of Wells, "date" but do not become "dated" in the sense of obsolete. A past-future can be just as futuristic as any other. And Tomorrow can still start in 1970.

DRILLING A CORE SAMPLE: THRILLING WONDER STORIES, SUMMER 1945

There are now certainly far too many issues of science fiction magazines in existence for anyone to have read them all. The past of our field is, for so many readers, a great unknown. So if we pick up an old issue at random and read it all the way through, this can be like drilling a core sample from the glacier to check out the weather half a million years ago. Or, in this case, 69 years ago. The selection of the Summer 1945 *Thrilling Wonder* is not entirely random. It is the one with Jack Vance's first story, "The World-Thinker" given second-place billing on the cover. Given the recent discussion of Vance (and this story) in *NYRSF*, it's an obvious choice.

I don't need to show you a copy of the cover. In this internet age, anybody can find that image with a couple of clicks. I am sure there are online archives of pulp covers. My first thought was to go to eBay, where I found two of them.

The Vance story is certainly the most important and interesting item in the issue. The editor at this point would have been Sam Merwin, under whose auspices *TWS* (as it was fannishly known back then) was to experience a sudden growth-spurt in the direction of maturity and, along with its companion, *Startling Stories*, begin to give John W. Campbell his first serious challenge by about 1948. This is Merwin's third issue. His predecessor, Oscar J. Friend, had left with the Fall 1944 issue. So Merwin would have edited Winter, Spring, and Summer 1945. There is some possibility that he inherited the Vance story from Friend, but I don't think so, given that Merwin waxes enthusiastic about it inside and gives it, for a first-time effort, considerable pride of place on the cover, when there were other, recognizable "big names" in this issue who aren't on the cover at all.

Whoever found "The World-Thinker" in the slush-pile must have realized at once that this was a more than commonly talented writer. The writing is smooth and sometimes ironic. The narrative really moves in the finest pulp, page-turning manner. Some of the story is formula, but some of it is genuinely imaginative. Our hero, Lanarck of the Tellurian

Corps of Investigation, somewhat of a maverick and on the outs with his boss, is sent to recapture an escaped convict, a "girl" (her age is given as 21), Kenna Parker, who has busted out of the Federal Women's Camp in Nevada and escaped into space. Of course she's beautiful. More interesting is that she's intelligent and probably has her own side to the story. She's a "scientist's daughter" of the standard model. Her "crime" was refusing to turn over the equations left behind by her late father which, if in the wrong hands, would enable an enemy to generate a balonium pulse and make every atomic power plant or engine in the Solar System explode. ("Balonium" is my coinage, not Vance's: that element or field effect which suspends the laws of nature as necessary for the plot.)

Off Lanarck goes, pursuing her over interstellar distances. His detectors must be really good, because he follows her all the way to a distant planet where he finds her spaceship parked next to a building. He lands and goes inside. Then the story gets more than slightly interesting, as within dwells a super-being, Laoome, effectively a god, rather like the whimsical, not-too-bright gods we see on *Star Trek* sometimes (for instance, Q). Laoome has the remarkable ability to think whole worlds into existence, or destroy them as fancy dictates. These worlds are inhabited, because an uninhabited one, he explains, would be less interesting. Do real, sentient beings die every time Laoome destroys one or are they just dream-phantoms? That issue has to be put on hold because Ms. Parker has been allowed to escape into one of these thought-worlds. Lanarck goes in after her. There is hugger-mugger, a switcheroo as the "girl" he thought to be Ms. Parker turns out to be someone else, and then a crisis. It seems that every once in a while Laoome has a kind of seizure, which has very severe effects on the worlds he creates. One of these occurs. Reality itself begins to break down. It is a very Philip-K-Dickian moment as our hero has to escape in his spaceship with *two* women aboard, one of whom is a "phantom" and may not be able to exist in the external universe. Does boy get girl at the end, as formula requires? In all too many pulp stories of this period, the "girl" exists primarily as a reward for heroics well done.

Actually, no. The ending is hardboiled. When they get back to where Laoome lives, Lanarck steps inside and kills the mad, destructive god, explaining that the creature was totally amoral and "the galaxy is a cleaner place" without him. When Kenna Parker asks if that was the right thing to do, Lanarck just shrugs. No wedding bells in this picture. (Oh, incidentally, she burned the formula.)

Mark von Schlegell, writing about Jack Vance in *NYRSF 309*, remarks on the C.L. Moore influence here. Yes, that is precisely what Northwest Smith would have done. I think I see another influence too.

Laoome reminds me of one of those bumbling, not-very-bright demiurges or cosmic bureaucrats one encounters in James Branch Cabell novels, for example Koshchei the Deathless in *Jurgen*, who created the Judeo-Christian Heaven for the satisfaction of Jurgen's grandmother, but doesn't have a very good grip on things. Did Vance read Cabell? Better to ask, did any fantasy reader in his generation *not* read Cabell? Is it possible not to detect a very Cabellian voice in the Cugel the Clever stories? What Vance has done here, intriguingly, is bring about an unlikely fusion of the Cabellian roguish wit with a hardboiled pulp style like something out of Raymond Chandler.

Of course you can read the Vance story elsewhere. It has been reprinted several times. The reason one has a copy of the Winter 1945 *Thrilling Wonder Stories,* much less reads it cover-to-cover is for context. That's why we drill these core samples. In what kind of a science fiction magazine, in what sort of a science fiction field, did that story first appear?

The cover on the Winter 1945 issue, by Earle Bergey, shows a typical "Bergey babe" in the arms of a spaceman, as the two of them float weightless in a spaceship control cabin. He is wearing a serviceable red jumpsuit with a rather Flash-Gordonish, riveted leather belt. She is wearing one of those skimpy, possibly-metallic costumes ladies wear in typical Earle Bergey cover paintings. And high heels. You would think she is a fugitive Las Vegas showgirl who is possibly having second thoughts, because, while the spaceman is gazing upon her intently, she is staring straight up past him as if thinking, "How did I get myself into this?" Bergey was not always the best at conveying emotion through facial expressions.

This illustrates a scene from Murray Leinster's "astonishing complete novel" entitled "Things Pass By," which runs all of 22 pages if you subtract the illustrations. The same scene is repeated in black and white inside, possibly by Bergey, though the illustration is not accredited. (I would actually guess early Paul Orban.) On the inside illustration, she is slightly more sensibly clad, though still in heels, and she and the hero are actually kissing.

The Leinster "novel" is not good, but it has points of interest. The Things which pass by possess an almost mythic grandeur. They are probably spaceships, but we're not sure, something, anyway, created by immeasurably superior intelligences, which are driving through space near to the speed of light which, as most SF writers have always conveniently ignored, would mean that they have gained an enormous amount of mass; 12 solar masses, we are told. If a whole fleet of these goes through the Solar System the resultant gravitational disruptions ("cosmoquakes") will destroy Earth, for all the inhabitants of those ships will no more notice than would the soldiers in a column of tanks notice if they happened to run over an anthill.

Fortunately the world is saved by one Dirk Braddick. Almost nothing more needs to be said, because that is what super-scientists heroes are expected to do. Braddick is an Inventor in the classic Doc Smith mode, even by 1945 a relic of an earlier era of science fiction. Braddick claims that his primary interest is psychology, specifically the nature of the research process, but working alone in his private laboratory, without assistants or an apparent source of income, he produces wonders. In an earlier story, "The Eternal Now" (*TWS* Fall 1944) a chap named Brent invented a "mass-nullifier" which turns into a "time-field" by accident. Braddick, following this up has invented some "power tubes" which give the Atomic Power Company a monopoly on power generation. This leads to something modern readers might well understand:

> …But it was not an amiable corporation by that time.
> It was too big to be human. Its higher executive positions were places of power and riches practically equal to the head-ship of nations. They were the subject of such feverish ambition as no other "private" employment ever fostered.
> …the little men in its organization, hoping feverishly for promotions, developed a cold-blooded ruthlessness for the purpose of impressing their bosses.
>
> (pp. 16-17)

This ruthlessness includes, blackmail, murder, kidnapping people and holding them in private prisons, and more.

Meanwhile, the Earth is threatened with destruction. Only Dirk Braddick has any idea of what is going on, though orthodox scientists scoff at him. He is in a feud with the Atomic Power Company, which can only think about the bottom line. He makes a deal with them, turning over his patents in exchange for a quick loan of a couple of the company's "mass-time field power units" (which Brent invented) because he needs to use them as a space-drive, which everybody "knows" is impossible. Conveniently Braddick has also invented and built something very much like an enormous 3-D printer, which spits out a completely functional, plastic spaceship in a few hours. All Braddick has to do is install the power units, wire the balonium cables from the whatsit through the thingamajig…you see, Dirk Braddick *is* one of those super-Edisons of early science fiction who can not only build a spaceship in the back yard single-handed just in time to save the world, but *design* the ship from blueprints, prove to be an expert in everything from power-generation to astro-navigation, *and* discover several revolutionary new principles of basic science every morning before breakfast.

Did I mention the Girl? The Girl actually dropped in, literally, by parachute, some while ago. Her name is Jane. She is twenty-something, pretty, scared, on the run, and possibly amnesiac (or faking; this is not quite clear). Dirk takes her in and gives her shelter. (But where did either one of them come up with that ridiculous costume? To be fair, it is not described in Leinster's text.) She almost develops into a character. She proves capable of doing far more than standing around waiting to be rescued. She has technical training and makes an excellent laboratory assistant. She even drafted the blueprints for Dirk's revolutionary new spaceship which he manages to pop out of the oven—er, I mean "construction machine"—in the space of three days, working without sleep.

He is not entirely superhuman. When he finally dozes off, the baddies are up to mischief. Braddick had asked for one Corporate technician to help him with the power plant, but got two, one of whom is quite clearly an assassin, whose job is to kill Braddick as soon as he is no longer useful. This assassin has slipped outside and signaled two Corporation helicopters, who immediately start bombing the place. But when our hero wakes up, this is all going on in slow motion, because the masstime thingy has slowed down time. The assassin is about to be killed by his own employer's bombs, and our hero, thinking he will have cause to regret it, risks everything to save him. (He does have cause to regret it, because the bad guy, desiring only to prove himself indispensable to the Corporation, makes more trouble later.)

Off everybody goes into space. The "impossible" space drive functions perfectly, by, as far as I can make out, pushing against itself. (An early version of the infamous Dean Drive…? Just kidding, I think.) The world is saved. Those vast intelligent, fantastically ancient, almost Cthulhuoid beings within the 12-solar-mass spaceships that have been causing all the trouble? We never meet them. Our hero runs a wire around one of their scout ships, gives a sharp tug on the whoozis, and pops the thing out of existence, possibly into a higher dimension. He hadn't even thought of what he was going to do up to the moment he took off. There was no plan beyond go out and meet the massive unknowing Things and hope he could think of something. So he just jerry-rigged saving the world, quite literally on the fly. One more scientific revolution, whole new vistas of physics opened up, and he didn't even have time for breakfast.

It ends happily. The aliens change course and Earth is saved. Jane proves to be Jane Brent, cousin to our hero's late colleague and now rightful owner of the Atomic Energy Corporation. She and Braddick get married, though why remains a mystery, other than that formula demands it. (The Girl as reward for heroism well done.) I mean, he has *no* human qualities whatever. I've actually now read and written enough fiction to understand precisely why Leinster's characterization in this instance is so flat. Dirk Braddick has no psychology, no inner life at all. He seems to be a total loner, with no friends, family, lovers, etc. Other than his late colleague (Brent) he does not seem to have ever interacted with a human being. Of course, in real life there are reclusive geniuses, but real ones have some feelings about being alone, maybe some embittering trauma which has made them give up on mankind, or else they're just so socially inept that they can't make contact. But Braddick doesn't have any feelings about that either. He isn't a sociopath either, just a blank.

About the rest of the fiction in the issue, not a lot needs to be said. Most disappointing is "The Deconventionalizers" by Edmond Hamilton, a well-established name by this point, who would surely have been mentioned on the cover if the editor had not valued the Vance story so extraordinarily highly. Hamilton had done pioneering work since the late 1920s, some of it even good. He had also written most of the Captain Future novels, for a companion magazine to *TWS*. Here we see him, intriguingly, departing from space opera, with a story about how people threaten the staid, conformist society of 1945 America by dressing strangely, behaving naughtily, etc., while listening to the strangely popular "non-tonal" or "unmelodic" music that has suddenly become all the rage. It's a little too early for rock-and-roll, but this story hints at the kind of satire which would be done far more effectively in the digest magazines of the 1950s, particularly *Galaxy*. The shame is that Hamilton throws it all away on a gimmick. The subliminal effect of music was indeed the cause of the uninhibited behavior. It's a plot by Martians to undermine Earth society, so that Earthmen won't someday come barging onto Mars. But, alas, as soon as the humans have become non-conformist, they no longer follow fads, and so lose interest in the music.

"The Shadow Dwellers" by Frank Belknap Long is, candidly, awful. A stranded human couple make like Tarzan and Jane in the jungles of Venus. They've lost their memories and reverted to primitivism, but are still much superior to the cringing, blue-skinned natives. They recover their memories and find their spaceship. Meanwhile they've taught the natives how to make themselves bigger and stronger (and smarter?) by eating cooked meat, since such a thing had never occurred to the previously vegetarian Venusians before. Frank Belknap Long was a colleague of Lovecraft's, who wrote some distinguished work as a young man back in the 1920s, and occasionally competent work scattered throughout a long career, but this adds absolutely nothing to his reputation. It is however better than "The Purple Dusk" by Leslie Northern, which I found unreadable and soporific in the extreme. Something about war on Venus.

Our hero is called away from a date with his best girl because his commander needs to send him on a mission. I never did figure out what the point was supposed to be. The Day *Index to the Science Fiction Magazines, 1926-1950* tells us that "Leslie Northern" may have been a house name, but it was very likely in this instance Frank Belknap Long again, wasting pages senselessly.

Much more bearable is "Percy the Pirate" by Henry Kuttner, not exactly major Kuttner, but a quite readable story, in the mode of his "Hollywood on the Moon." A movie publicist is given the job of staging a publicity stunt in space to promote a movie about an infamous space pirate, using that pirate's own reconstructed ship. Before you can say "Argh! Matey!" we learn that the real pirate, allegedly dead but very much alive, the Blackbeard of his day (minus beard, in disguise) has infiltrated the extras and taken over the ship. It's no longer a stunt. Like the historical Blackbeard, the pirate is almost a reasonable chap. He likes his loot and means to have it, but doesn't kill people if he doesn't have to. He's actually rather personable.

Now you might wonder what makes this story science fiction at all. As it could as readily involve a movie about a smuggler, a sailboat in the Caribbean, etc. That's where the particularly wonky "science" comes in. The pirate ship is dead black, you see, so it is invisible in space. It can easily evade the Patrol. When they find themselves surrounded, the pirates lie low on an asteroid, which has a lake on it—not of water, but of "copper sulphate solution." Our hero slips outside in a spacesuit (holding his breath because he has no oxygen tank) rigs up a wire, then comes back inside, turns on the juice, and electroplates the ship, whereupon it is a burnished bronze color and the Patrol can see it. The pirates escape in black-colored lifeboats, though the hero is secretly glad they did.

By the way, there is a Girl in this one, too, a starlet named Mona. Her key—unscripted—line is "Oh, Jerry, you were wonderful. And I'm going to faint." Our hero catches her and kisses her. The only person unhappy with the outcome is the hero's boss, the director, who regrets missing a chance to film the real pirate for the movie. Our hero slugs him. (Is Kuttner kidding throughout? Was this story intended to be satirical? We hope so.)

So, what do we conclude from our analysis of a science-fictional core sample from 1945?

More context here. *Thrilling Wonder Stories* was a middling science fiction magazine for the period, by no means the worst (that must surely have been the Ray Palmer *Amazing* which had just inflicted the Shaver Mystery on the world in its March 1945 issue), and by no means the best, which everyone acknowledged to be the John Campbell *Astounding*, then in mid-Golden Age, serializing Van Vogt's *The World of Null-A* in mid-1945, and also publishing episodes of Asimov's Foundation stories and The "Baldy" stories of Henry Kuttner which would constitute the very respectable fix-up, *Mutant*. Sturgeon's "Killdozer!" had appeared in November 1944, and C.L. Moore's brilliant "No Woman Born" had appeared in December. It was still very much Campbell's decade. That *TWS* would someday even come remotely close to challenging *Astounding*'s monopoly on the adult SF market would have seemed unlikely in mid-1945.

In fact *TWS* was still in what editor Merwin (or maybe it was his successor, Samuel Mines) would later refer to as its "knee-pants" era. The letter column was conducted by Sergeant Saturn, who was your Host rather the way Zacherley or Doctor Shock used to be hosts for horror movie marathons on TV. Sergeant Saturn babbled on in an almost baby-talk lingo and called his readers "kiwis" or "pee-lots" (pilots) while chugging down massive quantities of his favorite space-booze, xeno, which was handed to him by his alien assistants Snaggletooth and Frog-eyes. While the "Sarge" was none-too-soon to be consigned to the great xeno brewery in the beyond, it hadn't happened yet.

Despite the juvenile tone, many of the correspondents in the letter columns of this period seem to be adults, servicemen. (There was still a war on. The Summer 1945 issue would have appeared in the spring, about the time the fighting in Europe was coming to a close; but the war in the Pacific was going full blast. This issue features a War Bonds ad asking the readers to help Admiral Halsey fulfill his desire to ride the Japanese emperor's horse.)

More interestingly, some of the letter-writers are women. Under the headline SHE LIKES 'EM BRAWNY Muriel Gida of Monterey, California writes:

> Dear Sarge:
> I've decided that the only way to do this is to dash in—announce that I am a *feminine* fan—and hope for mercy. There have been so few letters from women published in THE READER SPEAKS that I have a darkling suspicion you send them threatening notes a' la Black Hand—or is it freshly severed warty ear? Come on—'fess up—do you really *want* female fans writing and criticizing?
>
> (p. 8)

Maybe so, because there are two other letters from women in this issue. Muriel Gida, probably kidding, asks for "a big, brawny MAN on the covers" to go along with all those scantily-clad Bergey girls.

Rather obviously the perception and role of women in SF is one of the things that has changed the most in the last 69 years. Much of what you've heard about the magazines of the period is true. It was not exclusively a boys' club, but sometimes it must have felt that way. There had been a Leigh Brackett story in *TWS* about a year earlier ("The Veil of Astellar" Spring 1944), but the magazine's most prolific female contributor, Margaret St. Clair, was not to appear for almost another two years, and it would be a couple more years before Marion "Astra" Zimmer (later known as Marion Zimmer Bradley) became a leading letterhack and fan personality, before she became a professional writer. In its more grown-up phase, *TWS* published Katherine MacLean's famous "The Diploids" (April 1953).

I think that what we can see in this more or less randomly selected pulp from the middle 1940s is the first faint stirrings of something that would become the maturation of science fiction. Notice that, as per pulp convention, the young woman in the stories is always called a "girl." (I have never read pulp romance fiction. Were 20-something male characters in love-story pulps called "boys"?) What is more interesting is that in the Vance and Leinster stories, the "girl" is actually an intelligent, effective character, with a mind and agenda of her own. For all she may fill the traditional "prize" role, the "girl" in Leinster's "Things Pass By" also ends up as the head of the largest and most powerful corporation on Earth, firing the crooks and cleaning up the place. She does not plan to retire and become a housewife. It may be that the content of these stories was starting to change before the language did.

There were quite a lot of conventions that had to be dropped if science fiction was to grow up. Such lazy stories as Frank Long's "The Shadow Dwellers" and also Kuttner's "Percy the Pirate," are set in the old, standard Solar System. The idea behind the purely generic sort of pulp fiction, you see, is that it followed a set of easily recognized formulas, so that the reader, realizing what kind of story it was, could immediately get his bearings. All the planets of the Solar System had humanoid races. There were squat Jovians, often lizard-like Venusians, and so on. Venus was a swamp or jungle, Mars a desert which not-coincidentally very often resembled Arizona. Moons and even asteroids were islands, usually inhabited, which is why space pirates could hang out on them. Thus jungle stories, westerns, sea stories, etc. could be turned into science fiction with the addition of one-man spaceships, "visiscreens," a few ray-guns, and little else. Primitive aliens are still generic "natives," even if blue or green.

This is the universe of Captain Future. It is also the universe of Ray Bradbury's early science fiction, including *The Martian Chronicles*. Roger Zelazny paid one last, nostalgic visit to the old Mars in "A Rose for Ecclesiastes" in 1963 and to the old Venus in "The Doors of His Face,

The Lamps of His Mouth" in 1965. Gardner Dozois recently made an even more anachronistic, retro-visit in an anthology called *Old Mars.* If you want to see where that Mars and that Solar System began, read about the first year and a half of the Clayton *Astounding Stories of Super Science*, 1930-1931. This was the first real *pulp magazine* of science fiction. Gernsback's magazines before that (*Amazing Stories, Science Wonder Stories*) were not regarded as pulps, but more in the low end of the popular science category. But Clayton's *Astounding* was an out-and-out pulp. (One of the last living voices of the era, Bob Madle, once told me what his reaction and that of the early SF fans was: "'Oh, no! They're going to do a *pulp magazine* of science fiction!' It was like your sister had just become a prostitute.") An out-and-out pulp needed out-and-out formulas, standard settings. Even as there was a standard Old West that anybody could set a western in, a standard South Seas, a standard North Africa (for Foreign Legion stories, a flourishing genre at the time), a standard Jungle, and so on, there had to be a standard Outer Space. And so there was. The standard, "old" Solar System was invented in the Clayton *Astounding* in very short order. It was the very stuff of *Planet Stories.* It was still very definitely prevalent in *Thrilling Wonder* in the middle 1940s. There were still traces of it in John Campbell's *Astounding*, but not as obviously.

In 1945, it was just barely becoming possible in science fiction to move beyond formula plots, stock characters, and formula settings. Not every writer achieved this or even tried to, but, little by little, it was allowed. What we find in our core sample would not have been recognized at the time. Its significance is only visible in retrospect.

ROBERT BLOCH AND THE DEATH OF SCIENCE FICTION—1951

Magazines are all about context. It's fun to go through old issues and read things that no one else has read in a long time. Sometimes you discover lost gems, but even if you don't the context adds an extra dimension. It's one thing to read a story reprinted in an anthology or collection, quite another to read it as it originally appeared.

The cover of the October 1951 *Other Worlds Science Stories* doesn't seem all that promising. The painting by H.W. McCauley shows one of those statuesque, scantily-clad ladies characteristic of the less progressive SF magazines of the period. She is holding a pistol of some sort and what might be a wand or scepter. Little more than knee-high to her are two elderly, semi-naked troglodytes, sort of what Santa Claus elves would have looked like in Fred Flintstone's day. The one in the foreground is holding a club and pointing. There is a fallen pillar in front of the three figures, to the far right of the painting, suggesting that they are among ancient ruins.

The feature story is "I Flew in a Flying Saucer" by Captain A.V.G.

And now some context: What this would have meant to an experienced science-fiction reader at the time is "more of the same crap." *Other Worlds* was Ray Palmer's magazine, the one he started, along with *Fate,* when he left the editorship of *Amazing Stories* in 1949. Palmer had been one of the first SF fans, and when he took over *Amazing* in 1938 there were high hopes for him, which were quickly dashed as he turned the magazine into a morass of juvenile, formula fiction, at precisely the time when John W. Campbell was producing a golden age in *Astounding.* Palmer's rationale was that Campbell had the adult market sewed up, so *Amazing* was aiming at a younger and less sophisticated sort of reader. He was certainly successful financially, even if very little of what he published proved to be of any lasting interest. Little of it has been reprinted, whereas *Astounding* material from the same era has been anthologized again and again, reworked into classic books, and possibly reached millions of readers since. Palmer's *Amazing* produced no *Foundation Trilogy* or *Slan* or *Revolt in 2100,* much less a "Thunder and Roses" or "Vintage Season." But if you judge editorial genius on the basis of copies sold, then Ray Palmer was the greatest science fiction magazine editor of all time. He achieved a circulation no one to this day has ever topped and, given the condition of fiction magazines at present, no one is ever likely to top. Keep that in mind the next time someone tries to justify editorial policy with numbers.

Palmer's *Amazing* outsold Campbell's *Astounding*. Part of the reason was that he commissioned a whole series of new Edgar Rice Burroughs stories and got the great J. Allen St. John to illustrate them, but his real breakthrough was the Shaver mystery. By the best account (see "Profit Without Honor" by Palmer's successor, Howard Browne, *Amazing,* May 1984), in 1944 there came into the editorial office a six-page crank letter from one Richard Shaver who claimed to have positive proof that degenerate little men called "deros" dwelling beneath the Earth's crust armed with ray machines caused most of the world's problems. Browne, who was Palmer's assistant at the time, read the letter aloud for laughs and tossed it in the wastebasket. Palmer insisted it be run. The response was astonishing. Thousands of people wrote in who had heard voices or discovered menacing things in caves. Palmer ordered more material from Shaver, rewrote it heavily, and ran it. The key document in the "Shaver Mystery" was "I Remember Lemuria!" (March 1945) which was later republished as a book. Palmer devoted an entire issue to Shaver in 1947. The quality was appalling, the content ridiculous, but sales reached astronomical levels. The gimmick was that this material "disguised as fiction" contained a core of reality, that there really *were* deros, plus a vast paranoid conspiracy to prevent the awesome truth from getting out.

Appreciate that this was a couple years before anyone had heard of flying saucers. The Kenneth Arnold sighting, Roswell, the Men in Black, contactees, abductees, extraterrestrial anal probes, etc. were all in the future, but Palmer had tapped into the same phenomenon before it had a name.

It was surely the biggest embarrassment in the history of science fiction, prior to the advent of Dianetics in *Astounding* in 1950. Reportedly, a motion was introduced at the 1947 Worldcon in Philadelphia to petition the Post Office to ban *Amazing* Stories from the mails on the grounds it was injurious to the mental health of its readers.

The only reason Shaver and the deros are not more remembered today is that this belief was subsumed into flying-saucerdom with the enthusiastic support of none other than Ray Palmer, who through *Fate* magazine became virtually the second father of the UFO after Kenneth Arnold, a St. Paul figure whose sudden conversion caused him to carry the faith to a tens or even hundreds of thousands of new believers.

After Palmer resigned from *Amazing,* Browne took over, wrote off a big chunk of Shaver inventory "because it stunk up the place," and went back to publishing fiction as fiction. But Palmer, in *Other Worlds*, because he was also the publisher, could do whatever he wanted. He hadn't given up on this sort of thing.

Hence the flying saucer cover story on the October 1951 issue. It's the first part of a serial, "as told to Ray Palmer." "Captain A.V.G." provides an introduction which must have seemed very familiar to Palmer's readers: this story is part fiction, part truth, and the Captain must protect his identity in case things become "serious."

The cover painting very much suggests the imagery of the Shaver Mystery, as, in addition to deros, the mythos also included sexy female "titans" who could grow to enormous height because they lived on sunless worlds where there was no baleful sunlight to stunt their growth. (The trouble started when our sun ran out of carbon and degenerated the deros. Trust me; it *doesn't* make any sense.)

This issue also contains not one, but *two* stories by Richard Shaver, one a 7000 word piece called "Journey to Nowhere," and a 20,000-worder, "Lightning Over Saturn" by Shaver and Chester S. Geier, a long-time Palmer loyalist.

There is a real, genuine science article by Willy Ley in the issue, but otherwise a glance at this issue's message to experienced SF readers in 1951 was, indeed, surely, "More of the same crap."

All this is context. I do not digress. What's more intriguing in this issue is a story by Robert Bloch, "The End of Science Fiction." Bloch was another long-time Palmer regular, whose Lefty Feep stories had been such a joy in the Palmer-edited *Fantastic Adventures,* a companion to *Amazing*. He had contributed to *Amazing* too, but had always kept well clear of Shaverism. Palmer, who was no fool for all he may have been a lunatic, valued Bloch for his brisk narrative style and for his humor.

"The End of Science Fiction" is one of Bloch's fannish stories. It is not as well-known as his "A Way of Life" (*Fantastic Universe* October 1956) which is about a post-holocaust society based on SF fandom brought to crisis by the unearthing of some actual fanzines, which prove to be filled with trivia. In fact it has only been reprinted twice, in a French collection in 1984 and in the very limited *The Fear Planet* in 2005. But it fits perfectly into *Other Worlds*. Despite his having alienated so many purists over the years (I believe it was Damon Knight who remarked that in Palmer's hands *Amazing* had died and been reborn as a dung-beetle), Palmer's magazines were among the most fannish of the time, with coverage of conventions, fanzines, etc.

"The End of Science Fiction" tells how Robert Bloch attended the 10th World Science Fiction Convention in New York. (In reality the 10th worldcon would be held in Chicago in 1952, about a year after this story came out.) He is met at the train station by a geeky fan:

> "Pardon me, but are you Robert Bloch?"
> "What did you expect?" I asked. "A gorilla?"
> "No—it's just you don't look the way I expected you to look—I mean—"
> "I understand," I shrugged. "It's true I used to have two heads, but one of them was amputated last year. I carry it in my suitcase. Want to see?"
>
> (p. 86)

Bloch is then rescued by his agent, Larry Fisher. Some real names are quickly dropped as the two of them reach the convention hotel:

> Otto Binder and some of the New York gang arrived about five, and then Ackerman called—just in from the Coast—and Bob Tucker came up looking for a deck of cards.
>
> (p. 87)

This sort of thing leads the reader, then or now, to wonder who some of the other characters "really" are. The guest of honor at the convention is Richard Ormsbee, an enormously successful science fiction writer. Bloch knew him as a fan, but "Then he turned writer and in a few years his reputation was established not only in the field of fantasy but beyond. He sold to the slicks, turned out books, did radio and TV work, and at the same time managed to retain his warm and unassuming friendliness." (p. 87)

Who is this? Heinlein? He's got a moustache like Heinlein but much of the background doesn't fit. Bradbury? Doesn't fit either. Very likely a composite then, a necessarily fictional character considering what happens to Richard Ormsbee by the end of the story.

What happens is this: Ormsbee is missing. He turns up in Bloch's suite, and confides to him with much dread and trepidation what he proposes to tell the fans in his speech the next day. Science fiction must cease. Writers must stop writing. Publishers must stop publishing. All science fiction books and back-issue magazines must be burned. Why?

It seems that Ormsbee's copy of Lovecraft's *The Outsider and Others* has been stolen by aliens, along with other SF books and magazines. He hears an inhuman voice trying to lull him to sleep at night, and realizes at once that it must be Lovecraft's "Whisperer in Darkness." He sees a glowing silver cylinder floating in the sky outside his window, obviously a spaceship. (The Lovecraft reader will also recall that in "The Whisperer in Darkness" the aliens from Yuggoth carried off human brains in silver cylinders.)

Ormsbee goes on, in language reminiscent of a Ray Palmer editorial:

> "Suppose, for the sake of argument, that this is the truth behind the so-called Flying Saucers, as has often been suggested. Grant that it's true. Outsiders with a superior intelligence arrive on this planet—what will they do?"
>
> "Wreck the Empire State Building," I sneered. "They try it in every story."
>
> "Exactly!" Ormsbee declared. "It's from those stories that they get their information!"
>
> "Now wait a minute—"
>
> "Don't you see?" he persisted. "Picture these aliens...arriving through a gap in the continuum of space and time. They have no direct kinship with humanity or human thought. The strongest link would naturally be through the minds of those who are at least conditioned—however unwittingly—to the possibility of their existence. To be specific, the writers of fantasy and science fiction, whose brains can conceive of such beings."
>
> (pp. 91-92)

The reason, Ormsbee insists, that science fiction must cease forever is that it is giving the alien invaders ideas. They use science fiction stories to scout out the territory and discover human stratagems, strengths, and weaknesses.

This all seems like raving madness, of course. Ormsbee leaves. The following morning, however, he does not deliver the speech he's rehearsed to Bloch. Instead, very stiffly, in an almost inhuman tone, he sneers at his audience:

> "You pitiful, deluded ones, who don't even dream of what goes on under your very noses, who sneer at Fort, scoff at the few thinkers who dared speculate on the truth... Still, you have unwittingly served your purpose. Ignorantly, you have opened the way to the very abysses of which you complacently scribble in your childish fantasies—"
>
> (p. 94)

This causes considerable consternation among the conventioneers, until suddenly a building attendant interrupts and insists that the fans get that damned gigantic silver cylinder off the roof before he has the lot of them thrown out. Bloch leads a charge to the roof. Half the convention follows, thinking this must be some kind of gag and not wanting to miss it. They get there just in time to see the silver cylinder, a spaceship, disappear over the horizon.

Someone realizes that Ormsbee is missing. Bloch, who knows his

Lovecraft and remembers how "The Whisperer in Darkness" ends, rushes back downstairs, fully expecting to find the rubber mask which an alien used to impersonate Ormsbee.

But the aliens haven't plagiarized Lovecraft exactly. Bloch finds, not a mask, but the corpse of Richard Ormsbee. The face has been neatly sewed up to conceal where the brain was removed. Inside the skull is the mechanism which had animated the corpse and presumably transmitted the speech from the spaceship on the roof—a mechanism of no earthly manufacture.

The story ends with suitably Lovecraftian italics. In fact the whole thing, beginning as Robert Bloch's reluctant confession of the truth after some period of time, is a parody of a typical Lovecraft story. Think of not just "The Whisperer in Darkness," but, in particular, "The Shadow out of Time."

* * * *

This is an amusing piece by any standard. It's still very readable and deserves to be reprinted. I point out that on considerably less specifically appropriate content than this one has, many stories have been dragooned into the Cthulhu Mythos and included in anthologies of such.

But what really makes it is context. It must have been absolutely hilarious in *Other Worlds* in 1951, with all that Shaver material, the flying saucer serial, and Palmer extolling the "mystery" in his editorial in the same issue. This was actually part of Palmer's charm, although it is precisely what got him into trouble later with the Saucerian faithful and pretty much written out of their history, despite his important, founding role in the UFO movement. Palmer liked to occasionally wink at his audience and hint that maybe, just maybe, he was kidding after all.

He never lost the ability to make fun of himself, to mock what he otherwise presented seriously or, in this case to allow Robert Bloch to do it.

RUSTY'S SPACESHIP FLIES AGAIN

It *is* enough to make me feel old, the realization that I've just gone back to the very first science fiction novel I ever encountered and that encounter took place more than fifty years ago. Fifty-two years ago, to be precise. When I was in the third grade, and therefore eight—this would have been late 1960 or early 1961—the teacher read the class a chapter of a science fiction book as a special treat in the last fifteen minutes or so of each school day, as we waited for the bus. For decades thereafter I didn't know the title or author, but I could remember that it was about some children (I didn't remember the characters specifically) who built a wooden spaceship in the back yard, rather the way many kids used to build tree houses. The boy in charge of the project had found a "heat shield" in the city dump, which he nailed onto the front of the vessel. Shortly thereafter, an alien came to claim this, explaining that the mysterious disk was a "flying saucer" on which the ill-tempered ruler of the planet Eopee sometimes banged his cup. When he did, it went flying through space. This alien had been sent to fetch it. Now that it was nailed onto the front of the spaceship, he had no choice but to bang the "cup" on the "saucer" and take the ship and the children into space with him. But, alas, he could not remember where Eopee was! So they went on a tour of the solar system looking for it, until at the very end the alien remembered (or recited) a bit of verse:

> *O messenger from Eopee*
> *From Andromeda galaxy ...*

At the end of the story the kids ended up back home and their mother assumed it was some game they were playing. Of course she did not believe a bit of their adventures.

I think even at the time I knew that should be "AnDROMeda," not "AndroMEda," and that either the pronunciation was wrong or something was wrong with the meter. I'd been taught to read on Dr. Seuss and had some (non-technical) idea of what meter was.

Decades later, I found the book, which proved to be *Rusty's Spaceship* by Evelyn Sibley Lampman (Doubleday, 1957). This is one of two children's science fiction books written by Ms. Lampman, the other being *The Shy Stegosaurus of Cricket Creek* (1955). There is a short biography of this author in the second volume of Robert Reginald's *Science Fiction and Fantasy Literature* (Gale Research, 1979), which tells us that Lampman was born in 1907, was a radio continuity writer and later full-time writer, and wrote in fields other than science fiction, and won a Dorothy Canfield Fisher Memorial Children's Book Award in 1962 for something called *City Under the Back Steps* and a Western Writers of America Spur Award in 1970 for *Cayuse Courage*.

Now at the age of sixty I have actually read *Rusty's Spaceship*. I find that my memory of it was fairly accurate. There are minor details I had wrong. The spaceship with built in Rusty's garage, not back yard, and the alien wielded, not the planetary ruler's cup, but another "saucer" which, when folded up like an umbrella, was a bit more practical for the purpose. Otherwise it was as I recalled it, the tour through the solar system, a scene in which the hero has to crawl out on the hull and strike the "saucer" on the nose to get the spaceship moving, etc., the conclusion with the disbelieving parent. I had even remembered the two lines of verse correctly.

The hero is a boy about ten or maybe a little older. He is accompanied by his friend Susan and their dog Cookie. This is not a teen book but a pre-adolescent book. Rusty is of the age where he has previously been perfectly happy to play with the tomboyish Susan, but now he's beginning to feel it an affront to masculine pride to carry on as before. She feels that the boys are excluding her. She is the last to be picked on a team for sports, and so on. But in private, in the garage, Rusty reverts to their former relationship and proudly shows Susan his latest creation, which he christens the *Terra Terror 1*.

Then the alien arrives, disguised in a hat and fur coat swiped from a clothesline. This is Tiphia, who, despite the feminine ending on the name, is male. Tiphia is a first-time junior messenger from Eopee, sent on his first mission to retrieve that saucer. He is desperately eager to prove himself capable, for all he forgets things sometimes. But he does endlessly praise the ineffable wisdom and goodness of his planet's ruler, the great Gwump, from whom all blessings flow, and if he sounds a little bit like a Chinese Communist extolling Mao Zedong, well, that is surely my adult perception adding something in retrospect that isn't really in the book. Here is a typical example of one of Tiphia's ditties:

> *In Eopee there is no greed,*
> *You wish aloud for what you need,*
> *And if you're too polite to say,*
> *Why, Gwump will grant it anyway.*
> *All hail, Eopee, hail!* (p. 152)

Physically, Tiphia looks rather like a green lizard that walks upright and has rather human-like arms, but no claws. He is conveniently telepathic, and even more conveniently dispenses pills which relieve the children of all need for breathing (though they still must wear clothespins over their noses to control the impulse). Thus, wearing dark goggles to block out the unfiltered sunlight, they are ready to soar off into space.

Needless to say, the level of scientific accuracy in this book is nowhere near the Hal Clement level, or that of the Heinlein juveniles. Sometimes the "science" is downright frivolous, as when, after a narrow escape, the children look back on the surface of Mars and realize that the "canals" and seasonal dark areas are actually swarms of billions of ants. Mercury is locked with one face toward the sun. They land on the hot side, and the dog's license melts right off its collar, and the children's shoes begin to smoke, but otherwise they are unharmed. Venus proves to have rather comfortable temperatures beneath its cloud cover, and the place is inhabited by rather imaginatively conceived semi-gaseous creatures no more substantial than soap bubbles. Mars has its ants. That Jupiter has a cold surface and thundering rivers of liquid methane is not a totally obsolete notion for the late '50s, and was certainly not unknown in the respectable, adult science fiction of the decade, or in the art of Chesley Bonestell. The spaceship then lands *on* the rings of Saturn, which are described as billions of tiny moonlets packed together like pebbles on a beach. The Eopeean messenger's handbook warns against landing on Saturn itself. We find out why. It is hypnotic. Everyone whirls around the planet, staring at it, hypnotized into seeing whatever they most desire, until an escape is effected.

Where Ms. Lampman falls down badly is basic physics. She does not seem to understand acceleration or gravity at all, thinking the latter something that ends when you leave a planet's atmosphere. Thus, in the space between planets, the occupants of the *Terra Terror* float weightlessly, but as soon as they enter an atmosphere, they thump to the floor.

Needless to say, it is absurd to hold a book like this to a hard-SF standard. That's not what it's for. It is a piece of whimsy, ideal for a third grade teacher reading to her charges in 1960. The teacher probably didn't understand the science either. This was the era of "duck and cover" air raid drills, which the kids did not take very seriously, particularly when the very same teacher explained that if the Russian pilot dropped his atomic bomb right on our school, you could forget it, but if he dropped it on the Treadway Inn (a large establishment about the equivalent of two city blocks away), you might have a chance. Well, at age eight I already knew something about World War II, and I knew what had happened at Hiroshima fifteen years earlier, and that the blast radius of an A-bomb was measurable in *miles*, not yards. Admittedly, I probably didn't know any more about acceleration and gravity than my teacher did. This was the tail-end of an era of innocence, when kids' stories, which used to be outright fairy tales, maybe even with fairies in them, now looked to outer space and other planets, but were still a species of fairy tale, not quite taken seriously. Yuri Gagarin and Alan Shepherd were about to go up. The "technological Pearl Harbor" of the Sputnik launch had already happened, though I had no awareness of it. Hearing *Rusty's Spaceship* was, I think, the first time I had ever encountered a story of interplanetary travel, and it came right at a time of endings and beginnings and was, in a subtle way, a life-changing event.

The story also has, I should mention, a socially progressive conclusion. Rusty gets over his incipient male chauvinism, determined that, however much the other boys in the neighborhood might object, Susan will be allowed to join his Space Patrol, even if she is a girl, because she's the only other person he knows who has any experience out there. Could the notion of a female astronaut be far behind?

DYING IN AN ECSTASY OF BLOOD: THE HALF-REMEMBERED PERVERSITIES OF DAVID H. KELLER'S "THE REVOLT OF THE PEDESTRIANS" (1928)

The subject came up in an interview I was doing with the eminent critic John Clute. He argued that science fiction "in its days of pomp" tended toward simplistic engineering solutions to problems, without regard for side effects and unintended consequences. Had there ever been so much as an illustration of a futuristic city prior to about 1965, he wanted to know, which depicted a traffic jam? Had anyone ever thought about how transportation would utterly change America? Well, one could glibly repeat (although I didn't) the Heinlein quip about how the science fiction writer's job is not so much to predict that the internal combustion engine would revolutionize transportation, but to predict how it would change mating habits. Not so much the traffic jam, but necking in the back seat at the drive-in. (Hey, does anybody remember drive-ins?)

Maybe that's another simplistic example. I brought up David H. Keller's "The Revolt of the Pedestrians." We discussed it at some length, though in a rather theoretical way, since at that point at least, John had not read the story at all, and I had not read it in at least twenty years. (Read the interview for that. It will be in *Orson Scott Card's Intergalactic Medicine Show* and will doubtless eventually find its way into one of my *Speaking of the Fantastic* books.) It's a transportation story, said I, albeit as perverse as anything ever written by Poppy Z. Brite. It sounds like a dystopia, said he, and it would have been read as a dystopia in 1928, not as an extrapolation on the future of transportation.

Then I went and reread it. The experience occasions all sorts of meditations on both the selective nature of a reader's memory and on the nature of science fiction itself.

Let me try to focus a little bit. David H. Keller (1880-1966) was one of the stars of the Gernsback Era of SF magazine publishing. He did appear elsewhere, notably in *Weird Tales*, but as a science-fictionist he was almost exclusively a Gernsback writer, for *Amazing Stories* and later for

Wonder Stories. His work was primitive, but it contained novel ideas, and is occasionally reprinted today. For all he lingered in fandom as a celebrity into the 1950s, his career was effectively over when Gernsback was forced to sell *Wonder Stories* in 1936. He continued to appear for a while in increasingly marginal markets, but he did not survive the John W. Campbell revolution of the late '30s.

However, when his published first story, "The Revolt of the Pedestrians," appeared in the February 1928 *Amazing*, he was far in advance of most science fiction writers. Unlike other newcomers of the period, he was no naïve kid in highschool or barely out of it, such as G. Peyton Wertenbacker, Alexander M. Phillips, or Jack Williamson. He was a mature man, 47 years old, with much experience in the world. He was a physician by profession, also a practicing psychiatrist (I am not sure the distinction between the two was quite so clear in those days) who had done work with shell-shock victims in World War I, then been on the staffs of mental hospitals in Illinois, Louisiana, Tennessee, and Pennsylvania. He had written numerous professional medical articles. In his earlier career, apparently, he had been a rural horse-and-buggy doctor.

I'm not *that* old, but I grew up reading David Keller's work, because the time at which I discovered science fiction magazines was a golden age of reprints. The first *Amazing* I ever bought (April 1967) had a Keller story in it. His work was appearing regularly there, and also in *The Magazine of Horror* and its companion, *Startling Mystery Stories*. Before long I had encountered two of his novels, *The Metal Doom* serialized in *Fantastic* and *The Abyss* in *The Magazine of Horror*. Both are catastrophe novels of what we would later think of as the John Wyndham sort, in which civilization is brought to the brink of extinction, then saved at the last minute; though Keller had the annoying habit of just letting his menaces fade away, rather like the ending of *The War of the Worlds* but with no philosophical resonance. Not very good at endings, I concluded.

I must have read "The Revolt of The Pedestrians" for the first time in *Amazing* for December 1966 (I had discovered back issues very quickly), and probably read it again in Keller's Arkham House collection, *Tales from Underwood* (1952), not a rare or expensive book in those days. I certainly read about "The Revolt of the Pedestrians" in commentary of the period, particularly that of Sam Moskowitz. It is safe to say that this story, along with Keller's other notable Gernsbackian hit, "The Stenographer's Hands," *used* to be a classic. There was a time when it was regarded by SF fans (and by Hugo Gernsback, whose opinion still carried some weight) as an ideal and important "scientifiction" story by a major writer. But that time has long passed. That John Clute hadn't read it startled me for a moment, but it makes sense if I consider that he's older than me, and if in 1967 one were paying more mature attention, not merely to literature in general, but to the actual cutting edge of science fiction, which would have been found in *F&SF, New Worlds,* and Judith Merril anthologies, rather than grubbing about in Sol Cohen and Robert A.W. Lowndes reprint magazines and turning into a teenaged SF antiquarian, it was entirely possible to miss "The Revolt of the Pedestrians" altogether.

Keller was a "classic" author for first-generation SF magazine readers, the ones who started reading about the time he first appeared, in the 1920s. Someone, it might have been either Lowndes or Robert Madle, remarked that in those days, when you read most pulp science fiction—A. Merritt or Doc Smith or Edgar Rice Burroughs—you knew it was lightweight and juvenile, but Keller's work had the feel of real, adult, serious literature. Yet the generation that followed didn't feel that way. In fact Keller became something of a kiss-of-death for would-be SF publishers. At least two imprints in the late 1940s (The Avalon Company and New Era) published one Keller book, then went broke, because *even then* Keller was a nostalgia item for older fans and there just weren't enough of them.

But it is interesting to go back to "The Revolt of the Pedestrians" now. It turns out that John Clute and I are both right. The story *is* I maintain, a transportation story, written within just a few years of the time in which Henry Ford began mass-producing the Model T and putting America on wheels, but it is certainly, and very strongly, a dystopia. In the opening paragraphs, a refugee Pedestrian woman, one of the last of her kind, is fleeing along with her young son. She is deliberately run over by a car and killed. Within are a rich woman and her small daughter. The chauffeur apologizes for the bump. The rich woman's little girl asks if Pedestrians feel pain. The mother explains, no, not really, they're not human.

A long expository lump follows. Slush-pile readers will recognize instantly that hook/backfill structure so common in bad science fiction to this day. There's a brief scene to snag your interest, and then, usually on page 2, the author cuts in and says "And now a history of the world to this point."

Keller's history of the world tells us that as the automobile became more common, it became first dangerous, then illegal to walk about. Society became obsessed with speed. People spent all their lives in their cars, even indoors, in small vehicles that sound like amusement-park bumper cars or handicapped carts. Eventually, the legs of Automobilists, as the majority came to be called, withered away, through what seems to be speeded up evolution. (It is not an artificial modification.) Cities were adapted entirely for vehicular use, without sidewalks or stairs, but with spiraling ramps inside the tall buildings just in case the elevators ever failed. But they don't. This is a well-run, if unpleasant society. No one is actually very happy, just speeding about frantically. The air is toxic from gasoline fumes. The Automobilists' idea of a day in the country is racing along highways past endless billboards. (A remarkable, satirical jab for 1928, you must admit.) Their economics are an odd mixture of "socialism," in which everyone is guaranteed meaningless make-work jobs, maintenance for their cars, paper clothes (4 suits a year), and tasteless food which comes in bricks with the nutritional content stamped on the side, and the worst sort of oligarchical capitalism, in which a handful of hereditary millionaires manipulate the now meaningless forms of the United States government. We meet one of these power-brokers, who makes presidents and owns presidents, but would never deign to actually have one in his family.

Meanwhile Pedestrians have been demoted from freak status to menace. The Pedestrian Extermination Act is passed, which explains why the chauffeur only apologized for the bump, and of course did not stop.

In time, Pedestrians are believed to be extinct. We see a family of stuffed specimens in a diorama in a museum. In the next display there's a stuffed family of (presumably obsolete and extinct) American Indians in a wigwam.

But Pedestrians are not extinct. It transpires that the small boy whose mother was run over in the first scene survived and grew up amid a hidden colony of Pedestrians in the Ozarks. He is Abraham Miller, the first of a line of sworn avengers against the Automobilists, whose slogan is, "We will go back." These feral Pedestrians are described as "paranoiac in their hatred," which is only to be expected since their ancestors were hunted like vermin.

The plot shifts gears. We meet William Henry Heisler, the rich man who makes presidents, in his mansion along the Hudson. He has a shameful family secret. His daughter, Margaretta, has *legs*. She is an atavism. Her father is too indulgent to do much about this, so she grows up as a "savage," fond not merely of running, jumping, and swimming, but even of shooting wild fowl with arrows and eating *meat* rather than prescribed ration-bricks.

(If you're thinking this is starting to sound a bit like *Brave New World*, published four years later, you're right. This and several other Keller stories—particularly "A Biological Experiment," which is about babies mass-produced in factories—very definitely do anticipate Aldous Huxley. Does this lead me to a fit of Moskowitzian source-tracing in which I "prove" that Huxley must have been reading *Amazing Stories*?

No, but the ideas were clearly in the air at that time.)

Suddenly, in *steps* Abraham Miller, great-grandson of the original, now militant leader of the Pedestrians (all three hundred of them), who presents an ultimatum to William Heisler and his colleagues and rivals. For all the tiny remnant of the Pedestrians eschews most technology and power beyond that of muscles, wind, and water, they have somehow made a massive breakthrough, discovering a new "electro-dynamic force" which has allowed them to build a *balonium generator.*

No, Keller does not call it that. I do. *Balonium* is one of the essentials of science fiction, and has been since the very beginnings of the form. It is that substance or field-effect which suspends the laws of nature as needed for the plot. H.G. Wells's "cavorite" was pure balonium. Keller's balonium not only shuts off all electrical power, but somehow removes all electricity from the environment. Not even steam-engines will work, we are told. Presumably fire still burns and water still boils…but no, it makes no sense, and the effect is permanent. Once the Pedestrians throw the switch, the power in all the world's cities goes off, and it cannot be restored, ever.

This is seen as a good thing, which suggests, I dare say, a certain moral immaturity typical of early science fiction. Yes, the nasty Automobilist oligarchs do mockingly refuse one final offer of peaceful co-existence from the Pedestrians, but then the Pedestrians actually throw the switch, condemning billions of human beings to a slow and hideous death. There are briefly-described scenes of apocalyptic horror as the helpless, legless population of New York City crawls and wriggles over the Manhattan bridges in search of food, already snarling and snapping at one another like dying, cannibalistic beasts.

What we don't get is any sudden shift like the one at the end of Richard Matheson's *I Am Legend*, in which the last "normal" human in a world of vampires realizes that *he* is now the monster. What we have instead is an example of a classic pulp SF motif which bothers me at least as much as engineering solutions without side-effects seem to bother John Clute. If I may add another term to the collective critical vocabulary, this is a *Feel Good About Genocide* story, in which the desirable and necessary solution to the characters' problems is the total extermination of every last one of *them*. Jack London wrote a FGAG story, "The Unparalleled Invasion" (1910) in which the White nations of the world handily wipe out the Chinese with germ warfare. The racial extermination motif survives as late as Heinlein's "Sixth Column" (1941, a.k.a. *The Day after Tomorrow*). But also think of all those space operas of the Super Science era of the 1930's, by Doc Smith, John W. Campbell, and others, in which super-scientist heroes blow up several planets before breakfast and the resultant disturbance doesn't even give Obi Wan Kenobi a headache. In the climax of his final novel, *Skylark Duquesne* (1965, and admittedly an anachronism by then) Smith topped 'em all and destroyed an *entire galaxy*, billions of worlds inhabited by intelligent beings wiped out largely because they were ugly. I admit that the one thing that leaves me uneasy about Tolkien is a similar attitude toward Orcs. For me Card's *Ender's Game* rose above the level of juvenile space opera and got genuinely interesting precisely when it came to this point, then backed off, and began to ponder the implications. But so much SF, alas, from David H. Keller onward (including, particularly, Heinlein's *The Puppet Masters* and *Starship Troopers*) never achieved this level of sophistication. The enemy is merely the Enemy, with no possible merit or viewpoint of its own, and no redeeming or redeemable characteristics. So three hundred Pedestrians exterminate many billions of Automobilists, somebody rescues the leggy Margaretta, and all is right with the world. In the end, we see stuffed Automobilists in the museum diorama.

But wait, I forgot to tell you about the *really perverse* part. If Poppy Z. Brite at her most deliberately wicked had written for Hugo Gernsback's *Amazing Stories,* what would the result have been like? Kind of like this:

Living among the Automobilists all this time has been a spy, a young man trained from boyhood to take female roles. He's got legs, but must have had them all this time scrunched up under his body in a modified cart. How he manages that without serious bodily damage we may wonder. How he goes to the bathroom we will not ask. In any case, this professional transvestite has been working as a stenographer, since, even though this is centuries in the future after mankind has experienced a major evolutionary shift, social roles have not changed much. There are still chambermaids and cleaning women. Stenographers are women.

This spy is young enough that he hardly has down on his cheeks, i.e. a teenager. He is also "patriotic" and of necessity "celibate." But romance has blossomed. He has started to fall in love with one of his (genuinely female, but legless) colleagues. This is "something twisted, a pathological perversion," especially when "when he might, by waiting, have married a woman with columns of ivory and knees of alabaster." That he might have loved her for *her* rather than for the mineral content of her lower limbs doesn't seem to have occurred to anyone. She, thinking him a woman, hints at "the new love between women," which leaves him bewildered, although her caresses and kisses he does understand in a vaguely heterosexual way.

It gets worse. Once the lights have gone out and everybody is doomed, this young man, now in unfamiliar male attire and *walking*, slips off to see his lady-love, offering to rescue her from the urban holocaust and live with her in the country. Her response:

> She laughed hysterically, said she would marry him, go wherever he wanted her to go, and then clasped him to her and kissed him full on the mouth, then kissed his neck over the jugular vein, and he died, bleeding into her mouth, and the blood mingled with rouge made her face a vivid carmine. She died some days later from hunger.
>
> <div align="right">(<i>Tales from Underwood</i>, p. 40)</div>

To which we have to say, *"Whoa!* Is Keller really aware of the sexual subtext here?" It is pretty obvious that Gernsback, and most of his readers, were not. There were certainly no letters in subsequent issues of *Amazing* complaining about this sadistic, lesbian-erotic filth....

That was the part of the story I remembered after all these years. I had entirely forgotten Heisler and his atavistic daughter. I remembered the story of the boy/girl spy, his tragic sexual awakening, and his gory, perverse end. In fact I remembered it slightly better than it actually is in the text. In my version, the girl dies in ecstasy, drowning in his blood. Not quite. She starved a week later, lingering over this last memory of her gender-ambiguous beloved. Maybe she was just after one final snack at his expense, but I rather doubt that's all there was to it.

Is my dirty mind running riot? Could Keller, a mature psychiatrist with extensive experience working with the insane, however Freudian and socially reactionary he might have been, have not known that there was an intense, erotic horror story going on here? Or was it just something he tossed off without thinking it through? Keller as a writer was never noted for his subtle characterizations.

So this young girl finds herself in a scene of utter despair and catastrophe, where she and everyone she has ever known and loved is about to die, as the escape ramp and streets are already crammed with useless cars and crippled, dying people sinking into utter bestiality; *in this context* her destroyer appears, transformed before her eyes into something more bizarre than the Creature from the Black Lagoon, and this monster wants to *marry* her and offers her a sunny life as a cripple on a farm raising baby geese ("...that would come to her chair when she cried 'Weete, weete.'"), and then all her passion and dread explodes at once, resulting in the hideous climax (in more than one sense of the word).

The jaw drops, the mind boggles, finding such stuff in a Gernsback magazine. The *Hot Blood* anthology series has nothing on it except more explicit detail.

There are several lessons for authors here, and for critics. The first is that future generations may not remember from your story precisely what you expect them to. The general concept, the neat science-fiction idea, is one thing, and that the literary historian may note in a reference book, but what the reader *remembers* is the horror, and the charged, perverse eroticism. Stories, even science fiction stories, are not about ideas. They are about images and feelings and experiences. This story is not about how, abstractly, a combination of social and economic factors turned the world into a vast highway system of whizzing go-carts (but with no traffic jams). It is about terror and misdirected love and lust coming together in the darkness of a dystopian apocalypse.

I am sure that's not what Gernsback had in mind at all, for his clean, wholesome magazine which was supposed to inspire young people into careers in science.

Am I misreading this story? I don't think so. I think I'm just reading it differently, from the perspective of 2011, not that of 1928. I am distracted from the main thread of the story and fixate on what is essentially a subplot because *that* contains powerful material that Keller either didn't notice or refused to come to terms with. A story like this can easily misfire, and become something quite different from what the author intended. Your future readership is going to surprise you that way.

Had "The Revolt of the Pedestrians" been better written, had it encompassed a broader sense of humanity, it might have gained some dignity and risen to the level of genuine tragedy. As it stands, 83 years later, it is merely grotesque. I am afraid that time hasn't been kind to much of David H. Keller's work. Such pieces become freak-show exhibits, stuffed specimens in some bizarre diorama.

But they're not devoid of interest.

Huxley, Aldous. *Brave New World.* London: Chatto & Windus, 1932.
Keller, David H. "The Revolt of the Pedestrians." *Amazing Stories,* February 1928. In *Tales from Underwood.* Sauk City, WI: 1952.

RANDALL GARRETT'S "THE QUEEN BEE": THE MOST SEXIST SCIENCE FICTION STORY EVER PUBLISHED?

Wow, I realized. I'm holding history in my hands.

What I was actually holding, while sorting through some magazines I intended to put on eBay, was a copy of the December 1958 *Astounding Science Fiction*, which would seem to be a typical late '50s issue. The cover shows a normal-looking, middle-aged man, obviously a salesman, displaying various colorful garments. The difference is that he's sweating and is held up by a personal antigravity unit, while his customer is so short and squat he looks like a beachball with a head and limbs—though still one of those muscular, roughneck characters we see so often on the covers of *ASF* during this period. We're obviously on a very high-gravity planet. In the background is a vast trading ship, and lots of squat customers crowd around. It's shopping day on a frontier planet. The caption reads "Fundamentals Don't Change." The painting, by Emshwiller, doesn't illustrate any story, but it does in its way tell us something about the late *Astounding* (soon to be *Analog*). The magazine was turning didactic. Editor John W. Campbell, Jr. liked to use it as a platform for illustrating principles, rules, and theories.

But what is a lot more "historic" in this issue is Randall Garrett's novelette, "The Queen Bee." Or I should say "the infamous 'Queen Bee,'" because this story has a reputation. I haven't been able to find much mention of it in the critical literature, but this story has a considerable word-of-mouth buzz. It is widely reputed to be the single most sexist story published in the entire history of science fiction.

Reader, I just *had* to investigate.

Not a literary or scientific masterpiece, I can tell you up front.

The opening line reads: "The problem was, what were they going to do with Elissa Krand?"

The story goes roughly as follows:

The interstellar liner *Generatrix* suffers a catastrophic gobbledygook breakdown when the technobabble drive overheats, rendering the vessel uninhabitable. Seven people, four men and three women, make it into a lifeboat, which gets pretty hot too. One of the women, the problematic Elissa Krand, immediately gets hysterical, so Peter Branson, the ship's navigator and the only officer present, does his duty and manfully (if "reluctantly") slugs her, because that's what you do with hysterical women, right?

Not a promising start. We're only a few paragraphs in. Then it gets so hot that it's very likely that "evaporation of perspiration" will become "absolutely necessary on every square centimeter of skin surface." More technobabble follows as everybody discusses parabolic orbits and such, because that's what you do in a hard-science story when not slugging women, I guess. The lifeboat can't launch for several minutes and it gets even hotter in there, so Branson orders everybody to take their clothes off. "Evaporation of perspiration," you know. It's already too hot to touch the walls without burning yourself. But I can't help but wonder where all that evaporated perspiration (i.e. water vapor) is going to *go* and why the close confines of this small vessel don't just turn into a sauna.

Another of the women starts to get hysterical, but before anybody has to slug her, the lifeboat is fortunately launched. Everybody has been standing around, unable to touch the walls, or presumably chairs. How come they didn't all go tumbling with the inertial jerk of the launch?

Well, never mind that. They land on a convenient planet. "Lucky!" one of the men exclaims. "You wouldn't find a planet like this in a dozen tries!" Apparently so. It's one of those *Star Trek* planets that looks like a particularly bland patch of Earth and is usually inhabited by a dozen people with funny facial makeup. This one is uninhabited, save by our castaways, but they are conveniently provided with every castaway comfort, including breathable air, running water, edible fauna, no nasty bacteria, and no aggressive critters that an Earthman with a blaster can't handle. There are even edible berries.

The only problem is that apparently the society the characters come from has no interstellar communication worth mentioning, because these folks are stuck there *forever.* For reasons that are not 100% clear, at least to me, they have no hope of being rescued or discovered for hundreds of years. Apparently it is the custom to send routine passenger liners through regions of space too large and too remote to be worth exploring first or patrolling later.

I think you can see where this is going. It's time to be fruitful and multiply. In fact, sexual mass-production is required *by law,* by something called Brytell's Law, which is as authoritative as Newton's Laws of Motion, we are supposed to believe. What you do in such a situation is colonize the planet. Since inbreeding is a potential hazard, this is no time for soppy personal or emotional considerations. Everybody, we are told firmly, ceased to be an individual as soon as they landed on the planet.

The Law, which concerns itself with breeding protocols, is quoted:

> Article IV… In such a case…the women must be isolated. All precautions must be taken as to prevent any confusion as to parenthood.
>
> Article V: In an ideal situation, each female would produce at least one female child and one male child by each male.
>
> (p. 76)

In other words, everybody is to screw in rotation to spread the available genetic material around as much as possible.

Mind you, these people are not the last survivors of the human race or anything like that. There is a flourishing human society on many planets of the galaxy. Admittedly, if everybody does nothing and they just grow old and die here, leaving the last survivor all alone, that would be pretty dismal. But that's a personal consideration, and we don't have time for such nonsense, do we? It is apparently regarded as everybody's patriotic duty to Humanity to claim and colonize this planet.

But the difficult Elissa Krand asks a sensible enough question, "Are we cattle?"

Branson isn't tolerating any dissent:

> "It's the Law that has populated the galaxy. It applies to First Colonists and shipwreck survivors alike. No one—I'll repeat that—*no one* is exempt from it."
>
> (p.78)

The characterization of Elissa Krand is a very hostile one. She is a snooty, high-class bitch, arrogant enough to speak her mind and defy ex-navigator Branson. She is diagnosed by the team's medical man as an "androphobe," which in case anybody is wondering, is Greek for "one who fears men," although in the course of this story she doesn't seem to be afraid of anyone. Worse yet, she seems to be that most terrifying of figures, a woman with confidence and brains, a high-level corporate executive trained in "manipulative economics"—admittedly not something much needed in this x-rated Boy Scout situation. She has no practical skills at all. Besides running multi-billion dollar corporations, all she knows how to do is design party dresses. You know, frilly girly things.

So Branson assigns her to dig a latrine. You may wonder why, with only seven people and the entire planet to poop on, a latrine is immediately necessary. The only answer I can think of is humiliation. It is a way to put the uppity broad in her place.

When one of the other two women, who have otherwise gone along with the program, gets a little out of hand, her assigned mate has to smack her too. That's what real manly men do in survival situations. No time for sentiment or softness.

Things go from bad to worse. Elissa Krand will *not* cooperate. She won't do her work. She refuses to take orders from anybody. She persists in helping herself to the irreplaceable steaks from the freezer. She won't eat the native meat. Finally, to get her way, she murders the other two women, so that *she* now has the only, utterly indispensable set of ovaries on the planet. She knows the men can't kill her. Brytell's Law forbids it. She hopes that she will then be able to blackmail the men into waiting on her hand and foot, as if she's "Queen Bee."

If this story has a generally-applicable moral it is that you should be careful what you wish for. Remember that an actual queen bee doesn't live a very interesting life. All she does once the hive is set up is lie around and produce eggs.

The story now moves to its infamous conclusion. Elissa Krand thinks she's won. She is contemptuous when the men go through the motions of a "trial." What can they do? Ah, but there's one angle she didn't think of. There's this discredited medical technique, you see. The doctor is to give her a lobotomy, so that she will be no more than a zombie, with no personality or will at all. But her reproductive organs will be just fine. She becomes a breeding machine. A year later the result is a nice baby girl.

II

Ladies, I mean female readers of *NYRSF*, have you thrown up yet?
Is this *the* single most sexist story ever published in science fiction? Yes, very likely.

We certainly have to admit that if we apply the reverse-gender test and imagine a story about a man who won't cooperate so that the women kill him and keep his gonads alive in a laboratory, the result would never have sold to John W. Campbell's *Astounding*. This may suggest a certain pro-male bias in at least some areas of the science fiction field, at least in the late 1950s.

In many ways, this story is hard to account for. Randall Garrett's other work is pleasant and lightweight, and he is best-known for the Lord Darcy series, about a detective in an alternate world where magic rather than science was developed. He was a competent entertainer and a bit of a hack, one of the people who wrote for *Amazing* when it was done on an assembly line by a handful of writers, and, more to the point, somebody who used to race with Robert Silverberg to see who could regurgitate a John Campbell editorial and sell it back to him as a story in the shortest amount of time. (Legend has it that one of these two got the story into print within six months of the original editorial. I'm not sure who.)

But Randall Garrett was no lifelong misogynist. He was apparently a rather jolly fellow, alternately bawdy and pious, who, because he had once been an Episcopal priest, remarked upon seeing a fan in a Friar Tuck costume, "There but for one letter goes the story of my life." He married writer Vicki Ann Heydron.

I think the answer begins with John W. Campbell, and what *Astounding* had become by the end of the Fifties.

The magazine was in steep decline, not economically, but *artistically*. Yes, that *matters*. If anybody whines, "It sold *more copies* than any of the competitors so it must have been the best!" reply firmly, "You mean to say that Ray Palmer was the greatest science fiction editor of all time, right?" It was Ray Palmer's *Amazing* of the Shaver Mystery, not the *Astounding* of the Golden Age, which achieved the highest circulation any science fiction magazine has ever reached in the entire history of the field. If circulation figures equal greatness, Ray Palmer was the greatest. No doubt about it.

Campbell, who had twenty years earlier raised science fiction out of the mire of routine pulp and almost single-handedly *created* modern science fiction and published virtually all the SF stories that the Baby Boom generation grew up reading—stories that stayed in print for decades and were later read by millions of people all over the planet in dozens of languages—was well past his prime by 1958.

For one thing, he had turned into a pseudo-science crank, fully as credulous as Ray Palmer, beguiled first by General Semantics, then the Bates Eye Exercises, then Dianetics, then psionics, then the Hieronymus Machine, dowsing, and the Dean Drive. He refused to believe that tobacco caused cancer. He was convinced it was the fumes from the match, so he smoked with a cigarette holder, to keep the match far away. He had *lots* of crazy ideas, and he forced them on his writers, alienating in the process most of his best contributors. L. Sprague de Camp testifies in his autobiography that his friendship with Campbell cooled considerably over Dianetics. Campbell probably didn't like it either that de Camp had published an article in one of the competing magazines entitled "Pfui on Psi." (*Fantastic Universe,* April 1957.)

The others drifted away, Heinlein, Tenn, Leiber, Sturgeon, Clifton, and many more. Damon Knight (who also stopped writing for *Astounding*) later remarked that Campbell's next move was a shrewd one. He gathered together a team of hungry, second-rate writers who had few prospects elsewhere—writers like E.B. Cole, Christopher Anvil, and, very likely, Randall Garrett—and used them as mouthpieces for his increasingly preachy, crackpot magazine.

Of course no such generalization is absolute, and one can only note that Katherine MacLean's classic "Unhuman Sacrifice" had appeared in the issue of *Astounding* right before "The Queen Bee" (i.e., November 1958), and also in the December issue is a pretty good novelette by H. Beam Piper, "Ministry of Disturbance," plus the conclusion of an amusing, certainly harmless short novel by Poul Anderson, "A Bicycle Built For Brew," about a beer-powered spaceship (published as part of an Ace Double as *The Makeshift Rocket.*) But the preachments were becoming more common.

The problem was that Campbell had lost interest in storytelling. He wanted to start fights. Barry Malzberg tells us in *Engines of the Night* how as a young, eager, novice science fiction writer he got in to see the Great Man and was dismayed by how bigoted, out-of-touch, and just plain contrary Campbell seemed to be. ("…arguing with him had made me sick," writes Malzberg, page 75.) Then, as they parted, Campbell sort of winked at him and said, "Don't worry about it, son. I just like to shake 'em up."

In other words, rather like a political talk-show host of today, Campbell had become, not an editor of stories, but a professional controversialist who used stories as a mechanism for "shaking them up."

How much do you want to bet that the basic idea for "The Queen Bee" came from Campbell, not Garrett?

Certainly science fiction is *supposed* to be provocative. No one would deny that. But provocation is supposed to lead to genuine insight, and in that department "The Queen Bee" falls apart for a whole variety of reasons.

What we're seeing here is the Campbell *Astounding* imitating itself. This is a failed attempt at another "The Cold Equations." Both stories are about characters in tight spots making tough choices based on laws of the universe which respect neither persons nor gentler emotions. Tom Godwin's "The Cold Equations" (*Astounding* August 1954) has certainly started enough arguments in its time, and may be the most talked-about single story in the field. As an aside, I'll opine that the arguments about the sexual politics in "The Cold Equations" seem overrated. The story would have worked out the same if the stowaway who must be ejected into space were a boy. Maybe some of the dialogue would have been different, and there might have been some thwarted buddy-bonding, but it would still have been a story about an innocent who blundered into a situation he didn't understand and nothing could have prevented the kid from going out the airlock at the end. It's a story about the fatal mistake of a *child*, and the word "child" in many languages, including English, is neuter.

Maybe the reason "The Cold Equations" works is that despite numerous contrivances to get into its situation—and it is very contrived—the basic theme, that the physics of mass, thrust, and ballistics cannot be argued with, rings true.

"The Queen Bee," when you really think about it, is, if I may use an esoteric, quasi-academic, technical term here, bullshit. Brytell's Law is a social code, not a scientific principle at all. Elissa Krand could readily have asked who the hell gave Mr. Branson any authority at all, because here, on this unsettled planet, nobody has jurisdiction. A genuine physical law, like one of Newton's, applies anywhere, because that is just how the universe works. But a human social code only applies because people agree that it does. It has no objective validity at all. One of the follies that Lazarus Long warned us against in his *Notebooks* was mistaking your opinions for the laws of the universe. John W. Campbell, in his decline, committed this error frequently.

What if the people stranded on the planet had been a bunch of Catholic monks and nuns? Would they have made babies non-stop or would they have just accepted that it was God's will that all of them live out their lives in this remote place, in solitude and prayer? Working from a different social premise, they would have come to an entirely different conclusion than Garrett's characters do.

The rational, humane solution to the problem of Elissa Krand, if she truly refused to contribute to the wellbeing of the castaway party and continued to make everyone's life miserable, would have been exile. Tell her, "Fine, if you do not want to be part of our group, go off and live by yourself. Become a hermit." Yes, they'd lose one set of female equipment, but they'd still have two others, which is twice as many as they have at the end, the way things work out in the story.

Besides, does anybody really believe you can breed an entire planetary population from a single human female? That, at the end of the story, is precisely what the characters are trying to do.

All contrivances aside, does this make any sense? I submit that it does not and that's not what the story's about anyway. Its core message is a truly appalling one: *All a woman's good for is breeding anyway. That's why she exists. Get used to it sister.*

As I've suggested, no male writer or reader is likely to accept that a man, when push comes to shove, is no more than a set of gonads and the means to protect them, so why should a female writer or reader be expected to put up with this?

Did Joanna Russ write *We Who Are About To* in white-hot rage in response to this specific story? Certainly she read the magazine science fiction of this period as a young woman. Her book is quite obviously an angry deconstruction, if not of this story, of the clichés behind it. Why *is* it so necessary to populate one more chunk of rock with humans, if the human race is not facing extinction? Why *does* it matter all that much? Can't somebody opt out if they choose to? Maybe Brytell can take his precious Law and shove it.

III

I never met John W. Campbell, but as far as I can tell from available reports—and I have spoken with people who knew him well—he wasn't a rabid misogynist any more than Randall Garrett was. He was hardly John Norman, who has put together an elaborate "philosophy" of female subjugation that he apparently believes with all his heart.

Campbell liked to start arguments, to force people to re-examine their assumptions. Did he believe what he preached? Not always. One of the sordid ironies here is that the editorial in the December 1958 issue, "Political Science," is one of a distasteful series in which he hints to the reader that, you know, maybe slavery is not such a bad idea after all. Sure enough, within a few months, Garrett had sold that one back to him as a story. (It's called "The Destroyers" and it's the cover story on the December 1959 issue.) But for all that he came out in favor of George Wallace for president in 1968, I don't think John Campbell believed in slavery.

Actually the most striking thing one discovers by looking through subsequent issues of *Astounding* is that for all "The Queen Bee" rated second in the Analytical Laboratory reader poll published in the February 1959 issue (rating stories published in the December 1958 issue), there are *no* outraged letters about this story published in "Brass Tacks." Either none were received or Campbell did not choose to print them. Correspondents in the February 1959 issue are babbling about the Hieronymus Machine, which was a "psionic" device which "worked" just as well with or without its wiring present. They aren't talking about the Garrett story in subsequent issues either. I went through all the 1959 issues to be certain.

There was no controversy. Only silence.

Two interpretations remain open to us. The first is that readers just accepted the premise of the story without question, being sufficiently unenlightened in that unenlightened time that the natural inferiority of women, who exist only as breeding machines for real people...er, I mean, for men...was taken as a given. But if this were the case, you would expect readers to have written in to praise Garrett for "telling it like it is." Apparently they didn't.

My best guess is that they shrugged it off as more Campbell crap and ignored it. The story's "infamous" reputation only developed later, and slowly. The story in retrospect came to typify everything female readers could possibly find offensive in science fiction, but at the time nobody took it seriously.

It's not a realistic story, after all. It's phony realism. When I was at the Clarion Workshop in 1973 someone coined the phrase "the I-crawled-on-my-bloody-stumps-and-kicked-him-in-the-balls school of realism," meaning that sort of supposedly gritty, grueling, grim sort of story that is usually written by very young writers in imitation of Harlan Ellison, in which the attempt at unflinching candor about life's harshness somehow goes over the top and becomes ridiculous.

"The Queen Bee" certainly has elements of that, but Garrett was not a novice writer in 1958. This isn't a naïve story. It's a lazy one. Call it "cigarette realism," after that cliché in 1940s and 1950s *noir* detective fiction in which descriptions of people smoking cigarettes could be used not only for padding, but as a substitute for more complicated character interaction. You know, the guy in the trench coat offers the dangerous babe a cigarette, mutters some trivial dialogue, and the scene is set, just like it's been set in hundreds of other similar stories.

The "realism" of "The Queen Bee" is like that. It's a set of stock assumptions and stock situations, with a lot of string-pulling to get it to work (sort of), but for all its pretense, there's really no thought content at all.

So there was nothing to talk about.

Maybe it's true, as the December 1958 cover suggests, that "fundamentals don't change," but, alas, this story didn't manage to address any of them.

CITED:

Randall Garrett. "The Queen Bee." *Astounding Science Fiction* December 1958, pp. 70-96.

Barry Malzberg. "John W. Campbell: June 8, 1910 to July 11, 1971." *Engines of the Night.* Doubleday, 1982. pp. 71-76.

NOTE, JUNE 6, 2012:

Of course we are not, in the logical part of our brains anyway, entirely surprised by the news of Ray Bradbury's passing, human mortality being what it is. The man had been in poor health. He was nearly 92. The last time I saw him in person, at the World Science Fiction Convention in Anaheim in 2006, he was specially driven to the convention center and wheeled in by his support staff so that he could give (still in finest form) one of his rousing public talks. You had to get a ticket for an autograph because the demand was so great. He signed for about an hour afterwards, then succumbed to exhaustion and went home. Nevertheless it is difficult to grasp, emotionally, that we are no longer sharing the universe with this literary giant, this legend, this magician of story. He has been a constant presence for all my life, and I am sure he has been like that for most of you, enriching us all. There is no more Ray Bradbury. It is as if the sun has gone out. He leaves a very large hole in American literature, which can never be filled.

Any number of memorials and tributes will follow in the next few days, weeks, and months. But here is something I wrote about Ray while he was very much still alive.

HOORAY BRADBURY

As I write this, news has come that Ray Bradbury has won a special citation from the 2007 Pulitzer Prize committee "for his distinguished, prolific, and deeply influential career as an unmatched author of science fiction and fantasy."

Wow. One of ours wins a Pulitzer, an award usually reserved for mainstream types, and given out with an implicit denial of the importance of such "genre" fiction as science fiction and fantasy. Another *Weird Tales* alumnus makes good.

But seriously, folks, and all "Hooray for our side" self-congratulation aside, this citation gives us cause to stop and consider why Ray Bradbury *is* a very special person, not just to *Weird Tales* readers or even to Baby Boomers, but to just about any reader of American literature who has been awake for the past sixty years.

Ray Bradbury is one of ours; there is no denying it. He made his reputation, first, in *Weird Tales* in the early 1940s, with many of the stories we now read in *The October Country*: "The Wind," "The Scythe," "The Jar," etc. He is certainly the magazine's second-most famous contributor, right after H.P. Lovecraft. If HPL got it into Library of America first, that may have been because he was born earlier and had a head-start —and died wretchedly at the age of 46, which added something to his posthumous mythos, whereas Bradbury, who is still with us at the age of almost 87, seems to have had a glorious and joyous career.

Bradbury became, very suddenly, one of the very best writers ever to appear in a pulp magazine. That a 22-year-old writer, with only a conventional high school education could have produced such masterpieces in such short order will doubtless have future scholars pondering whether the works attributed to Ray Bradbury were really written by Sir Francis Bacon, Edward De Vere, or Sir Walter Raleigh—but *we* know better, even as we know that the only outward sign of genius is genius, and that the only way you could tell that this particular highschool-grad, movie fan, and would-be science fiction writer, circa 1940, was anything special was that he started turning out things like "The Wind," "The Jar," etc. and produced *The Martian Chronicles, Fahrenheit 451, The Illustrated Man,* and *The Golden Apples of the Sun* within a decade.

He wrote a lot more and continues to write, but I will venture to say that if some malign time-traveler were to go back and prevent the appearance of everything Bradbury published between about 1943 and 1953, the remains of his work would be that of a talented, but frequently second-rate writer. (Some people rate *Something Wicked This Way Comes*, published in 1962, with Bradbury's best; I do not.) Some of his more recent work has been, well, not up to his highest standards. I couldn't finish the novel 2002 novel, *Let's Kill Constance.* Many of what we have seen in recent collections may be old trunk stories from the 1940s, some of them pretty good, some of them not, none at Bradbury's highest level.

But never mind that. William Shakespeare wrote *Titus Andronicus,* and that isn't very good either. What matters is how good a writer is at his best, and Bradbury at his best has been very fine indeed. What a miraculous decade he had! That it came early in his career does not really matter. The important thing is that it came at all. Many writers, indeed, may find themselves in the shadow of their world-famous younger selves, but I can only say, speaking as a writer myself, "I only wish *I* had such problems." I once asked the late Jack Williamson what it felt like to be best-known for work you've done 40 or 50 years ago (in Williamson's case, I meant *The Legion of Space, Darker Than You Think,* and *The Humanoids,* all published between 1934 and 1948) and he just laughed and said, "It's great to be a classic!"

I don't doubt that it is. Most of us are never going to get the chance to find out from personal experience. I am glad for Ray Bradbury that he's had such a long career, and certainly no one has the right to say, "Ray, you're not quite sparking the way you did in 1943, so stop." No, what a writer does is write. As long as he has anything at all to say, he should go on writing. Besides, another miracle might happen. Look at the career of Mark Twain, an undoubted genius, though his genius is not manifested in everything he wrote. Twain had long stretches in which he wrote huge amounts of material of varying degrees of merit, but nothing great, and then, randomly, something like *The Adventures of Huckleberry Finn* or *A Connecticut Yankee in King Arthur's Court* bobbed to the surface. Toward the end of Twain's life there was "The Mysterious Stranger," as great and profound as anything he ever did, indeed, something he wrestled with and never quite finished in his lifetime, written from the perspective of everything he lived through up to that point. Ray Bradbury at 87 might still surprise us.

I want to put in a word for late Bradbury. Some years ago an editor whispered to me, half laughing but shaking his head sadly, that he had received a story from Bradbury's agent which implied that the old war horse was long overdue for the glue factory. "It's about this old man who gets an erection for the first time in years and spends the rest of the story talking to it."

I found that story. I liked it. It's called "Junior," and it's in *The Toynbee Convector* (1988). I would agree that it was entirely inappropriate for the editor's magazine (which was devoted to fantasy) but the description was not entirely accurate. It's about a man who has his first erection in years and summons over all his old girlfriends to reminisce and say goodbye to "junior." It's a funny farewell to youth, decorum be damned, with the raucous sensibility of an underground comic. This from a man who has been criticized for being a professional 11-year-old and writing countless imitations of his younger self.

One of the things I have admired about Bradbury is his willingness to take risks, and be outrageous, rather than just settle back into being what is expected of him. Throughout his later works there are occasional stories like that, usually not fantastic, but about life itself, and a clear indication that Bradbury was not just coasting, and often very adult in texture and content, not quite what you expect from the writer we all read for the first time at about age 14. Go read "Long After Midnight," the title story in the collection of that name. This one is more middle-period Bradbury than late, first published as "The Long after Midnight Girl" in Ralph Ginsburg's cutting edge and banned magazine *Eros* in 1962. It will blow you away.

We do inevitably return, though, to that Golden Decade which makes Bradbury so special. I like to use "The Wind" (first published in *Weird Tales,* March 1943) in my writing classes (I teach for an adult-education night school) for its technical excellence, not just the spare precision of the prose but because this story, which is mostly in dialogue (told through phone conversations) handles point-of-view so well that you always know where you are in the story. It's also wonderfully atmospheric (almost a pun in the instance of a story about a man stalked by a sentient wind) with a nicely understated climax. It was published over sixty years ago and the only thing really dated in it is a reference to a ten-cent cigar.

Analysis cannot account for a miracle. Genius occurs within the head of the genius, where nobody else can see. But if we try define what the young Bradbury did right, which suddenly unlocked such an outpouring of wonderful stories, I think we can identify two areas in which he broke away from the pulp conventions of the time, which are still worth emulating.

First, he realized that much of the best writing occurs outside of "the field." This was particularly true in the late 1930s, when the teenaged Bradbury churned out reams and reams of reportedly awful fiction, and was modeling his work on what he read in *Thrilling Wonder Stories,*

Planet Stories, and *Astounding,* or maybe *Argosy* (which serialized Edgar Rice Burroughs' *The Synthetic Men of Mars* in 1939). He has since made the observation you may have to write a million words of junk before you write anything good, and seems to have personally put this to the test. But he also spent a summer reading, not pulp magazines, but Ernest Hemingway and Thomas Wolfe, and the result showed—quickly.

The other thing he did, even more important, I think, was reach into himself for honest emotions, rather than adhere to tried-and-true formulas, or—a common fault in science fiction, then and now—try to contrive clever gimmicks and twist-endings rather than tell honest, emotionally valid stories. He found something true within himself, and got it on paper, and the result hit the pulp field like a hurricane. Wow. However fantastic the dressings, here was something *real.*

And he became a part of our lives. I suspect virtually everyone reading this essay read some Bradbury when they were young. A lot of you may have been inspired to become writers because of Bradbury. This is a not uncommon admission among my colleagues. He wrote works—most of them between 1943 and 1953, but not entirely—which have survived, and remained vital and are likely to touch hearts and minds for decades, if not centuries to come.

That's why Bradbury won a Pulitzer. He really *is* special. I am unashamed to confess that the only time I was ever tongue-tied when meeting a writer, it was when meeting Ray Bradbury. Other writers are colleagues. They may be senior colleagues. They may be people whose works I admire and grew up reading. But Ray Bradbury is a *legend.* He is *Ray Bradbury.* Nothing more needs to be said, or can be.

WHY STANLEY G. WEINBAUM STILL MATTERS

It has often been remarked that if Shakespeare's career had only lasted as long as Christopher Marlowe's—about five years, seven plays and a few poems—no one would have paid much attention to him. The *Henry VI* plays? *Two Gentlemen of Verona*? Even a genius sometimes needs a little while to get up to speed.

Consider that Stanley G. Weinbaum revolutionized the science fiction field in fifteen months. That was all the time he had.

I shall digress. It is necessary to first lay down the principle that good writing is good writing and bad writing is bad writing, regardless of when they are done, and it is never correct to excuse bad writing on the grounds that it is old-fashioned or "standards were lower in those days." The first bit of context we have to keep in mind is that contemporaneously with any wretched "classic" of pulp SF you care to beat up on—let's say Hall and Flint's *The Blind Spot*, which seems pretty indefensible—there was very good writing going on somewhere. *The Blind Spot* appeared in *Argosy* in 1921. It is undeniably ghastly. But writers as diverse as James Branch Cabell, Ernest Hemingway, Lord Dunsany, and F. Scott Fitzgerald were all doing good work about then. So decent writing was to be had *somewhere*. It wasn't as if deft observation of human nature and the well-balanced sentence had to be re-invented.

Nevertheless it is true that Stanley Weinbaum's career (1934-1935) occurred during a time in which the standards of science fiction were *much* lower than they are today, and, frankly much lower than they had been a couple generations earlier. He appeared as a blinding flash of light in the midst of a literary dark age, which I have dubbed the Great Retarded Period. Gone were the days in which science fiction was published routinely in the best magazines and had to meet the standards of same, as when Fitz-James O"Brien's "The Diamond Lens" appeared in *The Atlantic* (1858) or H.G. Wells's *The War of the Worlds* was serialized in *Cosmopolitan* (1897). Somewhere in the early 1900s, under the stultifying influence of Henry James, who in a famous debate with H.G. Wells forcefully opined that the only "real literature" was the kind that he wrote, i.e. closely-detailed stories of real life set in the present, the mainstream became very uneasy about imaginative content. A certain amount of satire was okay, and Lord Dunsany's fantasies could still be published in *The Atlantic* because he was exotic, foreign, and respectably literary, rather like Borges in *The New* Yorker decades later, but most other imaginative writing was relegated either to the nursery or to the pulp magazines, and, as anybody who has examined pulp magazines from the beginning (the first real pulp being the October 1896 *Argosy*) knows, the pulps did not encourage polished and subtle literary masterpieces.

So the Great Retarded Period has its beginnings in the Munsey pulps in the early 20th century, where standards often plummeted to appalling depths, but things got worse when the first product actually marketed as *science fiction* was Hugo Gernsback's *Amazing Stories,* which began with the April 1926 issue. In orthodox fannish histories, this event is called "the birth of science fiction." The truth is a lot more complicated. Gernsback himself, the field's alleged "father," was a contradictory, even enigmatic figure. You can find a good portrait of him in Mike Ashley's portion of the Ashley/Robert A.W. Lowndes book *The Gernsback Days* (2004). Gernsback was a strange combination of visionary, entrepreneur, incompetent, and crook. He was the first person to see *some* use for what he originally called "scientifiction," as educational pro-science propaganda, and he figured out how to market it. Unfortunately, he simply was not a literary person at all, and seems to have been completely insensitive to what we would today call "literary value." He also did not believe in paying his writers except, all too often, under threat of lawsuit. (Ashley confirms that there was a New York lawyer named Ione Weber who specialized in Gernsback debts.) Probably the most important original story Gernsback published in *Amazing* was H.P. Lovecraft's "The Colour out of Space"—certainly it was the most sophisticated, and the only one to be found nowadays in a Library of America volume as canonical American Literature. How did Gernsback treat this major new contributor? He paid him, reluctantly, well after publication, a fifth of a cent a word, a rate so insulting that before long HPL and all his circle referred to Gernsback as "Hugo the Rat."

Unsurprisingly, the real *pros,* the top science fiction writers of the day, such as Ray Cummings, Murray Leinster, Ralph Milne Farley, and A. Merritt, may have been reprinted in Gernsback's various publications, but they did not write original stories for him. Who wanted a fifth of a cent on threat of lawsuit when *Argosy* paid one to two cents a word on acceptance, very reliably? This was the same Gernsback who reprinted many stories by H.G. Wells until he stiffed *Wells* once too often and lost him as a contributor.

The result was that the actual science fiction magazines, *Amazing* and *Wonder Stories* particularly, were a backwater *within science fiction.* Their contents were largely written by amateurs. With Gernsback's self-published gadget-catalogue disguised as a novel, *Ralph 124C41+* set up as an example of what "scientifiction" was supposed to be, the "literary" standards dropped as far as it was possible to go without printing utter gibberish. Most of the non-reprint content of the early *Amazing* was decidedly sub-pulp. The writers did not have—or need—the routine storytelling skills required by, say, a western or adventure story magazine. William Clayton, of Clayton magazines is reputed to have described the contents of *Amazing* as "unspeakables written by unmentionables" before he founded the first professional (i.e. pulp level) science fiction magazine, *Astounding Stories of Superscience*, in 1930.

To be fair, it must be admitted that Gernsback had one strength: he was genuinely interested in new ideas, much more so than the pro editors. *Astounding* in its first three years, edited by Harry Bates, tended toward formula bang-bang stories, the kind in which there is so much action that nothing happens. While some creative stuff did appear in *Argosy*, the editors there tended to favor the Burroughsian interplanetary romance, which was getting stale by the early 1930s. They weren't pushing for new ideas either.

The only other science fiction editor at the time was the very stodgy T. O'Conor Sloane at *Amazing* (which he had taken over after Gernsback lost control and switched to *Wonder*). While some science fiction appeared in *Weird Tales*, it had a different slant. Therefore, for a certain type of writer—the visionary science-hobbyists, not necessarily storytellers—Gernsback may have been the only game in town.

End of digression. Into this context came Stanley G. Weinbaum like a blinding flash of lightning out of a clear blue sky. His "A Martian Odyssey" appeared in *Wonder Stories* for July 1934. Instantly, readers knew that here was a writer who was different.

H.P. Lovecraft best articulated what was so special about this story and its author:

> I saw with pleasure that someone had at last escaped the sickening hackneyedness in which 99.99% of all pulp interplanetary stuff is engulfed. Here, I rejoiced, was somebody who could think of another planet in terms of something besides anthropomorphic kings and beautiful princesses and battles of space ships and ray-guns and attacks from the hairy sub-men of the "dark side" or "polar cap" region, etc. etc. Somehow he had the imagination to envisage wholly alien situations and psychologies and entities, to devise consistent events from

wholly alien motives and to refrain from the cheap dramatics in which almost all adventure-pulpists wallow. Now and then a touch of the *seemingly* trite would appear—but before long it would be obvious that the author had introduced it merely to satirize it. The light touch did not detract from the interest of the tales—and genuine suspense was secured without the catchpenny tricks of the majority. The tales of Mars, I think, were Weinbaum's best—those in which the curiously sympathetic being "Tweel" figure.[1]

If we go back and read "A Martian Odyssey" today and find it a little quaint, it is wrong to dismiss it, as it is to dismiss as hopelessly primitive a really well-made biplane you might see in the Smithsonian in an age of jetliners. You notice that the workmanship, with all those polished metal parts and taut wires, is actually very good and the design ingenious. Weinbaum, writing in the context he did, had to pretty much re-introduce everything: competent narrative, literate prose, and differentiated characterizations. During the Great Retarded Period of science fiction, nothing could be taken for granted.

If his jaunty style sometimes seems a little too glib and he uses too many said-bookisms, he is at least consistently readable, which cannot be said for many of his turgid contemporaries, and once you actually *read* "A Martian Odyssey" and its sequel, "The Valley of Dreams," you notice that Weinbaum doesn't just seem good because so much around him was so awful. He is genuinely good. He has science-fictional virtue almost to excess. He really *does*, as HPL noted, create an alien world in its own terms, where, for all the hero can establish a rudimentary communication with a Martian, Tweel, the creature's psychology remains an impenetrable mystery. We also encounter an apparently immortal silicon creature that spends millions of years building apparently useless pyramids out of its own excreta, and multi-limbed, barrel-shaped creatures of at least limited intelligence, which spend their entire lives gathering rubbish to feed grinding machines and every once in a while contributing one of themselves into the mix. There are also predatory plant-things which lure their prey to doom by projecting fantasies from out of the victim's mind. (Think how many other SF writers have made use of *that* concept.) The Martians, we are told, do not have sex or gender as we know it. On Mars, plant and animal life never differentiated. Pairs of Martians form a bud between them, which becomes a new individual. There is a suggestion that the unique psychology of the race stems from the physical conditions under which they evolved, that the dry, scarcity of Mars did

---

1   As quoted by Sam Moskowitz in the introduction to A Martian Odyssey and Other Science Fiction Tales, Hyperion Press, 1974; p. ix

not favor a dense population of aggressive creatures, as arose on Earth.

This was revolutionary stuff. Edgar Rice Burroughs's Martian princess, the "incomparable Dejah Thoris," is really just an ordinary girl if you overlook the fact that she lays eggs. But here was a writer suggesting that the way an alien thinks is not only utterly distinct from the way a man thinks, but rooted in the beginnings of a completely different evolutionary history.

There's also an almost Lovecraftian scene in "The Valley of Dreams," when the characters begin to explore a vast, ruined city and study the history of Mars (and the pre-history of Earth) as depicted in carvings on the walls. It's a creepy moment, which suggests Lovecraft's "At the Mountains of Madness," although influence is impossible in either direction, because the Lovecraft story was written in 1931 and not published until 1936. Just as a throw-away, Weinbaum suggests that his vaguely ostrich-like Martians must have visited the Earth in the ancient past and become the basis for the ibis-headed Egyptian god Thoth. (Again, think of what countless later writers have done with *that* notion.) His scientific speculations also scored one surprising bull's eye, when a character remarks that Mars has no "earthquakes." Now that NASA probes are actually crawling around on Mars, we have learned that the planet has no tectonic plates. Its crust is all one piece. No "earthquakes" indeed.[2]

It's also worth mentioning that Weinbaum, when he is not being brilliantly inventive or even borderline scary can be quite funny. Am I really the first critic to have noticed that the German member of the crew of the spaceship *Ares* is named Putz, and that Herr Putz is, well, a *putz*? If you think this is a coincidence, remember that Weinbaum was Jewish and writing shortly after Hitler had come to power. The Germany from which astronaut Putz hails is described as a dictatorship.

There are other funny and satirical bits, as Lovecraft noted. This tendency becomes more pronounced in later Weinbaum stories. It isn't too much of an exaggeration to say that he was the literary ancestor, not merely of Hal Clement, but of Douglas Adams.

The assistant editor of *Wonder Stories*, Charles Horning, who ran the magazine on a day-to-day basis, admitted that "A Martian Odyssey" had drawn more praise than any other story *Wonder* had ever published. How did Hugo Gernsback welcome and encourage his (or, actually, Hornig's) brilliant new discovery? The answer is quite shocking. It comes from the Ashley book. Hugo the Rat never paid Stanley Weinbaum a dime for any story Weinbaum published in *Wonder Stories*. Why there got to be a total of six stories is not clear. Possibly Weinbaum submitted them in close

---

2   For the absence of plate tectonics on Mars, see Mars: A Smithsonian Guide, by Thomas R. Watters (1995), p. 116 and following.

succession, still hoping to be paid, or he felt loyalty to *Wonder* despite everything, or the later stories were his rejects, which he just wanted published, regardless of whether he got paid for them or not.

The story of Hugo Gernsback, as told by Ashley, is a cautionary tale of a bright young visionary who came to America, the Land of Opportunity, to follow his dreams, then destroyed everything he touched by sheer, short-sighted greed. At the time when Gernsback paid Lovecraft that grudging fifth of a cent a word, he and his brother Sidney were drawing salaries of *one hundred thousand dollars a year*.[3] To grasp what this meant in modern spending-power, multiply that figure by twenty.

He paid Weinbaum *absolutely nothing,* presumably because Weinbaum, a newcomer to the field, did not know how to avail himself of the services of Ione Weber.

Unsurprisingly, Weinbaum, along with most of Gernsback's best writers, hightailed it out of *Wonder Stories* and into *Astounding Stories* as quickly as he could. While there might not be any plate tectonics on Mars, there was a tectonic shift of major proportions taking place within science fiction in precisely the year Weinbaum entered it, 1934.

Astounding Stories, the first professional-level SF magazine, had gone under with the collapse of the entire Clayton chain in early 1933. Fortunately it was sold to another, well-established pulp publisher, Street and Smith, and resumed publication late in the year. The new editor, F. Orlin Tremaine, was much more imaginative than Harry Bates. He emphasized "thought variant" science fiction. In other words, he was ready to complete with Gernsback on his own terms, for new ideas. He also demanded—and got—a higher level of writing than Gernsback did. The Street & Smith *Astounding* only paid one cent a word to Clayton's two, but it was still good money in an era when an office worker might earn $15 a week—if he had a job at all. Sell six thousand words a month and you could almost live on it.

This combination of reliable payment, new ideas, and better writing proved irresistible. *Astounding* had a spectacular year in 1934, publishing Jack Williamson's *The Legion of Space* and E.E. Smith's *The Skylark of Valeron,* and ending the year with the first installment of John Campbell's *The Mightiest Machine,* plus his classic story, "Twilight." By February 1935, *Astounding* had Weinbaum as a contributor. This was now clearly the dominant magazine in the field. Gernsback and T. O'Conor Sloane were blown away. Gernsback's *Wonder* had to sell out by early 1936. Sloane's *Amazing* limped on into 1938, but no one much cared.

While science fiction continued to appear in *Argosy* and occasionally

---

3   See Ashley, The Gernsback Days, Wildside Press, 2004, p. 131.

in other pulp magazines like *Blue Book* and *Top Notch*, something very important had happened with the transformation of *Astounding*. The SF in *Argosy* was becoming increasingly moribund—interplanetary swashbucklers, mad scientists threatening the world, more stories of future invasions of America as pre-World War II jitters began—and that in the other pulps tended to be quite conservative, aimed at readers unfamiliar with the form. For the first time, the real cutting-edge of science fiction was *in a science fiction magazine,* in the pressure-cooker environment of *Astounding*. Weinbaum was central to the scene, with more travelogue stories of other worlds, told in breezy prose. "Parasite Planet," "The Mad Moon," "The Lotus Eaters," and "The Planet of Doubt" were all very popular. His "The Red Peri" is more of a straight space-adventure, but it contained a scene of an unprotected character surviving for a short time in a vacuum which fascinated Arthur C. Clarke and is played out again in *2001: A Space Odyssey*. What was to become the Golden Age of *Astounding,* begun when John W. Campbell took over from Tremaine in late 1937, was right on the horizon. Weinbaum was poised to become one of *the* major figures of mid-20th century American science fiction, but for one thing.

He died of throat cancer December 14, 1935, at the age of 33.

* * * *

Weinbaum as a person doesn't come across very well from available sources. Colleagues who knew him liked him. He was college educated, trained as an engineer. He had read a lot of science fiction, both in the pulps, and the works of Mary Shelley, Conan Doyle, H.G. Wells, and others. He was clearly a smart fellow. In a brief autobiographical sketch (found in the Hyperion volume of his short fiction) he makes some very shrewd observations on the nature—and uses—of science fiction.

Like Lovecraft, Weinbaum was dissatisfied with most of the pulp science fiction he had read up to this point. He wrote:

> Here's the element that makes so much science fiction seem unreal. Half our authors use the word "scientist" about as the ancient Egyptians used "priest"—a man of special and rather mystical knowledge that has set him apart from the rest of humanity. In fact, as soon as the word is mentioned, one visualizes either a noble, serious, erudite, high-principled superman, or, depending on the type of story, a crafty, ambitious, fiendish, and probably insane super-villain. But never a real human being.[4]

He explains that science is "a road map, not a standard," and that ethical choices are made by people, not by science itself, which is neither

4   *A Martian Odyssey and Other Science Fiction Tales*, p. xxvii

a savior nor a destroyer, but a tool. Furthermore:

> ...because science fiction is not science...it is, or at least ought to be, a branch of the art of literature, and therefore can quite properly argue, reject, present a thesis, proselytize, criticize, or perform any other ethical functions.[5]

This was clearly a writer capable of ambitious, serious work. "If only he had lived," fans of the period lamented. Imagine what he would have done during the Golden Age! He was, as Isaac Asimov remarked, a Campbell-quality writer in the pre-Campbell era. I wonder what he might have been writing by the late 1940s, when *Astounding* was at its artistic zenith and publishing stories like C.L. Moore's "Vintage Season" and Theodore Sturgeon's "Thunder and Roses." What might have he been writing as the field entered a brilliance renaissance in the early 1950s? Imagine Stanley G. Weinbaum as a contributor to the early *Galaxy*. With a normal lifespan, he might well have remained active into the 1970s.

We are afforded some hints. Weinbaum may have found a perfect niche as a writer of funny-alien stories for *Astounding,* but he clearly had always aspired to write more than that. He had not quite sprung out of nowhere in 1934. Before "A Martian Odyssey" he had sold a romance novel to a syndicate under the pseudonym of "Marge Stanley." Sam Moskowitz describes it as "sophisticated." One suspects it was not. There was also early poetry, a libretto to an unproduced opera, *Omar the Tent Maker* (with music by his sister Helen), a rather bad novella finally published in 1950, "The Dark Other," and a serious, philosophical superman novel, *The New Adam*, which first appeared in 1939 and has had paperback editions since. This last is a bit turgid, but a substantial work, not pulp fiction at all.

With the funny alien stories, Weinbaum discovered a self-created formula which would sell. The SF pulps still wanted formula fiction. Even *Astounding* in the "thought variant" era wasn't going to let him stray very far. This he found out when he embarked on a novella, "Dawn of Flame," about an immortal woman of the future, with an emphasis on character and emotion. This, despite Weinbaum's celebrity, was rejected everywhere, for not being scientific enough. He tried again, rewriting it into a full-length novel, *The Black Flame*, the complicated history of which tells us and doubtless told Weinbaum some uncomfortable truths about the limitations of the science fiction field at the time.

The Black Flame should have been a pulp editor's dream. Not only was it by the hot writer of the moment, but it featured a man from the present who goes into the future via suspended animation, a revolt of the

---

5   *A Martian Odyssey and Other Science Fiction Tales*, p. xxviii

masses against a super-scientific elite, an immortal goddess/ruler rather like H. Rider Haggard's She Who Must Be Obeyed, super-weapons, an atomic bomb, and a love affair between the hero and the aforementioned immortal goddess, who in the end becomes a mortal woman.

If we go back to read *The Black Flame* today, particularly the complete version (first published by Tachyon in 1995) we discover that time has not been particularly kind to this novel. Sure, it's still entertaining and inventive, but the one way pulp science fiction (and much pulp fiction generally) tends to date more than any other is in its treatment of women, and, in particular, gender issues.

Weinbaum's fiction presents several super-women, the female space pirate in "The Red Peri," the super-evolved woman in "The Adaptive Ultimate," and, most especially, Black Margot of Urbs, the title character of *The Black Flame*. In all cases, the strong, assertive, powerful woman must be "tamed." She must give up what makes her special in order to regain (or retain) her "humanity." Black Margot, in the end, must renounce immortality in order to marry the hero, have children, and become a housewife. One imagines her working contentedly in the kitchen, with little flamelets tugging at her skirt.

Of course this perception is not unique to Weinbaum. Carl Jung called this character the "anima archetype" and he too cited Rider Haggard's *She* as an example. Such figures appeared in most of Haggard's enormously influential romances, and in the works of his imitators. They are to be found throughout the works of A. Merritt, and often in Edgar Rice Burroughs. (Think of La of Opar.) It all seems very quaint and politically incorrect today.

But in the science fiction magazines, during the Great Retarded Period, this was entirely too advanced, even downright threatening!

The Black Flame was rejected everywhere, even by Hugo the Rat's *Wonder Stories*. Charles Hornig's rejection must set some sort of record for sheer vacuousness. Moskowitz quotes him in the introduction to the Tachyon edition. Despite all the superscientific gadgets, Hornig complains that *The Black Flame* is primarily a love story, and "Love, to many of the young minds who read our mag, is a weakness in a man." Moskowitz notes that assistant editor Hornig was eighteen years old at the time he made this profound statement.

Let me suggest something subversive, or at least irreverent: if Weinbaum's idea of "love"—not a normal, mature relationship at all, but the conquest of a dominatrix by a he-man—seems immature by today's standards, but was too radical to be published at all in 1935, that is because the science fiction of the Great Retarded Period, particularly in the Gernsback magazines, was *pre-adolescent*. Sure, there had been science fiction or fantasy stories which sublimated teenaged sexual angst vividly before this one. One only need think of *A Princess of Mars* by Edgar Rice Burroughs. But as the field sank into Gernsbackian depths, even *that* level of sophistication was lost.

To be fair, *Astounding* didn't buy *The Black Flame* either, which seems an incomprehensible blunder, but the limitations of the "Thought Variant" era were showing.

John Taine, a writer of the period, once remarked that science fiction was one place where a beautiful girl could be "a damned nuisance." There was a strong feeling that "sex"—which usually meant considerations of gender relations, not pornography—had no place in the field. Weinbaum's fascinating alien creatures, the readers welcomed. But the idea that a character could be *driven by emotions* and possibly even motivated by sexual desire was entirely too frightening. At least that was Hornig's perception.

Yet *The Black Flame* is not an adult science fiction novel. It is a decidedly adolescent one. What Weinbaum was doing was pushing the magazine field out of the short-pants era, and *into adolescence.* There was, indeed, nothing in *The Black Flame* which was not routine in the pulps ten to fifteen years later. Then Philip José Farmer really blew everybody away with "The Lovers" in 1952, and adulthood loomed. But in the mid-1930s, *The Black Flame* was heavy stuff. If science fiction was ever to achieve maturity, it first had to move up to an adolescent level, as a necessary part of its development, even if over-cautious editors thought that their readers would find "love a weakness in a man."

As it turned out, the editors were wrong. Weinbaum's sudden death caused a flurry of memorial activity, the first time this had ever happened within the SF field. *Dawn of Flame and Other Stories*, published by a couple of fans in 1936 in an edition of 250 copies, was the first science fiction memorial volume. The demand increased for every last scrap of unpublished Weinbaum. "Dawn of Flame" was reprinted in *Thrilling Wonder Stories* for June 1939 and proved popular. Meanwhile, *The Black Flame* was used as the lead novel to launch a new magazine, *Startling Stories,* in January 1939. Editor Mort Weisinger rewrote the text considerably, shortening the first half to speed up the pacing, since otherwise we do not even meet the title character until about halfway through the novel; and also, incongruously, larding the first few chapters with a future slang that disappears later on. Even in this form, the novel was a huge success and came to be regarded as a classic. Maybe the SF fans didn't regard love as "a weakness in a man" after all. Weinbaum, like Philip José Farmer in 1952, had successfully expanded the range of what was allowable in science fiction. It was now possible to talk about emotions, and to consider character motivations in something that was beginning to approach the way human beings really act.

* * * *

If *The Black Flame* seems a trifle immature—consider: it is almost apprentice work. This was a writer whose entire career lasted fifteen months! In that short period he managed to revolutionize science fiction's notion of the Alien, and he left a legacy which three years after his death seriously pushed the envelope of the whole field. He wasn't one of those slow-developing types like, say, Shakespeare or Mark Twain, who took years to have any impact.

Think of what he could have done if he had lived!

BLOBFEST!

I touched the original Blob! It didn't even crawl up my hand or try to devour me. It must have been sleeping, lying contently in its 5-gallon drum where it has been residing (so its current custodian told me) peacefully since 1965.

I mean THE Blob, the title character and star of the 1958 cult film of the same title. *That* one. It wasn't like shaking hands with an old-time movie-star, because this particular star didn't have any hands. Touching it is not normally encouraged, but since I was a purported Gentleman of the Press (some people are easily fooled), present in my professional capacity, I was allowed. It was a bit rubbery under my fingertip, room-temperature and vaguely yielding. I did not press hard. No sense pushing my luck.

* * * *

But I am getting ahead of myself. What I am talking about is the 8th annual Blobfest, held in scenic Phoenixville Pennsylvania, at the Colonial Theatre, where a very famous scene from *The Blob* was filmed.

To fill in the background further, Phoenixville is a quiet little town about an hour and a half west of Philadelphia, four miles beyond Valley Forge. It is one of those old industrial towns along the Schuylkill River since turned to other purposes, unremarkable enough that for all I had been going to its outskirts for the past thirty years to visit a used-book store, I had never actually been into the town center until it occurred to me that Blobfest might be a suitably illuminating subject for one of these columns and an excuse to freeload a press-pass.

The Blob (shot in 1957, released in 1958, directed by Irvin S. Yeaworth Jr.) is the ultimate 1950's science fiction B-movie, about an oozing, gooey Thing that bursts out of a meteorite, oozes over the hand, then the forearm, then the whole body of a foolishly curious Earthling who first pokes it with a stick, and subsequently grows bigger and bigger and Can't Be Stopped until, at last, it is. But before that a bunch of hot-rodding, small-town teenagers led by Steven (later Steve) McQueen in his first starring role try to convince the authorities of the (literally) growing danger. But nobody listens to them because they're teenagers, and so the film gains a purported sociological significance (not to mention audience pandering) when, for once, the sort of wild, car-crazy kids who, in those dim days usually ended their high-speed adventures wrapped around telephone poles or otherwise messily demised in cautionary novels by Henry Gregor Felsen, are *right* and save the world. Or at least they make a significant contribution, as do the obnoxious cop everybody teases (who thinks the kids are jealous of his war record; but he proves an able marksman when one is needed), the high school principal (who defies decorum by actually *breaking* the school door open with a rock), and, last but not least (this being a 1950s monster movie), the U.S. military. When it is discovered that the Blob is repelled by cold and can be brought to bay with the aid of large quantities of CO_2-type fire-extinguishers (which is what they were breaking into the highschool to get), the military then transports the now inert Blob to the Arctic. It can't actually be killed you see, but, as McQueen portentously intones in the final line of dialogue, as long as the Arctic stays cold, it should stay put.

Can *you* say "global warming"? Isn't that an obvious opening for a sequel or another remake? (This film was remade once already, rather well, in 1988.) Once again, if we want to take it more seriously than it will really bear, *The Blob* assumes a whole new degree of relevance, as if the original allegory of how US society can pull together and overcome generational differences in a crisis were not enough.

More than that, *The Blob*, after all these years, is still cheesy fun. Not great cinema, but it moves well. Things happen fast enough that, while you're watching at least, you don't really care that this isn't *Citizen Kane*. Admittedly, if you look at it now, you realize that McQueen was the only actor in the cast who was obviously going somewhere. The others are routine B-movie character players. Most of the "teenagers" look to be about thirty. The role of the Blob itself is played by what I encountered in that five-gallon bucket—a large mass of silicone, acquired by the producer from Union Carbide, and dyed bright red. (This was one of the first *color* 1950s monster movies. The red made a difference.) The present owner of the prop (the eminent Blobologist, Wes Shank) bought it from the producer about 1965, and has been its keeper ever since. A chemist assured him that it is likely to retain its *blobbishness* for years to come, and so there it...sleeps.

Of course, as we all know, Hollywood seldom comes up with a new idea. There have been numerous blob and giant amoeba stories published in *Weird Tales* over the years, ranging from Anthony M. Rud's "Ooze," the cover story on our very first issue of March 1923, to Joseph Payne Brennan's celebrated "Slime," which inspired the Virgil Finlay cover that graced our March 1953 issue. But we must admit that *The Blob* rang in new changes on its amorphous theme by giving the story a distinctly late-1950's context. This may be one reason why the movie itself seems as unstoppable as its subject matter, fifty years later.

The reason it is celebrated in Phoenixville is that one of the most memorable scenes in the film takes place right in the Colonial Theater. After the teenagers have been scoffed at, ignored, and told to go home by the authorities, the Blob, which has now devoured several more hapless townspeople, comes oozing *right through the projection booth into the theater*—which must have been a wonderful novelty at the time, the cinematic equivalent of breaking the "fourth wall" of live-theater, involving the audience directly in the story, or at least pretending to. Of course, back in 1958, nothing actually came oozing out of that projection booth, in the Colonial Theater or elsewhere. It remained for schlockmeister William Castle to *really* involve the audience by such gimmicks as wiring the seats to give a mild electrical shock in *The Tingler* (1959).

In any case, it was great fun to watch the movie from the balcony, *right below that very projection booth.* I looked behind myself a couple times during the famous scene. No gelatinous monsters, but the little windows are configured exactly the same way they appear in the film, and the paint scoured from the walls might well be a sign of Blob-damage.

The other famous scene in the theater comes immediately thereafter, the "run-out," in which patrons stream screaming into the street. Nowadays, for Blobfest, this is lovingly re-enacted, with the help of the local police who close off the street, and a couple Blobfest staffers directing human traffic with glowing batons to avoid a pileup. I got to participate in this Friday night event. I had been in the balcony. It was announced that the lower theater was full, but it didn't look full, so I went downstairs, slipped in through a side door, and found that there was indeed room for one more. I may even have gotten on local TV for my trouble, because as soon as I emerged out onto the street I was face-to-face with a TV cameraman. Maybe as "press" I wasn't supposed to participate, but how else was I to report on the complete Blobfest experience?

Other activities Friday night included a screaming contest (won by a girl about five or six—the cute kid will get it every time), a tin-foil hat competition (some very elaborate creations, to prevent aliens from beaming mind-control rays into your noggin) and the showing of two award-winning amateur "blob" films. One looked to me like a typical high school effort, but the other was quite clever, a period "commercial" for Blob Jelly, which cheerfully assures us, "There's no trouble spreading it" on bread or anything else. There was also a Fire Extinguisher parade, in commemoration of how the Blob was brought to a halt before it could devour Steve McQueen and his co-stars in the nearby Downingtown Diner at the film's climax.

Saturday morning, Blobfest turned into a street fair, announced by a big banner as you drove into town. Several blocks of the town's main street were closed off. There was a large, inflatable Blob over the marquee of the Colonial Theater. Below that, you could pose with a cutout of the Blob. Rock bands played. Ghoulish goodies of all sorts were for sale, including such oddities as Turkish Dracula films. Inside the theater, there was a panel discussion featuring some of the people involved in the original film, including producer Jack H. Harris and co-scripter Kate Phillips (Kay Linaker), both of whom are now 94 and surely did not imagine that fifty years later they would be back in the same theater celebrating *The Blob*, with or without the presence of the Blob itself in a bucket upstairs. Another panelist was Howard Fishlove, a crew member on the original film, and an easy to spot extra in the famous "run-out." (The big guy in the white T-shirt.) Also present was the woman who (quite accidentally) tripped during the "run-out" scene. Fifty-years later she was presented with the Golden Crutch Award. There were also the inevitable lines for autographs. You could buy Blobfest T-shirts, posters, and pens. I even wandered into the projection booth whence the Blob oozed in the film. Also in attendance were a local scary storytelling troupe, the Patient Creatures. When I encountered a nearly 8-foot-tall Grim Reaper in the balcony, in the dark, I was able to say, "Ah, nice to see a familiar face." (We *Weird Tales* folks have connections, you know.) There were also characters from a local children's TV show called *Ghoul A-Go-Go*. I am not familiar with the show, but they had an impressively hulking hunchback. One other film was shown, *Angry Red Planet*, presumably because it has a (Martian) blob in it, but this is a film that is *so* low-budget that, next to it, the 1958 *Blob* looks as elaborate as the Peter Jackson *King Kong*. (They couldn't even afford matte-paintings. Mars seems to consist of black-and-white drawings.)

What is notable about all this is that Blobfest isn't just a gathering of film-buffs. It's a genuine community event. Most of the people there were way too young to have seen the film when it was first released, and *they* brought their children. There were whole families in Blob-centric costumes, particularly head-gear. The grandchildren or even great-grandchildren of the original *Blob* audience were being turned on to that throbbing red ooze. But for a couple of Phoenixville denizens I passed pitching pennies in a back alley on my way from where I'd parked my car, the whole town seemed to have turned out. It was a big deal. Maybe, you might say, that's the only thing this town has to celebrate, but that can't be the whole story. The film *Taps* was made in and around my (nearby) home town of Wayne, Pennsylvania and nobody much cared, save to be glad when the helicopters stopped flying low overhead at all hours. Certainly there were no commemorative street fairs. But as producer Jack Harris said on the panel, when someone asked him in 1957 why he was wasting his time on this junk, he replied, "This movie will outlast us all." Mr. Harris is still with us, but, undeniably, *The Blob* has lasted.

Why? We can only guess. Maybe we look back on it nostalgically, as typifying a more innocent time when it was still possible to believe that alienated youth, parents, teachers, police, and the military *could* join together to defeat a sticky menace from outer space. There is, admittedly, an appealing idealism there.

Maybe it's just an excuse to be silly and wear funny hats.

Or maybe it's because *not enough* people are wearing tinfoil hats and the alien mind-rays have taken control.

You'll never know…

EXCAVATING OURSELVES: A SHORT HISTORY OF ARCHEOLOGY-OF-THE-PRESENT BOOKS

I suppose the notion began around 1800, and specifically with Egyptology. That was the period in which, during Napoleon's sudden and uninvited visit to Egypt, the Rosetta Stone was discovered, and Europeans soon saw prints in books and magazines (particularly in French) of archeologists crawling over the broken and fallen colossi of a vanished civilization as they struggled to decipher mysterious inscriptions and puzzled over the purpose of many of the objects they found. It is the imagery of Shelley's "Ozymandias."

The notion, of course, is that one day in the far future such archeologists will be examining the ruins of *our* civilization, digging in the remains of New York or London and developing curiously faulty conceptions of what our epoch was like in all its grandeur.

Moralists are naturally drawn to this idea, as an illustration of the Biblical warning that all things of mankind are vanity and shall pass away. There is also the suggestion that maybe the past is less certain than we like to think, and much of what the archeologists tell us about remote eras is more the product of imagination than evidence, particularly in the standard default that explains anything you don't understand as "for religious purposes." (A quick aside on that: I read somewhere about a live-in history project in which people tried to recreate the lifestyle of prehistoric Britain. It was known that all the houses had a shallow pit of no apparent utility under the eaves by the front door. This was assumed to be of religious significance until the live-in experimenters discovered it was a handy place to keep the chickens out of the rain.)

Of course post-holocaust or post-civilization stories became commonplace. There's Mary Shelley's *The Last* Man (1826), not to mention Richard Jeffries's little-read but quite influential *After London* (1887), and even William Morris's utopian *News from Nowhere* (1890). The post-holocaust, complete with somber reflections on the ruins of (usually) New York became a standard pulp trope, with George Allan England's *Darkness and Dawn* (1914) being a notable early example from the Munsey magazines.

But none of these quite tell us what the archeologists *found.* This is the subject under discussion. It hearkens back to "Ozymandias" and those French Egyptologists. The earliest example I know of is J.A. Mitchell's *The Last American,* first published by the Frederick A. Stokes Company in 1889 and reissued, with revisions, in a deluxe illustrated edition in 1902, with color pictures by F.W. Read and designs by Arthur Blashfield. You can find the 1889 text reprinted as an example of "primitive" SF in August Derleth's *Far Boundaries* (1951), but the deluxe 1902 edition is the one you want. Now something of a crumbling, ancient artifact itself, the book more often than not turns up in rather poor condition, because the heavy, glossy paper used for the illustrated plates and pages tends to pull the binding apart. (I will mention to my fellow biblio-archeologists that I have been able to successfully repair one with the patient use of Sobo, a flexible, acid-free glue you can get in fabric shops.)

You want the illustrations because they are sometimes more effective than the text. There is a wonderful drawing facing page 88 of "A Street Scene in Ancient Nhu-Yok. We see a woman in a ballerina costume perched on tiptoe on the back of a galloping horse, a bearded, robed man with a halo carrying an umbrella, a man in a tuxedo wearing a feathered headdress, a classic Thanksgiving Pilgrim complete with musket, a naked Baby New Year in top hat, etc. The caption reassures us: "The costumes and manner of riding are taken from metal plates now in the museum at Tehran."

Why Tehran? It seems that in the year (old style) 2951, a Persian expedition has rediscovered North America. The Persians themselves have just come out of a long dark age, and are at a medieval level. But these are not "real" Persians. They are satirical figures, with funny names like Hedful and Nofuhl. Their vessel, which looks like a medieval cog, is the Zhotuhb ("Slow Tub") which took over a month to cross the Atlantic, guided by the steady hand of the excellent mariner Grip-Til-Lah. The head of the expedition and narrator of the story is a Persian admiral, Khan-Li, Prince of Dimph-Yoo-Chur. You get the idea.

The Persians land first in New York. They find the climate unbearably hot, except during one sudden and unequally unbearable cold-snap. This sort of rapid climate change, we are told, ultimately extinguished all human life on the continent, although the ancient Mehrikans had become decadent well before then. Some of their history is known. The Republic was founded by George-wash-yn-tun. The Protestant population was massacred in 1927, whereupon the Murfy Dynasty ruled until 1940. (The text in the Derleth anthology gives these dates as 1907 and 1930.) In any case, the explorers find a coin depicting Dennis, the last of the Hy-

Burnyan dictators dated 1957. By about 1990 the population was extinct. Of the character of the ancient Mehrikans we are told:

> Historians are astounded that a nation of an hundred million beings should vanish from the earth like mist and leave so little behind. But to those familiar with their lives and character, surprise is impossible. There was nothing to leave. The Mehrikans possessed neither literature, art, nor music of their own. Everything was borrowed. The very clothes they wore were copied with ludicrous precision from the models of other nations. They were a sharp, restless, quick-witted, greedy race, given body and soul to the gathering of riches. Their chiefest passion was to buy and sell. Even women, both of high and low degree, spent much of their time at bargains, crowding and jostling each other in vast marts of trade, for their attire was complicated, and demanded most of their time.
>
> (pp. 28-31)

The Persians have prejudices of their own, as they note with disapproval about ancient Mehrikan women:

> They strode public streets with roving eyes and unblushing faces, holding free converse with men as with women, bold of speech and free of manner, coming and going as it pleased them best. They knew much of the world, managed their own affairs, and devised their own marriages, often changing their minds and marrying another than the betrothed.... Brought up like boys, with the same studies and mental development, the womanly part of their nature gradually vanished as their minds expanded. Vigor of intellect was the object of a woman's education."
>
> (p. 43-44)

But, greedy and vain though they may have been, the Mehrikans also had a heroic side, at least when it involved defending their interests. Eventually the powers of Europe sent a vast fleet against them, but the Mehrikans sank it in an astonishing upset of a battle which would of course recall to Mitchell's readers Admiral Dewey's victory over the Spanish at Manila Bay during the Spanish-American War. (Indeed, the defeat of the Pan-European fleet is attributed by a Spanish admiral, Offulbad-shoota, to the work of the Devil.)

There are comic adventures, as one member of the crew encounters a nest of wasps inside the Statue of Liberty and another is chased out of the Fifth Avenue Hotel by a bear. There is one ghostly moment when a crewman dreams or has a vision of ancient figures at a formal party inside one of the hotels, and is offered a drink, and is apparently left drunk from the powerful liquor. At another point the expedition finds the beautiful, perfectly preserved corpse of a woman in a sealed, luxurious apartment.

The Persians marvel over the lost technology of the Mehrikans. They cannot fathom to purpose of the "monuments" in the river, which the reader discerns are the remains of suspension bridges. They find a cigar-store Indian and assume it is an image of a god.

Then they venture south to ancient Washington, DC and actually meet living Americans, the last three survivors of this otherwise lost race: an old man, a young man, and a beautiful maiden. Alas, after the Mehrikan has offered his Persian guests some more of that liquor the Persians clearly cannot handle, one of the Persians gets fresh with the maiden, a brawl ensues, and several Persians and all of the Mehrikans are killed, the younger man having proven quite a remarkable fighter despite his savage state and apparent physical degeneration, expiring under a statue of George-wash-yn-tun, which, at least in the dim light, seems to nod. Admiral Khan-Li can only order his men to collect more artifacts of scientific interest, and then depart. The skull of the last American is presented to the museum in Tehran.

This book was, by all indications, widely read in its time. Of course its time has passed, and we have a different perspective on it, even as the Persians do on the Mehrikans. We might find a hint of racism in its fears of an Irish takeover, and we are more approving of those intellectual, free-strolling women. But beneath the broad satire there is a sense of melancholy. Through both texts and pictures, we are given a vivid glimpse of our own civilization in ruins, picked over by scholars of the far future. Certainly Stephen Vincent Benet read *The Last American,* as he clearly replays parts of it in his story "By the Waters of Babylon" (1936), which at least used to be one of the classics of science fiction, for all it is less-known these days. There is even a scene in which Benet's post-holocaust savage, investigating the ruins of New York, finds a perfectly preserved corpse of an ancient "god" in a sealed, luxury apartment.

Next on the strictly archeological agenda is *The Weans* (1960) by Robert Nathan, the author of *Portrait of Jennie.* This had been published in a shorter form in *Harper's Magazine* in 1956 as "Digging the Weans," and was even adapted very effectively on a record by the folksinger-actor Theodore Bikel. The full-length, book version is very much "non-fiction," deliberately fusty, as if written by somewhat befuddled scholars of the far future. (Amusingly, Nathan himself posed for some of the photos of an elderly savant on the dig, in pith-helmet.)

This time the inquisitive explorers have come from Africa, from the civilized nations of Kenya and Uganda. The Great West or Salt Continent is completely uninhabited, we are told, but recently expeditions there have discovered traces of a lost people, who are known to scholarship as "Weans" because they called their land Us. In the southern part of the continent the term may have been "Weuns" or "Wealls."

Very little is known of this lost people, although modern science has determined a few basics:

> No Wean skeletons have survived, although a team of anthropologists...did discover several lumps of calcium in n.Yok which might possibly have been arthritic deposits. Nevertheless, the contemptuous claims by early Volgarian scholars that the Weans were, in effect, subhuman can now, in the light of recent findings, be summarily dismissed.
> (p. 13)

The Weans dwelt in great cities, one of which, possibly the capital, was called "Pound Laundry" (or possibly "Washing-Ton" although what, if anything, was ever washed there is unknown). Scholars are left to puzzle over such mysterious artifacts as an I LIKE IKE button and a relief showing beatnik trumpeters. The theory that these ancient people were related to the Brythons is based on the observation that the Brythonic glyph "bathe" and the Wean "bath" are quite similar, but this "necessarily comes to grief when one examines the glyph for 'that which rises'—the Brythonic 'lift' and the Wean 'elevator' having obviously no common root." (p. 14)

There is a lot less narrative here than in the J.A. Mitchell book, but the satire is sharp. Regarding the religion of the ancient Weans, which may have involved a divinity named Hedda or Lolly or Hatta, we are told:

> Nonetheless, the Wean Divinity, in whatever form, remained a Wean, and spoke the Wean language.
>
> Surrounded by infinite space, by endless galaxies, by stars and planets without number, these proud, simple-minded, and obstinate people continued to believe themselves the center of the universe and the particular concern of the Almighty.
> (p.22)

Nathan's Africans, like Mitchell's Persians, have their own prejudices. There is a footnote appended to the above which reads:

> "God is a Zulu."—Eretebbe.

As in *The Last American*, there is much criticism over the role of women in ancient Wean society. "Marriage," we are told, was a relationship usually of short duration and advantageous to women, since fragmentary writings relating to divorce "There is no evidence of the male Wean ever receiving anything in settlement." (p. 37). That the wife got to keep the "jaguar" suggests, a footnote tells us, some link to ancient Aztec or Mayan civilization.

Wean literature, such as it survives, is wholly incomprehensible:

> One of these scrolls appears to be an account of a god or hero named Finigan, or Finnegan; the size of the scroll and its rare state of preservation attest to its importance as a religious or historical document, but it is impossible to make out what happens to him. The second scroll is in what appears to be a metrical, or verse form known as a dylan: nothing can be gathered from it at all.
>
> (pp. 41-42)

Of course 21st century scholars may puzzle a bit over Nathan's text, though they are likely to conclude that 1960 is a little early for a reference to Bob Dylan, so this verse form alluded to must be that of Dylan Thomas. Likewise readers beyond a certain age may not fully understand the reference to the "hofa" ("a kind of boss") who "having triumphed over those who [did] oppose him, did bring together in union all that moved." (P. 29)

Even as *The Last American* is a product of the Gilded Age, revised to include allusions to the Spanish-American War, *The Weans* is a product of the 1950s, and the Cold War, reflecting the anxieties of its time. It is known that the Weans were opposed by a nation known as More We (or possibly "More Us" or "Usser"), there is also the possibility, based on some very abstract insect-like sculpture unearthed (and photographed; credit is given in the back of the book to Jean Paul Mauran), that they also fought wars against a totally vanished insect civilization. In any case, the Weans were probably destroyed in war. Nathan's final paragraph still resonates:

> But as to the history of these almost unknown ancestors of ours, no more is known than is known of the Romans and, later, the Brythons: they established themselves in the land by killing off the native tribes already there, and built their empire by the sword; when the sword rusted, they perished.
>
> (p. 55)

I think we're due for another such "archeology" book soon, one in which the bewildered futurians unearth everything from goth jewelry to relics of the computer age. What *would* relics of the computer age be like, after our electronic data devices are all scrap and dust? Would someone theorize that the remains of smart phones indicate the very purpose for which humans evolved opposable thumbs, or would they dismiss these artifacts as incomprehensible "religious objects"?

Meanwhile, the most recent example I can presently find is *The Motel of the Mysteries* by David Macaulay (1979). This is more of a picture-book than the other two, but it has much in common with both Mitchell's and Nathan's imaginings. In the year 4022, an amateur archeologist, Howard Carson, falls down a shaft and discovers a lost "tomb" on the uninhabited North American Continent. This time we know exactly what happened to the lost civilization. In 1985 an accidental reduction in the 3rd class postage rates caused a fatal deluge of junk mail, under which the entire civilization smothered. Since then, scholars can only chip their way through layers of *pollutantus literati* and *pollutantus gravitas* in hope of finding relics of this lost people.

Carson's find is extraordinary, an entire "motel" complex, in which there is one still intact, sealed chamber, which enables scientists to learn much about the mysterious burial rituals of the ancient Americans.

Macaulay puts all his emphasis on the element of archeological misinterpretation. The satirical parallels to King Tut are obvious. Howard Carson (i.e. Carter) even utters the famous phrase "wonderful things" to describe what he sees when the DO NOT DISTURB sign is removed from the ancient motel room doorknob and the door-chain is cut.

Within the "tomb" are two skeletons, one on the bed, the other in the bathtub, but of course Carson does not see it that way. There follows much learned exposition with excellent drawings (apparently by Macaulay) on every other page describing the alleged burial rites. The television is the "great altar." The toilet is the "sacred urn" into which, we are told, the chief priest would chant while mixing water from the sacred well with sheets of Sacred Parchment (toilet paper). The corpse in the "sarcophagus" (tub) wears a miraculously preserved "ceremonial burial cap" (shower cap). Plumbing fixtures are interpreted as musical instruments. And so on. At the back of the book there is even a catalogue of reproductions of these artifacts that you can get in the museum shop. Then there is a note that due to the sudden death of Howard Carson and some others and rumors of a curse on this "tomb," the site was resealed in 4046.

The Motel of the Mysteries is probably the least serious of these three "archeological" texts, basically an elaborate joke about how antiquities can be misinterpreted. It has considerably less social satire than offered by either Mitchell or Nathan, and makes less of an attempt to imagine what sort of future society would be making this discovery. If it has any other concern, it is not about the Irish taking over or the Cold War, but about the environment. We may not perish under a deluge of *pollutantus literati,* but we could still pollute ourselves into oblivion. This is as much an anxiety of our time (or the 1970s) as Mitchell's were of his.

Macaulay's book does deliver the same message as the other two, that the past is spied dimly through a murky glass, and our civilization, too, shall one day pass away. That is what all of these books have to tell us, that one day future archeologists *will* be poking among our ruins like those 19th century French Egyptologists among the Pyramids. Can we reasonably expect to be understood by the future, much less to justify ourselves to it?

WORKS CONSULTED:

Benet, Stephen Vincent. "By the Waters of Babylon." In *Thirteen O'Clock, Stories of Several Worlds.* New York: Farrar and Rinehart, 1937.

Derleth, August (ed.). *Far Boundaries.* New York: Pellegrini and Cudahy, 1951. (Contains the 1889 text of *The Last American.*)

Macaulay, David. *The Motel of the Mysteries.* Boston: The Houghton Mifflin Company, 1979.

Mitchell, J.A. *The Last American.* New York: The Frederick A. Stokes Company, 1902.

Nathan, Robert. *The Weans.* New York: Alfred A. Knopf, 1960.

THE WHOLE WIDE LOVECRAFT: AN HPL BIOPIC?

First of all, let me recommend that you rush at all possible speed to your local video store and rent Dan Ireland's *The Whole Wide World*, which is an absolutely splendid movie about the tragic romance of Robert E. Howard and Novalyne Price, starring Vincent D'Onofrio as Howard and Reneé Zellweger as Price, with a beautifully low-key screenplay by Michel Scott Myers, based on Ms. Price's memoir, *One Who Walked Alone*. You have to rent it because this picture lasted in the theaters about a day and it doesn't seem to show up on TV. I was even willing to take time out from the World Science Fiction Convention in Baltimore in 1998 to see it there, but, alas, the showing was apparently cancelled because of technical difficulties. So, while I have been aware of this film for two years, it's taken me that long to track it down and I am here to report old news.

The Whole Wide World is lovingly, touchingly done. It creates such a convincing image of REH in the mind that it may be a while before you can read Howard's prose without hearing D'Onofrio SHOUTING AT THE TOP OF HIS LUNGS in a Texas accent. Odd, I'd never really head that accent in Howard's writing before. Now it's inescapable.

But I digress. That *The Whole Wide World* was made at all must be accounted a small miracle. Consider that REH isn't exactly lionized in the general literary world. Conan is better known from comic books and Schwarzenegger movies than from Howard's own writings. Why Howard's personal life would be a suitable subject for a mainstream movie, and how and to what audience such a film should be pitched must have puzzled quite a lot of people in the movie distribution business. It must only be by the devotion of a handful of people who wouldn't give up that the film got made or distributed at all.

(If you want to read more about it, there's a very good piece about it in James Van Hise's *The Fantastic Worlds of Robert E. Howard*, a book I otherwise have some real problems with; but the material about the film, including interviews with the principals, is excellently done.)

We Lovecraftians are inevitably wondering: can lightning strike twice? Do miracles repeat themselves? Might someone someday do such a movie about "our" guy?

It's certainly possible. It would be, like *The Whole Wide World,* a small film, made by someone with both the talent to bring it off and sufficient devotion to the subject that he'd be willing to risk (probably) his own money. Lovecraft may stand a little higher than Howard in the literary world, if that can be measured by the number of critical books about him coming out of university presses, but he has the same problem as Howard: unknown to the general public and known even to much of the "fan" audience through distorted, trashy movies that run mostly downhill from *Reanimator* and do not appeal to the sort of folk who would want to see a movie about the romance of HPL and Sonia.

What?

Honest, I'm not just trying to rip off Michael Scott Myers, but I think he's shown us the way.

What is this movie about?

"It's about Lovecraft struggling to be a writer and get his stories published," says my friend and colleague, the illustrious Lee Weinstein.

"That's not enough," I reply. "What are you going to show? A guy sitting at a typewriter? It needs focus."

What is this film *about?* It's too general to say it's about HPL's life, too abstract to say it's about his career or his developing cosmicism. A movie has to focus on people in a way that will touch the audience's emotions, even, in the case of "based on a true story" flicks, the emotions of people who have never heard of the characters before. It has to have some kind of shape and form and rise to a climax at the proper place, while making a few interesting detours along the way, so that, by the time we're at least half an hour into the film, it's at least somewhat a different story from the one we thought we were going to get, and it changes its stripes again half an hour after *that*, before it comes to its gradually inevitable conclusion.

I think there would be very sound reasons—not just ripping off Myers—for a biographical picture about HPL to be told from the point of view of Sonia, based on her memoir, "Lovecraft as I Knew Him" (1949), with of course material drawn additionally (selectively, lest we get lost in detail) from the veritable mountain range of memoirs and reminiscences available, not to mention HPL's own letters.

A movie like this is going to need a lot of voice-over, in effect first-person narration. One of the things that I've learned about writing fiction for so long is that, no matter how much you like the first person or are good at it, the Remarkable Person Story—one in which the whole point of telling it is to express how extraordinary the subject person is—rarely works *in* the first-person voice of that extraordinary person. It makes him sound, if nothing else, egotistical. It also bogs down the narrative, as first person narrators writing about themselves tend to expostulate, rationalize, feel sorry for themselves, or otherwise fail to get on with the story.

This is why Conan Doyle shows us (with only a couple of pretty unsuccessful exceptions) Sherlock Holmes through the eyes and voice of Dr. Watson. Thus we are able to see the Extraordinary Person from the *outside* and still maintain the strengths and intimacy of first-person narration, and we gain plausibility (and a little humility) as the admiring narrator's purpose becomes to tell us why this person is so special.

The remarkable person I met and the remarkable things we did together and how it changed the both of us is such a basic story template that it will never go away. It has the added advantage that we may delve into the mystery of why so-and-so is so extraordinary, but the answer remains, as it does with Sherlock Holmes (or it would with Lovecraft) just a little bit incomplete. A resonance remains behind, which is always good. It also allows for a little bit of fakery on the part of the writer—to imply more than can actually be delivered. Doyle wasn't such a genius that he could actually present the mind of Sherlock Holmes. He could only hint, show a few glimpses, and imply a lot more. In other words, we cannot really imagine ourselves to *be* Sherlock Holmes (or, for that matter, Lovecraft), but we can imagine ourselves to have known him. That isn't *too* presumptuous.

Such, then, is the purpose of the secondary viewpoint character or secondary narrator.

Our secondary narrator would be Sonia, who I gather was (a bit like Novalyne Price) a headstrong, intelligent woman of some literary aspirations but not a lot of story-telling talent, who could never share HPL's total immersion in literary (or cosmic) matters but could appreciate them just enough to want more than she had and be attracted to a man who was, in her eyes, a literary master.

How does the story focus?

It focuses on the period of HPL and Sonia's acquaintance through amateur journalism, their courtship, marriage, and break-up, which is pretty much congruent with HPL's New York period. There would be a lot of bit parts and cameos in the party scenes and assorted gabfests (Kalem Club meetings, walking tours in the middle of the night), but the *plot* would have to center on Sonia's attempts to "humanize" HPL without really understanding him, and it would come to the conclusion that as she understood him better, she realized she could never really change him.

The tone would be quite different from *The Whole Wide World*. Robert E. Howard and Novalyne Price's romance ended in tragedy. Novalyne didn't know at the time (and Robert probably did) that their relationship was Robert's *only* chance, not merely at love, but at life itself. She alone might have been able to break his ties with his mother—at least stretch them a bit—and give him some basis for continuing beyond Momma's death. When this didn't happen, Robert's suicide became as inevitable as the fated doom at the end of a heroic saga, but, I think, a bit more pathetic. As one friend of mine commented on hearing about *The Whole Wide World,* Robert E. Howard sounds like the saddest figure in the whole history of literature.

Lovecraft doesn't. His life wasn't always *happy,* but there is no high tragedy in it, even in its ending, because all of us who aren't otherwise killed die of natural causes sooner or later, and Lovecraft's death had nothing whatever to do with Sonia. After HPL broke up with Sonia, life went on for both of them. They *could* live without one another, and did. She ultimately married again. He was complete unto himself, as doubtless she feared he had been all along.

The tone of the relationship was quite different. Howard was *angry*, expressing anger and romantic longings (and, arguably, sublimating his sex drive) in his fiction. Lovecraft was not. Once his own mother was out of the way (quite early on), he suffered from no overwhelming emotional anguish which drove and directed his life. Lovecraft had laughter in him, which Howard mostly lacked, for all he could write a few slapstick westerns. Howard seems to have been an obsessed, intense person. Lovecraft enjoyed japery. He could parody himself. His whole "Grandpa Theobald" routine, whereby he pretended to be an aged gentleman of the 18th century, was a game, done for his own amusement and that of his friends.

We also read in S.T. Joshi's *I Am Providence* that one of HPL's ways of showing affection for Sonia was to hook his pinkie in hers and vocalize, "Mmm-mmm!"

Imagine him doing that while Sonia tries to force another helping of eggs down him at breakfast, since she's trying to bulk out his gaunt and starved frame a bit.

Imagine the somewhat sheepish look on his face and the exasperation on hers as she is mock-horrified by the state of his wardrobe, having discovered that he doesn't seem to have bought a new suit since 1910.

And his waistline goes out, out, out, and eventually he can't fit into the shabby old clothes anymore.

That's funny. The audience is going to smile, then laugh.

Let me suggest, then, that the tone of this movie, most of the way through, would be one of romantic comedy.

Seriously. I mean it. In the sense of, not kidding.

There would be, of course, hints of the horrific nature of HPL's fiction, possibly with a scene or a voice-over of him reading some famous or blood-curdling passage, but it shouldn't be enough to spoil the light atmosphere. We might also hear him reading (and mock-depreciating) some of his verse. Both "The Rats in the Walls" and "To Mistress Sophia Simple, Queen of the Cinema."

The story is about this bright, energetic lady who knows quite a bit about the world already (she is, after all, twice married before and has a daughter) who takes it upon herself to "improve" upon this genius, HPL, to whom she is attracted, by whom she is often exasperated—but never offended, even when he makes the infamous remark to the effect, "Sam Loveman is such a great guy. Too bad he's a Jew," and she reminds him that she is Jewish too, and he replies that no, she is Mrs. H.P. Lovecraft, late of His Majesty's colony of Providence Plantations. Even HPL's racism becomes merely an exasperation, as it just shows how he is more caught up in his own imaginings than in reality. In such things, Sonia can't quite take him seriously.

Then the tone of the story darkens and becomes bittersweet as the marriage doesn't work out (though the scene of her retyping the lost manuscript of "Imprisoned with the Pharaohs" to his dictation on their wedding night is both tender and funny) as, just as she wants it to, his genius blossoms, but he becomes less and less a part of her life, more interested in writing or a night out with the boys than spending time with her. His letters, of course, are charming. Some sense of them would have to be conveyed on the screen, with voice-overs and occasional shots of his crabbed manuscripts, sometimes illustrated with the odd little drawings HPL occasionally executed.

But Sonia saw how, near the end of their marriage, when she had already lived apart from him in Chicago for a time, she re-established herself in New York and:

> That spring I invited Howard to visit me and he gladly accepted, as a visitor only. To me his nearness was better than nothing. The visit lasted throughout the summer, but I saw him only during the early morning hours when he would return from jaunts with Morton, Loveman, Long, Kleiner, some or all of them.
> (*Lovecraft Remembered* ed. Peter Cannon, p. 262)

That must have been heart-breaking for her.

After this point, the marriage (and our film) moves to its conclusion. Despite Lovecraft's numerous protestations to the contrary ("You do not realize how much I appreciate you, my dear."), the marriage is clearly doomed. The fateful meeting with Lovecraft's aunts, in which Sonia proposes that she rent a house in Providence, start a business, and they all move in together, and the aunts make it absolutely clear that Howard Lovecraft will not be supported by his wife *in Providence*, has an element of the grotesque and absurd, and the comedy is pretty bleak at this point, but it is still comedy.

Then we end, poignantly, on that night in 1932 when Sonia asked, "Howard, won't you kiss me good-night?" and he replied, "No, it is better not to."

Then fadeout, maybe with a final voice-over from Sonia, or credits.

It would work. It *could* be done. All we need is a bunch of people with the right talents and another small miracle.

JOHN W. CAMPBELL'S LOVECRAFTIAN TALE

Barry Malzberg remarks in his introduction to *A New Dawn*, the NESFA omnibus of John W. Campbell's "Don A. Stuart" stories—and he is almost certainly correct on this—that there will never be a biography John W. Campbell, Jr. The reasons are that most of the people who knew him are now dead, and, furthermore, it is impossible to separate the man from his work. Other than his early career as a science fiction writer, and his much longer one as editor of *Astounding*, there is nothing particularly remarkable about Campbell. His extra-literary life contains little drama. His involvement in science fiction *was* his life.

That being so, the best, and virtually the only source of information we have about Campbell's ideas, influences, and thoughts are his own writings, his editorials and occasional essays, and his letters. Like his older contemporary H.P. Lovecraft, he was a brilliant letter-writer, perhaps the greatest editorial letter-writer the science fiction field has ever seen. His specialty was starting arguments, without malice and in a sense of sportsmanship, which would stimulate new stories and new approaches from the recipients. Two volumes of his correspondence have been published to date.

The mention of H.P. Lovecraft is immediately relevant to the subject of this essay. What did John Campbell think about Lovecraft? He made himself clear enough in a letter to Robert Moore Williams dated August 14, 1952, explaining why the modern writer *shouldn't* lard on the adjectives:

> A good many years back, you started selling yarns that had a lot of "mood," and they went pretty well. They were, in a way, rather like the Gothic horror story "The Fall of the House of Usher" sort of thing, built up with *Roget's Thesaurus*, and various sources of adjectives. Lovecraft did the same kind. I did some of 'em myself. As of the time and the slant of the field, they were right.
>
> That was a dozen years ago, and the field's changed far and fast since then. We're older too, you and I, and we've got to change with the change.
>
> (*The John W. Campbell Letters*, Vol. 1, p. 66)

The remark, "I did some of 'em myself," is interesting, and is the key to much of what follows here. Campbell is at least acknowledging that his work, at one point, was somewhat akin to Lovecraft's.

Elsewhere Campbell commented on the sort of story he wanted for his short-lived fantasy magazine, *Unknown*, explicitly rejecting the old-fashioned, Gothic approach of the traditional ghost story (and, by implication, of *Weird Tales*). He makes a specific, unfavorable reference to Lovecraft ("I do not want the sort of stuff Lovecraft doted on.") in a letter to Jack Williamson from 1939. (Quoted in *The Annotated Guide to Unknown and Unknown Worlds* by Stefan Dziemianowicz, p. 14.)

What then is the Campbell-Lovecraft connection, if any, in the absence of direct epistolary evidence?

Campbell *must* have read both "At the Mountains of Madness" and "The Shadow Out of Time" in *Astounding* in 1936. He probably read "The Colour out of Space" in *Amazing Stories* in 1927, though that is less certain. We can be certain that he *did* read the two *Astounding* stories if we keep in mind that in 1936, science fiction was a very small field indeed. Hugo Gernsback, who had founded the first all-science fiction magazine, *Amazing Stories,* in 1926 and with it the consciously aware genre itself, lost control almost immediately, due to inept editorial policies and business practices so bad that there really was a New York lawyer who specialized in collecting Gernsback debts. (We have this datum from Mike Ashley's *The Gernsback Days.* Her name was Ione Weber.) Readers didn't want Gernsback's turgid science lessons disguised as fiction. They wanted stories. Authors preferred to be paid. So Gernsback was out. His *Wonder Stories* was dying in 1936, ending with the April issue, forced to sell out to a pulp chain and come back as the juvenile, formula-written *Thrilling Wonder Stories* later in the year. The original *Amazing Stories*, now edited by the aged T. O'Conor Sloane, was also very close to being on its last legs, so imaginatively barren and just plain dull, that for all Gernsback's shortcomings, it was clearly *Amazing Stories* which was third in a field of three. It too would sell out, in 1938.

Astounding Stories had seized the clear lead in science fiction in 1934, edited by the energetic F. Orlin Tremaine with an unbeatable combination of better (or at least more lively) writing, reliable payment, and a wider range of allowable imagination. Quite unlike the ultra-conservative Sloane, who didn't believe in space travel, Tremaine encouraged far-out speculations. The most extreme stories he tagged as "thought-variants," which proved very popular with his readers.

There was no question about it. For all *Amazing* and *Wonder* still limped along, and some science fiction was published in other pulps (notably *Blue Book, Argosy,* and *Weird Tales*), *Astounding Stories* was the place to be in science fiction in 1936. As is evident from interviews with writers of the period and memoirs and autobiographies, everything from Frederik Pohl's *The Way the Future Was* to Isaac Asimov's *In Memory Yet Green,* if you were a science fiction fan in 1936, that meant you read *Astounding.* You read every story, every month. You argued with other fans in the letters column, "Brass Tacks," making it a point to race your letter into the mails first, so it would be published as quickly as possible.

The professionals did pretty much the same. In this pressure-cooker environment, science fiction itself was like a heated, ongoing conversation at a closed party. Everybody had read the same things, discussed the same ideas, come down on one side or the other of the various controversies. This was a period in which the science fiction fan not only could, but was expected to, read everything published in the field. For John W. Campbell, as one of the top three writers in science fiction at the moment (the other two being E.E. Smith and Stanley G. Weinbaum), *not* to have kept up with the only science fiction magazine that mattered, to which he was a regular contributor, would have been inconceivable. (Incidentally, Campbell has a science article in the June 1936 issue, which also features "The Shadow Out of Time.")

So much for inference. We move on to hypothesis.

I suggest that John Campbell not only had Lovecraft in mind when he wrote his single most famous story, "Who Goes There?" (published in *Astounding*, August 1938), but that the story is a virtual critique of Lovecraft's "At the Mountains of Madness" (*Astounding,* February-April, 1936). It seems to answer reader criticisms of Lovecraft, almost point-for-point.

* * * *

Lovecraft's sudden appearance in *Astounding* was something of a fluke, and for Lovecraft, a miraculous bit of good luck. "At the Mountains of Madness" was written in early 1931, and was regarded by Lovecraft as a kind of magnum opus, certainly the most substantial thing he had written in years. It is his second longest fiction, surpassed only by "The Case of Charles Dexter Ward" (written 1927), which he had repudiated and probably never expected to see published. The rejection of "At the Mountains of Madness" by *Weird Tales* was a devastating blow, which Lovecraft felt had pretty much finished his career as a fiction writer. The manuscript circulated among his friends thereafter, and was eventually submitted to *Astounding* via the fan-turned-agent, Julius Schwartz, who reported that Tremaine bought the story without reading it.

This makes a certain amount of sense. Tremaine, although already the unchallenged leader in the science fiction field, sought to consolidate his position by attracting all of the important writers of the period into the pages of *Astounding*. He knew that Lovecraft was immensely popular in *Weird Tales,* and revered by some of Lovecraft's friends who were regular *Astounding* contributors (such as Frank Belknap Long and Donald Wandrei), so when Schwartz said, "I have here a 35,000 word story by Lovecraft," Tremaine allegedly replied "Sold!"

"At the Mountains of Madness" is problematical in the Lovecraftian canon. It is undeniably an important work. Some Lovecraft readers admire it immensely. S.T. Joshi calls it "a triumph in every way." Others are not so sure.

That the novella is densely written and slow, no one denies. It is the story, written in the form resembling a scientific report (although the narrator's intent is to reveal just enough to *discourage* further exploration), of an expedition to Antarctica, in which explorers from Miskatonic University discover the ruins of a vast, pre-human city half buried in the ice. They also uncover specimens of completely unknown life-forms, semi-vegetable, which resemble large, bat-winged cucumbers with a starfish-like head and a variety of tentacles. These creatures are clearly millions of years old. Their footprints have been found in stones from the era of the dinosaurs. Yet the "specimens" are surprisingly well preserved, and when disaster strikes a remote camp, where the complete "specimens" have disappeared, the more damaged ones are found ritually buried, and the camp has been smashed and all humans and dogs are either slain or missing, the explorers can only hypothesize madness, but any reader of *Astounding* knew perfectly well what had happened.

Here Lovecraft faced a problem inherent in any sort of genre writing. In the context of a science fiction magazine, *of course* we know that these ancient creatures have returned to life, but rational scientists in real life would be, at the very least, extremely reluctant to conclude that a million-year-old corpse just sat up on the dissection table; yet the *reader,* knowing that this is a science fiction story, becomes impatient. (Similarly, in a mystery story we *know,* merely from the fact that this is a mystery story, that the corpse must have been murdered, possibly well before a real detective could come to that conclusion. If you read a story in a ghost story anthology, you can be pretty certain that the thing bumping around in the attic *is* a ghost. An awareness of genre tends to defeat ambiguity.)

The narrator and a colleague take an airplane inland and discover the main city of the Old Ones, creatures that descended from the stars and colonized the Earth shortly after the planet cooled and before native life evolved. The Old Ones must be the most artistic species the universe has ever seen, because, over a period of several million years, they carved their entire history in fantastic detail into a series of reliefs which line the walls and corridors of their buildings. Furthermore, our heroes must be the most perceptive art critics and archeologists who ever lived, because in just a few hours, while making their way by flashlight through the ruins in an atmosphere of increasing dread, they are also able to interpret these carvings, which are not only the product of a hitherto unknown culture but of an unknown *species*, that the narrator can provide a vastly detailed history of the expansion and collapse of the Old Ones' civilization upon the Earth, complete with much about their government, biology, and culture. (For comparison, consider how much difficulty archeologists had making any sense at all out of Mayan or ancient Egyptian inscriptions.) This exposition goes on for many pages, until it almost seems that Lovecraft has abandoned writing a story altogether and is composing a pseudo-nonfiction treatise, rather like some of the works of Olaf Stapledon. (A writer Lovecraft read and admired, by the way.)

At this point someone at *Astounding* must have become alarmed, because the novella, as serialized, is heavily edited, his long paragraphs cut up into shorter ones in an attempt to give Lovecraft's prose a more conventional, jauntier pulp feel. (This outraged Lovecraft, who lapsed from his usual gentlemanly decorum in a letters to refer to "that goddamn'd dung of a hyena Orlin Tremaine," and ultimately came to regard the story as unpublished. A fully restored text was not published until 1985.)

Toward the end of the story, things do pick up. The explorers learn that the ancient city was built with the aid of *shoggoths*, protoplasmic beings bred by the Old Ones and controlled through mental powers. However, over time the shoggoths got out of control, grew crafty, and revolted against their makers. They became the horror that even the Old Ones feared. There is a powerful moment when the explorers discover "degenerate" examples of the ubiquitous wall carvings, which seem to be mocking parodies of the Old Ones' work, which we realize must have been done more recently by semi-intelligent shoggoths.

Also discovered are the missing Old One "specimens," headless and covered with ooze, plus a couple sledges and the carefully wrapped bodies of a missing expedition member and a dog. It is clear what has happened. The perfectly preserved Old Ones awoke, finding one of their number being dissected by the humans. In the ensuing chaos, they killed the men and dogs that confronted them, then gathered together one specimen of each species for further study, plus assorted human artifacts, bundled them on sledges and tried to make their way into the depths below the city, where (it is implied by the carvings) there is an opening to a vast sea beneath Earth, whence the last of the Old Ones have long since retreated. In an extraordinary passage, the narrator suddenly understands that these are not "monsters" at all:

> Scientists to the last—what had they done that we would not have done in their place? God, what intelligence and persistence! What a facing of the incredible…! Radiates, vegetables, monstrosities, star-spawn—whatever they had been, they were men!
>
> (*ATMM,* p.96)

Unfortunately the surviving Old Ones then fell victim to still-lingering shoggoths, which implies, to the two humans who have discovered this, that the strange sounds and strange odors wafting up from the depths below do not bode well. In one of Lovecraft's most effective passages of sheer fright, the two are chased out of the ruins by a barely glimpsed shoggoth. The narrator, flying the airplane, does not see the final horror, but his colleague, looking back, glimpses *something* beyond the even vaster mountains beyond the city, and is never quite right in the head again.…

This did not go over well with *Astounding*'s readership. While some letters in the Brass Tacks department praise Lovecraft, it is hard to find anything in the period which brought down such a deluge of complaint as "At the Mountains of Madness." Readers find the story tedious. They object to its total lack of dialogue. In the August 1936 issue, reader O.M. Davidson finds Lovecraft's work "too tedious, too monotonous to suit me," while admitting that the images of the Old Ones etc. will stay with him for a long time. Peter Ruzella, Jr. finds Lovecraft "trash" and begs for no more. Andy Aprea calls "At the Mountains of Madness" "drivel." In the June issue Robert Thompson had quipped, "I am glad to see the conclusion to 'At the Mountains of Madness' for reasons that would not be pleasant to Mr. Lovecraft." Cleveland Soper, Jr. declared that he would "never forgive" the editor for having foisted such unscientific "bunk" on the readership. Davidson had probably summed up the reservations of a lot of readers when he wrote, "If Lovecraft could only create real characters and action to go with his superb, but lifeless fantasy, he would put out some classics." And so on. The Lovecraft controversy sputtered through the rest of 1936.

Now it must be admitted that many of these readers do not seem to have been intellectual titans—indeed many of them trash Lovecraft and clamor for the return of the Hawk Carse, the worst, most formulaic space opera from *Astounding*'s pre-Tremaine days—but they *were* the people forking out twenty cents a month for the magazine, so the editor had to listen to them.

* * * *

One wonders: did John W. Campbell listen to them too? Did he read "At the Mountains of Madness" and decide to do it one better? Within the narrow confines of genre science fiction, an environment in which most of the writers know one another, they read one another's work, and ideas are exchanged freely, it has long been the tradition to write subsequent stories in answer to an earlier one.

It would have been an interesting challenge, if John W. Campbell, arguably *the* best science fiction writer of the day and the man who would soon completely reshape the field around his own vision of it (the result being subsequently known as the Golden Age of SF), decided to improve on Lovecraft.

Did he? Consider:

Where Lovecraft's opening is the sort of "Had I but known..." style of Gothic writing that Campbell warned his writers against:

> I am forced to speech because men of science have refused to follow my advice without knowing why. It is altogether against my will that I tell my reasons for opposing this contemplated invasion of the Antarctic—with its fossil-hunt and wholesale boring and melting of the ancient ice-cap—and I am the more reluctant because my warning may be in vain.
>
> (*ATMM*, p. 3)

Campbell's is a classic of vivid, you-are-there concreteness:

> The place stank. A queer, mingled stench that only the ice-buried cabins of an Antarctic camp know, compounded of reeking human sweat, and the heavy, fish-oil stench of melted seal blubber. An overtone of liniment combated the musty smell of sweat-and-snow-drenched furs. The acrid odor of burnt cooking fat, and the animal, not-unpleasant smell of dogs, diluted by time, hung in the air.
>
> Lingering odors of machine oil contrasted sharply with the taint of harness dressing and leather. Yet, somehow, through all the reek of human beings and their associates—dogs, machines, and cooking—came another taint. It was a queer, neck-ruffling thing, a faintest suggestion of an odor alien among the smells of industry and life. And it was a life-smell. But it came from the thing that lay bound with cord and tarpaulin on the table, dripping slowly, methodically onto the heavy planks, dank and gaunt under the unshielded glare of the electric light.
>
> (*A New Dawn*, p. 335.)

The situation in "Who Goes There?" is very similar to Lovecraft's. An Antarctic expedition has discovered *something* in the ice, which turns out to be an alien spaceship, millions of years old. But the hull is made of an alloy of magnesium, which bursts into flame when the explorers try to melt the ice with explosives. After a tantalizing glimpse, everything is destroyed, except this one specimen, which lies dripping on that table.

It took Lovecraft several thousand words to get to this point. Campbell has his "dead" alien in the second paragraph.

He does write atmospherically, as he remarked in that 1952 letter to Robert Moore Williams. He does not engage very much in adjectivitis, although we do find a few passages like this:

> It was lone and quiet out there in the Secondary Camp, where a wolf-wind howled down from the Pole. Wolf-wind howling in his sleep—winds droning and the evil, unspeakable face of that monster leering up as he'd seen it through clear, blue ice, with a bronze ice-axe buried in its skull.
>
> (p. 340)

Campbell's creature has less in common with the Old Ones than it does with the shoggoths. Indeed, it might be seen as an improved shoggoth, a "jelly-like protoplasm" with the disquieting ability to change its shape and to absorb and mimic any living thing, so that it can devour a dog—or a man—and then turn the victim's tissue into its own, the imitation being so good that it cannot even be detected under a microscope, but with an alien mind. Its ultimate purpose is to replace all life on Earth with itself. There is a strong implication that it did not build the spaceship it arrived in, but, like the Lovecraftian shoggoths mockingly mimicking the Old Ones, this creature has supplanted some technological species and then set forth into space in search of new prey.

Campbell's narrative style is seemingly as far removed from Lovecraft's as possible, for all that many of his aesthetic goals are quite similar. For the benefit of readers who complained about the lack of dialogue in Lovecraft, there is plenty of dialogue in Campbell. There is also physical action, beginning with the monster's almost-off-stage awakening, then several vivid battles with it.

Significantly, Campbell makes a distinct attempt to characterize the members of the expedition. Lovecraft's characters are complete ciphers, unimportant in Lovecraft's view in a story which is largely a static word-picture of vast, cosmic vistas. Campbell's characters are individuals, who argue, tell jokes, and respond differently to the mounting, increasingly paranoid crisis as the men realize that anyone among them could well be and probably *is* a monster from outer space. Two of them, in finest Lovecraftian fashion, go raving mad. The characterizations are not entirely successful, and the modern reader may still have trouble telling members of the large cast apart. A modern science fiction writer probably would have dealt with this problem by narrowing the viewpoint, so that everything is perceived through the eyes and mind of one person and the story is what these events meant to that person and how it changed him forever. This would have brought things into tighter focus, no doubt, but that is not the way pulp stories, which tended to be situation-oriented rather than character-oriented, were written in 1938, even by a writer as good as Campbell.

Again simplifying Lovecraft, Campbell leaves out the history of the aliens. We learn nothing more about the shape-changing monstrosity beyond the implication that it came from the distant stars, from a hotter world with a blue sun. There would, indeed, be no way for the human characters to have gained any more perspective, unless somebody had a long, telepathic rapport with the Thing, which would have slowed down the pace intolerably. Lovecraft, who was far more interested in sweeping visions of remote epochs, dealt more convincingly with the knowledge problem in his second *Astounding* story, "The Shadow Out of Time." There, a man learns the history of a pre-human civilization by switching bodies with an alien and living in the remote past for several years, which is a more plausible method than just looking at wall-carvings for a few hours.

But Campbell's focus is more on the present, on what the men have to do *now,* to save themselves and the Earth. (They have no doubt that if this creature escapes from Antarctica; all life on Earth is finished.)

Campbell builds suspense in steady stages, through a combination of action and logic. Every time the men think they have destroyed the monster, someone comes up with a logical reason why they have not. On this level, the story generally holds together quite well, although there is a seeming lapse when one fellow, who has gone mad and made a nuisance of himself with constant prayers and hymn-singing, is found dead with a knife in his throat. Somebody snapped. This ironically proves that the murderer is human. But then it is discovered that the corpse is a monster, and previously we were told that the best way to tell a human from a monster would be to shoot him through the heart. The monster wouldn't die so easily. So why is the "madman" dead—or is he?

The monsters can be killed with a combination of a blowtorch, electricity, and acid. An effective method for detecting them is found. It looks as if the humans have won, but then, to their horror they realize that one of their number, who had gone mad from fear and been isolated in a remote shack, has been left alone for a full week. They rush to the shack and discover that the thing within (yes, this was another monster, pretending to be an insane human) has been working unimpeded with available materials and developed an atomic power plant and an anti-gravity pack. In another half hour or so, it would have gone soaring off to South America and to world domination.

In this way the emotional structure of Campbell's story continues to resemble Lovecraft's. After everything has been revealed, there is one last fright—though with the essential difference that with Campbell it is a threat narrowly averted and with Lovecraft it is an even larger threat, still very much present at the end of the story. (One naïve *Astounding* reader called for a sequel to "At the Mountains of Madness" in which the second Miskatonic expedition destroys the monsters and discovers the wonderful lost civilization. No, I do not think that is what Lovecraft had in mind....)

* * * *

Had Campbell successfully "improved" upon "At the Mountains of Madness"? There is no question that "Who Goes There?" was an immediate success, far better received than the Lovecraft story by the readership, almost universally praised. It went on to become recognized as one of the great, early classics of genre science fiction. It has never been out of print since, and has been filmed twice. Its shape-changing monster, far more than Lovecraft's shoggoth, has spawned countless descendants in later stories, TV shows, and films.

There are undeniable flaws in the Campbell version, notably that the characterizations don't seem quite distinct enough for the reader to keep track of who's who, and that Campbell telegraphs his very effective punchline a few paragraphs earlier; but what he did, and did very effectively, was take the material of "At the Mountains of Madness," streamline it, and produce a more conventional story, with elements that would immediately seize and hold the reader's attention: the vividly concrete opening, the greater emphasis on human characterization and human interactions, and the physical action, while maintaining a great deal of atmosphere and suspense. He added the eerie, immensely dramatic notion that the monster could change shape and impersonate the man next to you, so that no one can trust anyone, and you could already be (though only one of the "madmen" might have come to such a conclusion) entirely surrounded by monsters, whose mock-humanity could, at any moment, literally melt away.

"Who Goes There?" like most Lovecraft stories, is primarily a story of cosmic fear. It has ideas in it, but its appeal is emotional. It is, indeed, one of the most effective blends of science fiction and horror ever written, a combination which, despite outsiders' ignorant notions that science fiction is all about monsters, is actually rather rare in the field.

"Who Goes There?" has a much stronger plot-engine than "At the Mountains of Madness." Where Lovecraft's story is more of a subtly disquieting tableau almost until the end, Campbell's *moves,* and builds its own unique, paranoid intensity. It was very much more the kind of story that *Astounding*'s readers wanted. Of course, as I have mentioned, the readers of *Astounding* in the 1930s were not necessarily intellectual or aesthetic titans. That a story was popular in a pulp magazine in 1938 is of no consequence. Trash is often popular for a short time. Even Hawk Carse was popular in his day. What matters is that the Campbell story has shown real staying power. "At the Mountains of Madness" has since been appreciated, too, for its richness and complexity, but it took decades for it to gain recognition. "Who Goes There?" was an example of what is usually an oxymoron, an "instant classic." What proves its worth is that it stayed a classic, for decade after decade.

So the question is not, "Did Campbell do better than Lovecraft?"—even if that was what Campbell was trying to do. This is more like the case of H. Rider Haggard's *King Solomon's Mines* (1885). Haggard wrote his novel after his brother bet him that he couldn't produce a book better than Robert Louis Stevenson's *Treasure Island.* It was a tall order. Did Haggard succeed? That is a matter of taste, but it is clear that Haggard *also* produced a classic, which has never been out of print after more than a century.

Keep in mind that in science fiction, particularly in the science fiction field as it came to be dominated by Campbell in the 1940s and later, was a form of dialogue between editors and writers, and between writers and readers. How many subsequent stories were written as "answers" to such controversial classics as Tom Godwin's "The Cold Equations" or Robert Heinlein's *Starship Troopers*? What the subsequent writer was supposed to deliver was not an insult, in the sense of the famous remark of Beethoven's, "I liked your opera. I think I'll set it to music." Instead he would say, as one colleague to another, "Your version has undeniable validity, but have you considered this twist, or that angle?" and, rather like a shoggoth reproducing by fission, a second, often equally potent story would result. That was what Campbell, as editor, encouraged in his writers, to the extent of farming out ideas to more than one writer. Distinct ideational threads can be discerned in Campbellian science fiction. For example, the whole series of stories and novels about super-scientific, fake religions as tools of social engineering can be traced ultimately to an unpublished novelet by Campbell (who had to give up his writing career when he became editor of *Astounding*) called "All," which he showed to Robert Heinlein. The result was Heinlein's *Sixth Column* (later reprinted as *The Day After Tomorrow)*, in response to which Fritz Leiber proposed that the only way to overcome the super-scientific "miracles" of the oppressive church would be through super-scientific "witchcraft."

He wrote *Gather, Darkness!* which Campbell also published. And these were only the most famous two. There were others.

So what Campbell was doing, whether deliberately or not, and I think it was very deliberately, was *engaging in dialogue with Lovecraft*. He was saying that, yes, "At the Mountains of Madness" was impressive, but wouldn't it be a bit more dramatic if the monsters were up-close and personal?

My guess is that if Lovecraft had lived a little longer, and still been around when Campbell actually became editor of *Astounding* in late 1937 (Lovecraft died in March), Campbell would have not only solicited material from Lovecraft but been trying to *provoke* stories out of him. It would have been a sign of the greatness of both Campbell and Lovecraft that this was so.

SOURCES CONSULTED:

Campbell, John W. Jr. *The John W. Campbell Letters*, Volume 1. edited by Perry Chapdelaine, Sr., Tony Chapdelaine, and George Hay. Franklin, TN: AC Projects, Inc., 1985.

_____. *A New Dawn: The Complete Don A. Stuart Stories.* Framingham, MA: NESFA Press, 2003.

Dziemianowicz, Stefan. *The Annotated Guide to* Unknown *and* Unknown Worlds. Mercer Island, WA: Starmont House, 1991.

Lovecraft, H.P. *At the Mountains of Madness and Other Novels.* Sauk City, WI: Arkham House, 1985. Corrected fifth printing. (Note: This is the first publication of the complete text of the title story.)

H.P. LOVECRAFT AND THE AMERICAN STONEHENGE: HOKUM, PSEUDO-ARCHAEOLOGY, AND THE IMAGINATION

America's Stonehenge! The very name conjures up vistas of huge, standing stone circles, almost unimaginable antiquity, lost civilizations, and maybe the occasional orgiastic human sacrifice, doesn't it?

It's obviously supposed to.

The real deal is not quite as impressive as that, but I will have to admit that it does not entirely disappoint.

And it's got something to do with H.P. Lovecraft. What more could you ask?

Lovecraft may have known of the place, although not under that name. If he ever visited, he did so privately, since it was not open as a tourist attraction until 1958. It was called Mystery Hill originally but, probably because there are dozens of Mystery Hills all over America, most of them places of natural optical illusions where cars seem to roll uphill, a more distinctive name was needed. "America's Stonehenge" better evokes imaginings of a hoary past, and, incidentally, sells more tickets. Whether what we see there is authentic is one question. Whether this site, a rumor of its existence, or similar sites scattered across New England inspired Lovecraft's fiction is, I think, the more interesting question.

Located in Salem, New Hampshire, not far from but not to be confused with the other Salem, America's Stonehenge is a roadside attraction, probably more appropriately listed in *Weird US* (where it is indeed listed) than in any serious archaeological text. I visited last July, on a suitably gloomy, overcast day, which may have helped contribute to the eldritch atmosphere. I was there precisely because of the alleged Lovecraftian connection, which, curiously enough, the fellow at the ticket office/museum did not know about, for all it could be a considerable source of publicity.

America's Stonehenge is on the site of a former farm. It occupies a wooded hillside. It is allegedly four thousand years old, but scientific difficulties begin immediately, if only because William B. Goodwin, the first "researcher" to purchase the place in 1937, and especially Frank Glynn, a president of the Connecticut Archeological Society in the 1950s, seemed determined to make the evidence fit their conclusions rather than draw their conclusions from the evidence, which would be the more proper way of doing things. Think of the proverbial Egyptologist who was caught filing something off a tomb so the inscriptions would fit his theory. At the very least, this is a highly contaminated site.

We know that it has been altered and changed over the centuries, including some removal of stones in the 18th century in keeping with the good old Yankee tradition of tax-evasion. (There was a tax on quarried stone in those days.) Then again, some of the structures have been built up. Some may have been used to hide moonshine in more recent times.

What remains is a series of very primitive stone structures, the largest of them like trenches lined with stones and roofed over with more. You can walk into a couple of the tunnels or caves. There is the celebrated "altar stone," which does indeed have a sinister-looking groove around the edge, and an obvious "drain." Around it, raised stones are placed to mark the movements of the sun, solstices, equinoxes etc. It has been carbon-dated, we are assured. Four thousand years old.

At the ticket office/gift shop there is a considerable amount of display that tries to convince you that this site was built by Phoenicians or Celts or other trans-Atlantic peoples—even medieval Templars, for all they are at variance with the 4000 year claim. (Well, maybe they worked on it later.) We are also told that runaway slaves on the Underground Railroad were hidden here. Why, some of their *very shackles* have been excavated and are on display in a glass case. That there could have been slaves hiding hereabouts is not impossible, but why they would still be wearing their shackles until they got as far as New Hampshire is not explained. (If you believe that, why, I have the *very dollar* that George Washington once threw across the Potomac, which I will show you for a price. Or would you prefer the third thighbone of the Apostle Peter?)

Actually, I think the documentary film shown in the little theater opposite the ticket counter may have let the truth slip out in a careless moment. There are, apparently, *hundreds* of such constructs around New England, few this elaborate, but stone "altars" and "tables" and upturned stones are found all over northern Massachusetts and into New Hampshire and Vermont. Lovecraft hinted darkly in several stories that these were used by native sorcerers too call down Things from the stars in orgiastic rites, and maybe the old New England witches had a hand in it, too. In "The Thing on the Doorstep" we are told that one such complex in Maine even features a pit of shoggoths. Well, why not? What's an eldritch structure like that without a pit of shoggoths?

With a little critical thinking, alas, most of America's Stonehenge falls apart. I am far more willing to believe in shoggoths than I am that Phoenicians crossed the Atlantic and built hundreds of these sites *inland* and away from rivers, then departed without any further trace. Of course true believers have manufactured "evidence" including a stone with an unconvincing "Punic" inscription on it, which is displayed in the gift shop/museum. Those Phoenicians must have *left all their tools at home*, too, because the stones in the structures show no evidence of being shaped by any means other than banging other stones against them, if they are shaped at all, and in real life the Phoenicians were quite a bit more advanced than that. (They were, after all, the folks who built Carthage.) The Celts, too, were sophisticated metal workers.

It's actually an old, racist assumption at work here. Very obviously, what parts of this and other such sites that are genuinely ancient were built by Paleo-Indians. Not necessarily the tribes that lived there when the whites arrived in the 17th century, but American Indians, nevertheless. But if they were "savages," then they couldn't have built such a thing, and therefore Phoenicians or Celts must have done it. That they could not have built such a thing shows that they were savages, and might be exploited. QED. Similar "logic" used to be applied to Great Zimbabwe, in Africa. I met a white South African couple in 1990 when I was in Rome, on a bus on the way to Pompeii. We got to talking because we three were the only English speakers present. They were vacationing in Italy because it was one of the few countries that would accept an Apartheid-era passport. They seemed to be completely ignorant of the history of their own country. They'd never heard of the Monomotapa Empire, and of course insisted that the blacks in their neighborhood were just too mentally primitive to conceive of building stone structures, so it had to have been done by King Solomon or the Egyptians or Arabs, etc. Needless to say, they had never read Sprague & Catherine de Camp's *Citadels of Mystery* (a.k.a. *Ancient Ruins and Archaeology*), which has a chapter on Zimbabwe.

But if we acknowledge that the "savages" are just as smart as we are, and that the ancient Britons were not the only people in the world to notice you can place stones to mark where the sun rises on certain days, then obviously ancient Indians *could* have done the same and they must have built anything that is authentic at America's Stonehenge. It occurs to me that a simple test should prove the antiquity of these stones, if antique they are. In 4000 years the Earth's axis has moved. The stones should all be *wrong*. Are they? If the North Star stone really points at the North Star, then it was placed there much more recently. I wonder if anyone has checked this. I regret that I did not innocently ask that question while I was there.

What *about* the Lovecraftian connection? For all Lovecraft had friends in this area, and visited several times, it is *not* clear that he ever beheld this particular spot. But he didn't have to. That does not matter. That the alleged "archeological site" serves up a large degree of hokum, is likewise irrelevant. It does matter that Lovecraft was aware of at least similar sites, and was, as Andrew Rothovius pointed out in his "H.P. Lovecraft and the New England Megaliths" (in *The Dark Brotherhood,* Arkham House, 1966), certainly the first writer to make use of them in fiction. This is how fiction differs from science. You don't have to be *right.* You just have to be entertaining. You are allowed to fabricate, elaborate, and lie. Good hokum is grist for the proverbial mill.

Let your imagination run. Ignore the pseudoscience and the fake "Templar stone" in the gift shop and even the weirdly unlikely Alpaca Habitat outside, which enables tourists to coo at the cute critters if they get tired of looking at stones. What is exciting about all this, what must have excited Lovecraft, too, is an appreciation that the New England landscape *is* ancient and as littered with mysterious traces of lost peoples as are, say, Arthur Machen's Welsh hills, or, for that matter Salisbury Plain. There *are* secrets to be unearthed.

Of course the site was used to call down Yog Sothoth from the stars. Only in the early 20th century did Wizard Whateley manage to duplicate the procedure, among the standing stones on Sentinel Hill outside of Dunwich.

CITED:

Andrew E. Rothovius, "H. P. Lovecraft and the New England Megaliths," in *The Dark Brotherhood and Other Pieces,* by H.P. Lovecraft and Divers Hands. Sauk City WI: Arkham House, 1966. Pp. 179-197.

Mark Moran and Mark Sceurman. *Weird US.* NY: Barnes & Noble Books, 2004. The entry on America's Stonehenge is on pp. 41-43.

WHY LOVECRAFT IS FUNNY

The H.P. Lovecraft Historical Society, those talented and twisted folks responsible for the recent silent film, *The Call of Cthulhu*, (see *WT* 343) recently sent me an absolutely delicious collection of goodies, which I must describe at length. I already had a copy of the CD of their curious musical production *A Shoggoth on the Roof*, but, in order that I might review it with the fullest possible appreciation, the good folks at HPLHS also sent me: 1) the libretto for *A Shoggoth on the Roof*, 2) the DVD of the "Documentary" about the alleged attempt to produce the musical in 1979, 3) two CDs of eldritch Yuletide carols, *A Very Scary Solstice* and *An Even Scarier Solstice*, complete with booklets of lyrics for both. The first booklet has an introduction by S.T. Joshi, the second by Ramsey Campbell. Both are wittily annotated.

A Shoggoth on the Roof is exactly what it sounds like, a musical parody of *Fiddler on the Roof*, with book and lyrics by He Who For Legal Reasons May Not Be Named, "restored" by Sean Branney and Andrew Leman. It is copyrighted 2001, but, if the back story is to believed, the work was written much earlier, by someone who may or may not have gone mad, who has been forced (mysteriously) to cut off all contact with Lovecraft fandom. In any case, *A Shoggoth on the Roof* is quite wonderful. It is *not* an amateur production made by a handful of fans of dubious musical talent standing around a piano. No, this sounds entirely like a *professional* musical. The singers can actually sing. The musical accompaniment and sound quality are excellent.

As for the script itself…well, it seems that Dr. Armitage of Arkham has three daughters, all of whom want to marry. The eldest is engaged to Wilbur Whateley, but she's fallen in love with Herbert West, the great reanimator. (He sings: "To life, to life, I'll bring them!/ I'll bring all these dead men to life!") The other two daughters sneak a copy of *The Book of Eibon* out of the library and summon up a byakee ("Byakee, byakee, fly me through space," to the tune of "Matchmaker"), then think better of it. Before long one is dating Old Man Marsh ("If I Were a Deep One…") and the other has caught the eye of the chief Cthulhu cultist. There's a zombie chorus, apparitions from beyond the grave, and classic Laurel-and-Hardy type comedy bits involving Randolph Carter and Harley Warren poking about in a crypt. Jilted, Wilbur Whatley shows up at the wedding anyway, reads from the *Necronomicon*, and Great Cthulhu rises from the sea...and *sings*. ("Do You Fear Me?")

The DVD "documentary" purports to be based on a mysterious old Super-8 movie film someone found on eBay, containing footage of a doomed attempt by the Other Gods Theatre Troupe of Los Angeles to actually stage *A Shoggoth on the Roof* in 1979. But it was not to be. A mysterious figure is seen in many of the shots. He blocks the camera with his hand at the end. The players went their separate ways. Some have disappeared or have gone mad. There are interviews with survivors, most of whom deny everything, including Stuart Gordon (the director of the film *Reanimator*) and actor Chris Sarandon. Of course we're being hoaxed. But where does the hoax leave off and the truth begin? What remains is one of the funniest pieces of Lovecraftiana ever. Listen to this a few times and you too will find yourself irresistibly singing along to such lyrics as these, from the opening number (to the tune of "Tradition"):

> *Who day and night must slumber in R'lyeh,*
> *Wave his tentacles, having nasty dreams?*
> *Who has the might, as master of R'lyeh,*
> *To drive humanity insane?*
> *Cthulhu! Cthulhu! Tentacles!*
> *Cthulhu! Cthulhu! Tentacles!*

Exquisite. You will go mad. Then everything will seem much, *much* clearer. *Trust me* ... Then next Christmas you can sing (or gibber) along with the two *Solstice* albums, which are, again, fully of professional quality, with excellent production values and instrumentation. I am sure you will enjoy "Freddy the Red Brained Mi-Go," "It's Beginning to Look a Lot like Fish-Men," "I Saw Mommy Kissing Yog-Sothoth," and numerous others, but the song that may truly knock you through non-Euclidian angles for its sheer audacity and complexity is "Oh Cthulhu" to the tune of "The Hallelujah Chorus" from Handel's *Messiah*, if only because it actually manages to make lines like "Ph'nglui wgah'nagl fhtagn" seem melodic.

Do yourself a favor. Go to the H.P. Lovecraft Historical Society website www.cthulhulives.org and check out all the wonderful stuff they have for sale. You will *never be the same*. I raise my pseudopods in salute to everyone involved in these extraordinary and delightful productions. I am impressed that for these people *no* detail is too trivial to get right. In the prologue of *A Shoggoth on the Roof* the Arkhamites are arguing whether the protective Elder Sign should be drawn as a star or more like a tree. The CD comes sealed with a little piece of tape, on which *both* versions are printed, just in case.

I am left with two more serious thoughts:

Would it actually be possible to stage *A Shoggoth on the Roof*, assuming no supernatural interference? I think so. The chief technical problem would be the climax, in which Great Cthulhu rises from the sea, devours much of the cast, and destroys Arkham. But I imagine a stage would have several layers of semi-abstract sets, kept in darkness much of the time. Scene-switching is done with a spotlight, so when the two daughters sneak out for *The Book of Eibon* they walk a few steps from their "bedroom," the light on the bedroom goes out, and another light illuminates a row of old books, which becomes the "Miskatonic Library." In various parts of the stage are flats suggesting crypts, or Arkham streets, illuminated when needed. Behind all this is an enormous head of Cthulhu, like something you'd see on a Mardi Gras float, and an equally enormous claw. Both have been on stage *throughout the entire play*, but hidden in darkness. At the climactic wedding scene, lights inside the Cthulhu head go on, the head rises, eyes blazing, and the first victim just happens to be standing in front of the claw. Lights go on and off as people scream, disappear. Cthulhu's singing is projected through a speaker inside the head. This is not multi-million-dollar Broadway technology I'm talking about. This could be done in a college theater.

The second serious thought I have is this: why does Lovecraft make us laugh? It is not merely because he is a great author, one of great solemnity. Poe is a great author, and while "The Raven" is endlessly parodied, he is otherwise not very funny. Sure, you *can* parody almost anyone. Leo Tolstoy is not a barrel of yucks, but Woody Allen managed to laugh along with *War and Peace* in *Love and Death*. You can do funny things with Shakespeare, like condense all his plays into a single 90-minute rendition, or perform *Hamlet* as a comic song ("And Fortinbras knee-deep in Danes lived happily ever after.")

But somehow Lovecraft seems *inherently* funny. It's not as if his work is actually ridiculous. Any sensitive and imaginative person has only to read the best of Lovecraft to see that this is a writer of genuine seriousness, with real philosophical depth, who is also authentically creepy in a way most would-be fright-meisters never will be. And yet…who can resist a good shoggoth joke, or a plush Cthulhu toy in an Elvis outfit? (Yes, a whole line of plush Cthulhu toys is commercially available from Toy Vault. They've also got a Nyarlathotep and a cuddly, stuffed shoggoth.) I myself have indulged in considerable Lovecraftian humor in these very pages, frequently in verse. Long time *Weird Tales* readers will remember "A Dunwich School Primer" (#315) or "What a Friend We Have in Dagon" (#324). I am responsible for *The Innsmouth Tab-*

ernacle Choir Hymnal and quite a bit more. I once assembled an entire *anthology* of Lovecraftian humor that I actually sold to a publisher in 1977. (But alas, the book seemed as eldritchly cursed as that production of *A Shoggoth on the Roof,* and it never appeared.) It was a great book, containing among other things "Riders of the Purple Ooze" by M.M. Moamrath, "Ralph Wollstonecraft Hedge: A Memoir" by Ron Goulart, and even "At the Mountains of Murkiness" a very early story (1937) by none other than Arthur C. Clarke.

Lovecraftian humor goes back to Lovecraft. He could write funny verse, including a screamingly good parody of T.S. Eliot's "The Waste Land" called "Waste Paper." When his young friend Alfred Galpin confessed how, on the eve of Prohibition, he slipped out into the woods and tasted the demon liquor, the Puritanical, but bemused Lovecraft immediately penned an entire short story, "Old Bugs," telling how, in the remote future year of 1950, the once promising young man met a sodden end. His writings are full of such japes, including a mock-biography of the learned Mr. Ibid, whom you see cited in so many footnotes.

More to the point, he would insert playful elements into even his most serious stories, in the reference to "The Commorium myth cycle as preserved by the Atlantean priest Klarkash-Ton" in "The Whisperer in Darkness." Particularly in his "revisions" (ghost-rewrites of stories by amateurs) he more than once slipped over the line into self-parody, and inserted all manner of dread allusions to extra-cosmic menaces and to forbidden tomes, just beginning with the abhorred *Necronomicon.*

This is getting closer to the core of the matter. Lovecraft's fiction and his Cthulhu Mythos always had an in-joke aspect, which he invited others to share, and which has perhaps preceded any appreciation of the more serious aspects of his work as he has continued to permeate popular culture to an extraordinary degree. The plush Cthulhu may reach some people first, then Lovecraft-inspired role-playing games, and only later the actual reading of his texts. Meanwhile other writers find it fun to slip Lovecraftian references into stories that are not otherwise Lovecraftian. Michael Crichton even included the *Necronomicon* in the bibliography of *Eaters of the Dead.*

But why do we *play* with this material? When you get right down to it, Lovecraft's outlook is extremely bleak and depressing. His fiction is all about how little humankind matters, and how absurd our pretensions are in a mindless and uncaring universe. His message is that we are not masters of anything, but represent only a brief and accidental episode of organic life, soon to be replaced by something else. Indeed, many of his protagonists go mad or turn suicidal with the realization of our true place in the scheme of things.

And this is *funny?* At the risk of seeming a show-off, I quote here one of my own most celebrated effusions:

> *A cultist, entranced by Cthulhu,*
> *Encountered a slavering ghoul who*
> *Said "Old Ones don't need me,*
> *they won't even feed me,*
> *and so, in a pinch, I guess you'll do."*

Yes, it's funny. But I wonder if at some level it isn't a very dark laughter, like that at the end of *Dr. Strangelove,* which, as you, recall, ends with a nuclear holocaust, the presumed extinction of the human race, and a romantic lyric, *"We'll meet again, don't know where, don't know when."* We laugh at doom, pain, the destruction of the Earth, and the sheer futility of existence.

If we are indeed doomed, if, on the cosmic scale of things nothing we can ever do will matter—remember that all the accomplishments of Shakespeare and Einstein will be entirely forgotten in a mere million years, an eyeblink in the face of Eternity—we can whine or rage or decry the injustice of it all. But that accomplishes nothing. If it's all the same, we might as well laugh, even as the best joke may well be made at the gallows.

Is it possible, then, that the reason that Lovecraft is funny is precisely because he is convincing? He speaks a terrible, compelling truth.

We might as well laugh.

WILLIAM BECKFORD, CALIPH OF FONTHILL ABBEY

The Vision is an early work by the author of the still-famous Arabian fantasy *Vathek*. It was written when the author was about 17 years of age, abroad for the first time to complete his education, in the midst of the "European tour" conventionally given to wealthy young men of the late 18th century. The story may have been intended to flatter one of his teachers, the St. Petersburg-born painter Alexander Cozens, who taught young Beckford art and encouraged his dabblings in the bizarre and fantastic.

All very interesting, you might say, a piece of juvenilia by a writer who later wrote an important book.

But William Beckford was no ordinary writer. He was, first of all, a genius in the strictest sense, an amazing child prodigy, who spoke French by the time he was three and was working on Latin and Greek by the time he was seven. Although he had no formal education at all, he ultimately mastered over half a dozen languages and became a leading connoisseur of art. More than that, he was a spectacular eccentric, an obsessive bibliophile and builder, who ultimately became one of the greatest aesthetes of all time. It is safe to say that if he had not existed, it would have been necessary for Oscar Wilde, J.K. Huysmans, or even Edgar Allan Poe to have invented him. The product of an era that expected and to some degree tolerated extreme behavior, he was a contemporary of Lord Byron and the Marquis de Sade, and even next to them he seems to be one of the most astonishing people to have come out of the Romantic Age.

Beckford was born in 1760 to an obscenely rich family. His forebears had made their fortune from slaves and sugar in Jamaica, where his great-grandfather had been governor and died in a brawl in 1711. The governor had two sons, one of whom was Speaker of the Jamaican Assembly but later stabbed a judge to death. The other son was himself murdered. The murdered man, Thomas Beckford, had already sired two sons, one of whom, William, the father of our author, was somewhat more respectable, twice mayor of London, and became a Whig M.P. noted for his radical views. Despite his overbearing ways and violent temperament (something none of the Beckfords seem to have controlled very well) the elder William, called Alderman Beckford, was a man of cultivated tastes, which his inordinate wealth enabled him to indulge.

From his earliest days young William was prepared to be the master of a great fortune. In 1770 his father died, leaving him, at age nine and a half, the owner of an estate worth over one and a half million pounds and with an annual income from the Jamaican slave plantations of seventy thousand pounds. By 1797, Beckford's annual income was one hundred and fifty-five thousand pounds. To put such figures in perspective, this is a period in which a laborer's salary might be a shilling a day, or, perhaps thirty-five pounds *a year.*

That's enough to go to anyone's head, and it went to young William's in a spectacular fashion. He was not the virile and domineering man his father was. He had no fondness for blood-sports, no interest in politics, and in fact all his life loved and got along with animals better than he did people. He was emotional, withdrawn, given to fits of temper, and notably effeminate in a way that only a rich boy who has never had to go to school with his peers can be.

In his late teens, he was taken on a tour of the Continent, where, in Italy, his homosexual tastes began to develop. His mother, fully as domineering as his father, tried to direct him along more conventional lines, but he resolutely failed to become a conventional man of his class. His one heterosexual affair seems to have been equally inappropriate, with Louisa, the wife of his first cousin. About the same time he developed, like Oscar Wilde, a catastrophic infatuation for a boy, the Honorable William Courtenay, later Viscount Courtenay and the 9th Earl of Devon, a.k.a. "Kitty." In 1784 there was the inevitable scandal, something glimpsed through a keyhole, a serious matter when sodomy was still a capital crime in England. But Beckford was a lot richer than Wilde and was never prosecuted. He also had the sense to go abroad. In fact no charges were ever brought, but his reputation was ruined by the time he was twenty-four, and he remained alienated from the "best" society for the rest of his very long life. This was one of the many things that made Beckford the strange, embittered man he became.

By way of a "normal" interlude, Beckford had married (by his mother's arrangement) Lady Margaret Gordon, the daughter of the 4th Earl of Aboyne in 1783, much to the confusion of Beckford, Kitty, and Louisa. Despite everything, Lady Margaret remained devoted to him. The couple had two daughters, both of whom married nobility. Lady Margaret died in 1785 of childbed fever after giving birth to the second of them. Beckford's relationships with his daughters were strained, often very difficult. He always had a cruel wit and a sharp tongue and he did not spare, especially, his older daughter. That his daughters never lived with him wasn't entirely his fault. A family conference had determined that he was entirely unfit to raise them, and they were taken away.

In 1782, when he was twenty-two, in the space of a few days, Beckford dashed off, in French, a first draft of the brilliant Arabian Nights romance, *Vathek*, which has insured his immortality. It has been enormously influential on subsequent writers of fantasy, notably H.P. Lovecraft and Clark Ashton Smith.

Even with *Vathek*, things did not go smoothly. While Beckford was still polishing the French version, his "friend" the Reverend Samuel Henley published an English translation of the work, "from an unpublished manuscript," without putting Beckford's name on the book. Beckford had to rush a French version into print to prove his authorship. (Henley's is still the standard English version, but since it is not by Beckford it has no particular authority. The novel is best read in the 1929 Grimsditch translation, which is based on a later, revised French text.)

Vathek is the story of a young caliph, heir to unlimited wealth and power, who sinks into utter, fantastic indulgence, and ultimately achieves damnation. It takes on a deeper meaning in consideration of the circumstances of its author.

Beckford's other literary productions include some travel books, the *Episodes of Vathek* (unfinished and not published until 1911), and miscellany. One of his editors has described him as "Spoiled, undisciplined, eager to display his artistic sensibilities, an artist so absorbed with his own image that he easily became one of the sublime solipsists of his age."

But, by the time he was thirty, his literary muse had pretty much left him. He was a widower, shunned by polite society, still fantastically wealthy, uninterested in (and doubtless unsuited for) a political career, with a great deal of time on his hands.

He then entered the most fantastic phase of his life. Beckford, who was largely a failure in his dealings with human beings, devoted the rest of his life to the creation and acquisition of beautiful things, which he, by and large, did not wish to share with the rest of humanity.

He became the supreme aesthete, a collector of rare books and manuscripts, and of great art. He owned paintings by such Renaissance masters as Titian and Raphael. He risked his life by going to France during the French Revolution to buy up rarities from the estates of guillotined aristocrats. When war broke out between England and France 1793, Beckford was in danger as an enemy alien, but a French bookseller friend let him work as an assistant in his shop in disguise for a time. (This was doubtless the only actual *work* Beckford did in his life.)

Back home in England, he began to express his aestheticism in building and in furniture design. He built an enormous palace for himself, Fonthill Abbey, which was a wonder of the age, perhaps the most fantastic English country home ever constructed, as large as a Gothic cathedral with a gigantic tower in the middle. (Imagine the usual proportion of the tower to the body of a cathedral, reversed so that the tower overwhelms the rest of the building.) That the place was virtually unlivable was beside the point. It was intended to create a sense of awe in the lucky few Beckford admitted into his abode. Every inch of Fonthill was to be exquisite, each piece of furniture designed and placed in the most artistic positions, the walls covered with the rarest paintings, the shelves filled with the finest and most expensive books in the most perfect bindings. When he heard there was fox-hunting in the neighborhood, Beckford, who still had a horror of cruelty to animals, built a 12-mile wall around his estate so no animal could be harmed on his grounds.

This isolation, and Beckford's tarnished reputation, gave rise to wild rumors, most of which seem to be untrue. It is unlikely there were vast homosexual orgies at Fonthill, if only because the hundreds of servants and staff would have eventually talked. It is not true that Beckford came to so loathe women that he had special alcoves built in the walls so that, should he pass a female servant in the halls, she could stand with her face hidden until he was gone. (In fact he had cordial relationships with several women throughout his life.) It is true that he had a dog called Viscount Fartleberry, and it is undeniable that he spent a fabulous amount of money *wholly on himself,* for his own private gratification. He would spare no expense to own precious things which had belonged to his enemies, particularly when those enemies took steps to prevent this from happening.

He was the richest commoner in England, who had the grandest house. Even in his youth, when he first journeyed to Europe, he went in such state that he was once mistaken for the Holy Roman Emperor travelling incognito.

Ultimately it all proved too much, even for Beckford. By the 1820s, his finances were precarious. Neglect of his estates and plantations (and possibly some dishonest managers) had greatly curtailed his income. He had to sell Fonthill Abbey and most of its contents, later proclaiming that once the gawking public had been invited in for the sale, the place had no more allure for him.

This actually proved a blessing in disguise. Not only did the proceeds of the sale keep Beckford for the rest of his life in the style to which he was accustomed, but in 1825 the architect's contractor made a deathbed confession: the foundations of Fonthill were not built according to specifications. Inferior materials had been used. The whole place was in danger of imminent collapse. Beckford informed the current owner, one Farquar (whom Beckford didn't seem to like and referred to as "Old Filthyman") of the danger. Farquar laughed and said the tower would last as long as he did and that was all he cared about. But, in fact, the tower collapsed that very year. Miraculously, no one was killed, though a servant was blown thirty feet along a corridor by an outrush of air. Fonthill today exists only in fragments of outbuildings and ruins.

Beckford moved to Bath, built another tower (albeit more sturdily this time) and lived until 1844 as a misanthropic recluse hoarding beautiful things, withdrawn in an aesthetic dream-world, obsessively designing and re-designing his domain when he was not driving hard bargains, buying and selling the most expensive and exquisite books, paintings, furniture, and art objects. Much of the contents of his collections can still be seen in various British museums, including the National Gallery.

Beckford may be best described as an unfulfilled genius, whose creative abilities only manifested themselves in a couple of brilliant moments, notably *Vathek* and a suppressed volume called *Dreams, Waking Thoughts, and Incidents* (1783). Beyond his youth, he expressed himself mostly through extravagance, making his own life, as Oscar Wilde attempted to do later in the 19th century, a fantastic work of art.

The Vision is an early, somewhat unformed work by this man, written when he was a spoiled, sheltered, troubled, and amazingly brilliant teenager. It was not published for the first time until 1930. In it we see his romantic sensibilities, his painterly sense of landscape and detail (acquired from Cozens, even if Beckford never actually became an artist of any merit himself), and his tendency toward Oriental exoticism, which would flower in *Vathek*. It is undeniably difficult in places, but intriguing for the glimpses it provides of the kind of artist Beckford was—and might have been.

WORKS BY BECKFORD:

Biographical Memoirs of Extraordinary Painters, 1780.

The Vision, 1777-78. First published with *Liber Veritatis* in 1930, ed. Guy Chapman.

An Excursion to the Grande Chartreuse in the Year 1778, 1783.

Dreams, Waking Thoughts, and Incidents, 1783. Suppressed. Reissued, much edited, in *Italy; with Sketches of Spain and Portugal,* 1834.

Vathek. Written 1782. Henley's English translation, published 1786. Beckford's French, published 1787. Revised, 1787, 1815. Translated by Herbert Grimsditch, 1929. Note: The peculiar edition in the Ballantine

Adult Fantasy Series, 1971, edited by Lin Carter follows Henley's English text, incorporates the *Episodes* where Beckford originally intended to place them, at the climax of the book, and also includes spurious material, including bridging passages by Carter and the completion of the Third Episode by Clark Ashton Smith.

The Journal of William Beckford in Portugal and Spain. Written 1787, published, 1954 ed. Boyd Alexander.

Journal of 1794. Published, 1961, ed. Boyd Alexander.

Modern Novel Writing, or, The Elegant Enthusiast, 1796. Published under the pseudonym Lady Harriet Marlow.

Azemia, 1797. Published under the pseudonym J.A.M. Jenks.

Recollections of an Excursion to the Monasteries of Alcobaca and Batalha in 1794, 1835.

The Episodes of Vathek, edited by Lewis Melville and published in 1911.

Liber Veritatis. Written circa 1830, published 1930.

ABOUT BECKFORD:

William Beckford by James Lees-Milne, 1979.

SOME ANCESTORS OF VATHEK

For all H. P. Lovecraft may have liked it, the literature of the eighteenth century seems to be little read in the twentieth. The Augustan Age of English letters was a golden age of satire, and satire does not age well. Even Jonathan Swift, I suspect, is more admired than read these days. The prose of the period contains a great deal of elegance and wit, but very little emotion. The verse is, to the modern ear, windy and stilted. The modern reader tends to prefer the later Romantics, or the Elizabethans. Tastes change with time. For all we know, the twenty-first century may prefer Pope to Shakespeare. But right now, the eighteenth century seems to be out.

In 1764 Walpole's *The Castle of Otranto*, the first Gothic, appeared. An explosion of ghastly, ghostly, wildly romantic tales followed. The sensibilities of these are a little more to the modern taste, but the Gothics aren't read much either, mostly for reasons of changing novelistic techniques, and the fact that, by any standard, most of the Gothics are simply awful.

William Beckford's *Vathek* (1786) stands as the most readable novel of its century, and also as a unique work of fantasy. Critics have long been trying to shoe-horn it into the Gothic school, but it never seems to fit. It is an extravagant romance based on the *Arabian Nights*, filled with magic, adventures in strange lands, supernatural beings, and, at the end, a descent into Hell. It has been enormously influential. Clark Ashton Smith obviously studied it closely. Peter Cannon's "The Influence of *Vathek* on H. P. Lovecraft's *The Dream-Quest of Unknown Kadath*" (*in H. P. Lovecraft: Four Decades of Criticism*) ably demonstrates another line of development.

The novel more resembles a modern, imaginary-world romance than a true Gothic. If you want to know what Gothics were like, read a few of the surviving specimens (perhaps *Otranto* or *Melmoth the Wanderer* or *The Monk*) or else consult Ann B. Tracy's *The Gothic Novel, 1790-1830* (University Press of Kentucky, 1981) which contains synopses of almost two hundred of them. You will be struck by how little Beckford's masterwork resembles the "other" Gothics. They usually take place in the European Middle Ages, or in eighteenth century Italy, and have to do with gloomy castles, wicked noblemen, dispossessed heirs, imperiled heroines, and the like. Probably only about a third of them have any fantasy elements.

The reason *Vathek* doesn't resemble a Gothic, I have since discovered, is that it isn't one. This is not to say that a whole new genre suddenly leaped full-grown from William Beckford's forehead. I have not come to any definite conclusions yet, but it looks to me as if *Vathek* comes at the end of a long tradition, that of the pseudo-Oriental moralistic tale. The element of parody, I would suggest, is stronger than often supposed. (In the same way that Lucian of Samosata's "True History" is not so much a pioneering work of science fiction, but an outrageous parody of a long tradition of fantastic travel tales.)

But first, Dear Reader, as it would have been fashionable to address you in those days, we shall have a digression on the history of the English magazine.

The Tatler made its appearance in English coffeehouses in 1709. The coffee house being the center of social activity for literary men, it was only natural that the first magazines should be distributed through them. Such magazines were apparently single sheets in tiny print, containing a single essay per issue, almost always unsigned, frequently under the auspices of an editorial persona after whom the magazine was titled. Lovecraft's amateur magazine, *The Conservative*, is very much in this tradition.

The Tatler, i.e. editor of the paper of the same name, was really Richard Steele, who was forced to discontinue in 1711 due to political problems. However, Steele soon teamed up with Joseph Addison and launched the enormously popular *The Spectator*, which came out several times a week for a total of 635 issues. Soon there came to be a host of imitators, *The Rambler, The Connoisseur* (an exception to the editorial rule, conducted by "Mr. Town"), *The Adventurer*, and the like. Copies of individual issues are now extremely scarce (I doubt there are many to be found outside of the British Museum and a few university libraries), but even as they were being published, they were quickly reprinted in book form. These rapidly became standard classics, and reprints of them, usually under collective titles like The British Classics or The British Essayists, are common from the first half of the nineteenth century. You can find them in college libraries, or even very cheaply in used bookstores and sales.

Another aside: My favorite (although horrible) book sale story involves a college library which was getting rid of all the old leather-bound books the librarians didn't want to repair. They were all five cents each. The dates of the books ranged from about 1580 to 1820. There wasn't much of literary interest, but I did snatch ten out of twelve volumes of *The Spectator*, two out of four *Adventurer*, and three out of four *Connoisseur*. "Oh," said the attendant. "We didn't know anybody would want them. We're already burned most of them!" More recently I was browsing in another college library and found a complete set of British Classics from 1827, all in their original bindings, in almost perfect condition. From all evidence, they'd never been checked out. Such has been my introduction to eighteenth century magazines. The competition, to put it mildly, is not fierce.

Imagine my surprise when I found fantasy fiction in these neglected tomes. Most of the contents of *The Spectator* and the like are comparable to the "Talk of the Town" section of *The New Yorker*, short pieces on manners, morals, literature, and anything else that might have been on the writer's mind. However, there was a small amount of fiction. *Spectator* 578 contains an untitled story of King Fadallah and his lover Zemroude, allegedly translated from the Persian Tales by a Mr. Phillips. (Zemroude's beloved comes to her in the form of a nightingale. This motif occurs in English ballads, so we might question the authenticity of the tale, but then, these motifs are so universal you never can tell.) Issues 584 and 585 contain a pseudo-biblical account of "Shalum and Hilpa," with a sequel, both by Addison.

The 1827 set contains *The Adventurer* complete, and this, I found, contained quite a bit of fiction. It bears further examination.

The Adventurer was largely the work of John Hawkesworth, although there were other contributors, including even the illustrious Dr. Samuel Johnson. Hawkesworth (1715-73) was born into an undistinguished family of religious dissenters, and doesn't seem to have had much education. However, he made up for it somehow, became a lawyer, got bored with that, and turned to literature. His first literary job was as a successor to Johnson, recording Parliamentary speeches for *The Gentleman's Magazine* (1744). Some years later, after Johnson's own *The Rambler* was defunct but still fresh in the public mind, he followed up with *The Adventurer*, which ran 140 numbers, of which he wrote about half. The ostensible purpose of this magazine was the moral and ethical instruction of the readership, and Hawkesworth was sufficiently good at it that the Archbishop of Canterbury bestowed a Doctor of Civil Law degree on him as a reward. This went to Hawkesworth's head, and he soon became arrogant enough to alienate most of his literary friends. However, his career continued, and included a "fairy entertainment" (apparently a novel), *Edgar and Emmeline* (1761), and an "Eastern Tale" *Almoran and Harriet* (2 vols., 1761). He translated *Telemachus* by Fenelon into English, a fantasy novel (sequel to the *Odyssey*) by a French bishop of Louis

XIV's reign. In 1773, the year of his death, he published an account of exploratory voyages, taken from the accounts of sea captains (including Captain Cook), which, much to his chagrin, was widely criticized for being too racy. As a result, his reputation declined.

Considering that *The Adventurer* was intended as a vehicle for moral instruction, the amount of fiction it contained is surprising. However, as Hawkesworth remarked in an early number, often a point can be made more memorable if linked to a vivid story. "Those narratives are most pleasing," he tells us, "which not only excite and gratify curiosity but engage the passions." Further, "…the most extravagant, and yet perhaps the most generally pleasing of all literary performances, are those in which supernatural events are every moment produced by Genii and Fairies.… It may be thought strange, that the mind should with pleasure acquiesce in the open violation of the most known and obvious truths.… But it is not, perhaps the mere violation of truth or probability that offends, but such a violation as perpetually recurs. The mind is satisfied, if every event appears to have an adequate cause…the action of the story proceeds with regularity, the persons act upon rational principles, and such events take place as may naturally be expected from the interposition of superior intelligence and power; so that though there is not a natural, there is at least a moral probability preserved, and our first concession is abundantly rewarded by the new scenes to which we are admitted, and the unbounded prospect that is thrown open before us." (Issue #4)

In other words, introduce the fantastic premise, then treat it realistically, with the characters behaving like real people so that the story makes an emotional sense. Hawkesworth's "moral probability" is very similar to the distinction made by Le Guin between the true and the factual.

For all he was part of a very different literary scene, Hawkesworth was a fantasy writer, almost in the modern sense. His professed didacticism is present, but his stories are more than sermons. He delights in exotic locales and supernatural devices. His "Eastern Tales" are actually a kind of imaginary-world fantasy, since to the Englishman of 1750, the Islamic countries were about as far away as Mars. Hawkesworth makes numerous errors in cultural details and attributes Christian teachings to Muslims, but then he wasn't writing about the real East (then, mostly the Ottoman Empire), but an imaginary one. This convention persists up until Lord Dunsany.

Hawkesworth also wrote "domestic" fiction, which does not concern us. His Eastern Tales are as follows:

"Imperceptible Deviation to Vice— Moral Use of Punishment— Remonstrances of Conscience Universal— Amurath, an Eastern Story"

(Issues 20-22):

Amurath, Sultan of the East, inherits the throne from his virtuous father. He is then visited by a spirit, the Genius Syndarac, who gives him a magic ring which will pinch his finger if he does evil. This way he can stay on the path of righteousness. However, the spiteful sultan soon resents having his every action controlled and becomes wicked out of sheer spite. He degrades his worthy vizier Alibeg and lusts after his daughter Selima. She disappears. Amurath becomes a tyrant in his rage. Tired of being tormented by the ring, he takes it off, whereupon the Genius appears, rebukes him, and turns him into a monster, half wolf, and half goat. He is captured and put on display in his own capital. His keeper beats him into submission, and gradually he becomes less fierce. He saves his keeper from a tiger and (as a reward) is transformed into a dog. Now given run of the palace, he learns that he is presumed dead and Alibeg is the new sultan. As a dog, he has a vision of a marble wall, on which is an inscription, "Within this wall liberty is unbounded…nature is not oppressed by the tyranny of religion, nor is pleasure awed by the frown of virtue."

He goes in. Within there is rape, riot and murder. Still as a dog, he comes beneath a window, through which come sounds of dancing and music, then cries of distress. A piece of meat is thrown out. He eats it, is poisoned, and dies. Now the Genius moves his soul into the body of a dove. Trying to escape from the strange land, he is overcome by a "sulpherous vapor" and alights at the mouth of a cave. Inside is a hermit, and, much to his amazement, the missing Selima. She confesses how she nearly gave in to Amurath's advances, then found herself in the riotous land. It was she who was almost poisoned with the treacherously supplied meat. The hermit explains the need for restraint. Amurath is returned to human form. He weds Selima in good faith, and they live happily and moderately ever after, having been returned to the kingdom by Syndarac.

(This is the best and most elaborate of the stories. Note the plot similarities to *Vathek*, which is also about a sultan given to wickedness out of sheer spite. *Vathek*, lacking a Genius to correct him, however, is not redeemed.)

"Religion the Only Foundation of Content" (Issue 32):

Omar, a holy hermit, meets Hassan, who is in great distress. Hassan, a poor man of Mecca, has been content in his labors for many years, until he is visited by the Caliph Almalic in disguise. The Caliph, seeing how well Hassan has adjusted to life, reveals who he is, and says that he was thinking of raising him to a high estate. Now, he understands, that is unwise. As soon as the Caliph leaves Hassan sorely regrets having missed such an opportunity. He becomes wretched, neglecting his work. The Caliph visits him again, sees what has happened, and makes him a hanger-on at the palace. Hassan lives in luxury until he finds himself jaded to every pleasure. Then the Caliph dies, and Hassan is kicked out by his successor. Having known luxury, he can't return to simple life, and is worse off than before. The hermit explains that only by religion can one be content. Hassan becomes pious.

"No Life Pleasing to God That Is Not Useful to Man" (Issue 38):

Mirza, a governor under the sultan Abbas Carascan, wants to resign. The sultan doesn't like the idea, but says he will consider. Three days later, Mirza says he will keep the job. Cosrou the Imam's account of a vision he had in the desert has changed his mind.

"The Folly of Human Wishes and Schemes to Correct the Moral Government of the World—The History of Nouraddin and Amana" (Issues 72-73):

Nouraddin the merchant falls in love with Amana the shepherdess. He carries her off to Egypt. The wedding is delayed. Meanwhile, Osmin, caliph of Egypt, has grown tired of his harem and proclaims that he who produces the most beautiful virgin within two days will be made third in the kingdom (after the caliph and his chief eunuch, Nardic). Caled, a disaffected servant of Nouraddin, tells Nardic about Amana. On the day of the wedding, the wicked Caled shows up with a royal order and makes off with the bride. She is presented to the caliph. She begs to be allowed to return to her lover but the enraged tyrant gives her three hours to submit to him, or else he will throw Nouraddin's head at her feet. A sympathetic eunuch advises her to agree, but ask for three days to prepare.

Meanwhile, Nouraddin in his despair wishes aloud that he could change places with Osmin, since the caliph has his beloved. A spirit, a Genius, appears and gives him a magic talisman, by which he can change into the semblance of the caliph and back again at will.

Meanwhile, further, the wicked caliph, spurned by Amana, wishes that he could take on the appearance of Nouraddin, so she would accept him. He is changed. Unfortunately, Caled the traitor, who now commands the guard, takes him for the real Nouraddin; they fight and both are slain. The real Nouraddin, disguised as the caliph, is poisoned by Amana. He changes back into his real form briefly, but dies as the caliph. His body is taken for that of Osmin. Amana is executed.

A holy hermit explains that virtue should suffer adversity, not presume to change it. Nouraddin and Amana were punished for presumption.

"Natural and Adventitious Excellence, Less Desirable Than Virtue—Almerine and Shelimah: a Fairy Tale" (Issues 103-104):

In "remote times" when fairies still intervened in the lives of men, a noble of the East, Omaraddin, has two daughters, Almerine and Shelimah. Almerine is blessed by a good fairy, Elfarina. She is beautiful and is destined to marry a prince. However, the evil fairy Farimina does her worst for Shelimah, making her ugly, and further cursing her so that every wish she makes shall have an opposite effect. However, the good fairy decrees that Shelimah shall be content with humble things and perceive them as greater than riches.

Shelimah is raised in obscurity. Almerine is the toast of society, but all this adulation makes her proud and discontented. She sees everyone and everything as inferior. Also, she falls in love with her teacher, the physician Nourassin. Now the prophecy about marrying a prince is a curse. When the caliph proposes, she is in despair. Nourassin gives her a poison so she can do away with him. It is fed to her by mistake. He mixes an antidote, but this makes her hideously deformed and leprous. Actually these are temporary symptoms, and she will recover, but she doesn't know this and confesses everything. The physician is exiled and she is cast out of the palace. The caliph now decides that beauty will get him nowhere, so he will marry the ugliest woman in the land—Shelimah. At the news Shelimah wishes that she might indeed be the ugliest woman in the kingdom. Her wish backfires, and she becomes the most beautiful. The caliph marries her anyway, and since her wishes never work out, she remains humble and content.

"The Value of Life Fixed on Hope and Fear, and Therefore Dependent upon the Will" (Issue 114):

A stranger comes to Almet the "dervise" seeking advice. He (the stranger) owns everything, has every wish fulfilled, but lives an empty life and is sure to be forgotten as soon as he dies. Almet tells of a vision he saw, of a man discontented amidst an apparent paradise and another, naked and seemingly wretched, happy in a wilderness. The first has everything, but suffers because he is afraid of losing it. The second has nothing, but hopes for a better future.

"Benevolence Urged From the Misery of Solitude" (Issue 132):

Carazan the miserly merchant is given a vision of the hereafter. Because he has valued money above mankind, he is to be cast into the outer darkness, beyond all stars and inhabited worlds. He is not even allowed the comfort of inhabiting a comet, which would bring him near mankind every few thousand years. An eternity of cosmic solitude awaits. Sure enough, he reforms.

The titles of these stories, by the way, come from the contents pages of the collected *Adventurer*. Quite possibly they were not titled as they originally appeared.

There is a little more fantasy in the magazine, one minor Eastern Story by Joseph Warton and two sketches by Hawkesworth, depicting the experiences of a flea and a louse respectively. Both are dictated to the Adventurer (i.e., Hawkesworth) in dreams. The flea episode is considerably the better, carrying the unfortunate narrator through many incarnations as various beasts, all of them ill-treated by mankind. It is rather like a shortened version of Dunsany's *The Strange Journeys of Colonel Polders*.

Hawkesworth's Eastern fictions aren't very good by today's standards, although "Amurath" has enough interesting episodes and striking images to be worth reading. The modern reader's main objection is that, like much eighteenth century fiction, the stories are told almost entirely in synopsis, rather than in dramatic scenes. This prevents the reader from vicariously experiencing the action. We only hear about it. Most of the fiction of the day is like that. When more dramatic narrative techniques were developed, however, there was no looking back. The synoptic mode is no longer used, except in some fables, where the outline of events, rather than the texture of them is what matters.

The importance of Hawkesworth's fantasy fiction is that they are part of what I am sure was a flourishing tradition. Somewhere around his time the moral fable was giving way to the romance. The *Arabian Nights* had been discovered by Europeans, mostly through a French translation in the early part of the century. Imitations abounded, again mostly in French, but quickly translated into English. I've found a few of these in used bookshops, in centuries-old editions. One particularly prized one is a volume entitled *Chinese Tales*, published by Walker and Edwards, 1817. This actually contains *Chinese Tales, or The Wonderful Adventures of the Mandarin Fum-Hoam* by Thomas Simon Gueulette (1683-1766) and *Oriental Tales* by The Comte de Caylus (1692-1765). Gueulette's China is about as authentic as Hawkesworth's Arabian "East". Further, a look in Reginald's *Science Fiction and Fantasy Literature, A Checklist* reveals *Fum-Hoam* published in London as early as 1725. Gueulette is also the author of *Mogul Tales, or, The Dreams of Man Awake* (1736) and *A Thousand and One Quarters of an Hour* (1716). This latter is sometimes reprinted in sets of the *Arabian Nights* as the most able pastiche.

Reginald does not list de Caylus. I don't know when he was first published in English, but this is hardly important, since any educated Englishman of the day could read French.

Hawkesworth was taking elements that were already standard in the literature of his day and using them for his own purposes. So far there has not been much research into the pseudo-Oriental fantasies of his era. I suspect I have uncovered the tip of an iceberg.

Suddenly *Vathek* can be seen in a different perspective. There was a tradition of Oriental fiction, most of it fantastic, for at least two generations before Beckford. He is at the end of a long line of development. Further, since these stories tended to be heavy-handedly moralistic and quite contrived ("Nouraddin and Amana" being the most extreme example) it is easy to see how Beckford, who was more akin in spirit to Oscar Wilde than Johnson or Swift or Hawkesworth, could find himself very tired of this sort of thing. It would look ridiculous to him. Therefore, in *Vathek*, he would try to create something far more extravagant than anything before him. Indeed he does. There is also an episode in which a holy man right out of Hawkesworth (in essence, a Christian monk/hermit transmogrified into a Muslim) comes to rebuke Vathek for his wickedness. But Vathek and his cronies kick him along the streets like a soccer ball, to the edge of town. It's a grotesque, comic scene. Beckford is giving the pompous fellow what he (as Vathek would say, anyway) deserves.

Vathek has obvious elements of parody in it. But because Beckford was a far more capable writer than most who went before, because he had absorbed the influences of the richer, more romantic Gothics, and because (I suspect) he got caught up in the richness and grandeur of his story, it is far more than a parody. He transcended what was by his time an already long-established and moribund genre.

BIBLIOGRAPHY

The Adventurer. 2 vols. Included in British Essayists. London: J. F. Dove, 1827.

The Spectator. 12 vols. James Crissy. Philadelphia, 1832.

John Hawkesworth (trans.). *Telemachus* by Fenelon (Del La Motte Fenelon, Archbishop of Cambray). W. Suttaby & B. Crosby & Co., 1807.

Thomas Simon Gueulette and The Comte de Caylus. *Chinese Tales* and *Oriental Tales.* Walker & Edwards, London, 1817.

William Beckford. *Vathek*, trans. by Herbert B. Grimsditch. Bodley Head, 1953. This is the preferred text.

Vathek has a strange history. Beckford, though English, wrote it in French, trusting a clergyman, Samuel Henley, to translate it into English. Henley published it in 1786, without putting Beckford's name on it. To protect his claim to authorship, Beckford had to rush a French version into print (1787). In the rush, he had to leave three episodes out. A revised text appeared later that year. In 1815 he published a second revision of the French version, still not including the episodes, which finally appeared as *The Episodes of Vathek* (1912). Lin Carter edited a version of the Ballantine Adult Fantasy Series with the episodes in place. Unfortunately, he followed Henley's text. Grimsditch's translation is based on the 1815 revision and is considerably superior stylistically. It was originally published by the Nonesuch Press in 1929.

M.R. JAMES AND HIS PLEASING TERRORS

I've had the privilege of seeing Montague Rhodes James in person twice now—or at least as close as is possible to attend upon a man who shuffled off this mortal coil in 1936. It isn't surprising, I suppose, that James, who was after all the 20th century's leading describer of things that don't stay dead, should have been brought back to life before my eyes. In this instance it was done by an extremely talented English actor named Robert Lloyd Parry, who appears on the stage in Edwardian garb, surrounded by minimal furniture and such small props as may become relevant: a glass and decanter, a few books, perhaps what seems to be an ancient manuscript. He then tells—or recites and partially acts out—stories by James. It's a very sophisticated illusion, giving the impression of James himself before us, declaiming his stories and in turn assuming the role of his beleaguered protagonists.

So far I have seen Mr. Parry perform four stories, "Canon Alberic's Scrapbook," "The Mezzotint," "Oh, Whistle, and I'll Come to You My Lad," and "The Ash Tree." He groups them as two different shows, the first called "A Pleasing Terror" and the second, "Oh, Whistle..." I saw the first at the 2007 World Fantasy Convention in Saratoga Springs, New York, where I was chairman of programming and given the convention theme of "Ghosts and Revenants." Under the circumstances, when an actor, who was clearly a professional with good reviews, offered to put on such a thing, it was like being handed gold on a platter. I would have to have been an idiot to refuse.

I was a bit chagrinned that not a lot of people showed up that Saturday night of the convention. *I* came early, to make sure I'd get a seat at all. As it turned out, there were about three seats for everyone in attendance. Most people were at the parties. The more fool them. They missed something *spectacular*. While it is a general rule that you should never pass up a live theatrical event at a World Fantasy Convention because they are rare and certainly very special, this succeeded beyond my wildest expectations.

"...brilliant," I heard Christopher Roden remark. Roden and his wife Barbara publish Ash-Tree Press, and are both among the world's leading experts in all things Jamesian. That he used a modifier of which James himself would certainly not approve may be attributed to the difference between our time and James's, and the kind of amazed enthusiasm a Parry performance can arouse in a knowledgeable audience. Needless to say, when I had a chance to see Mr. Parry again, in New York, performing "Oh, Whistle…" at the 78th Street Theatre Lab under the auspices of The Open Book (a readers' theatre company founded in 1975 by Bill Bonham and Marvin Kaye), I of course jumped at the opportunity. The show will be gone by the time you read this, but if you should ever, anywhere, get the chance to see Robert Lloyd Parry doing M.R. James, go. Meanwhile, you can see brief clips of him online at http://uk.youtube.com/user/NunkieTheatreUSA. No filmed version of his performances seems to be generally available. I can't help but feel that the experience of watching him on the screen, however impressive that might be, would not quite have the same power as seeing and hearing him in person, in a closed, small room. But you have to make do with what you can get. A filmed version, if it ever becomes available, will be a must for any fan of the ghostly and terrible.

Who was M.R. James? I should hope I don't have to explain, but I suspect that for some people I do. This is not a put-down, but instead means that some of you have a wonderful discovery ahead of you. Certainly for anyone who aspires to *write* supernatural fiction, it is an essential discovery and part of one's artistic growth. I don't suggest that you have to go through a phase of writing James pastiches, but he is one of those writers, like Lovecraft and Poe, with whom the entire field is engaged in an ongoing dialogue. The book you want is simply called *The Collected Ghost Stories of M.R. James,* first published in 1931 and reprinted endlessly since. Or, if you are inclined to luxury, you can try to find the Ash-Tree Press version, *A Pleasing Terror,* put out by the Rodens, which is definitive, annotated, and contains much material not in *The Collected Ghost Stories,* including two extra stories, some fragments, a play, the entire text of James's rare juvenile novel *The Five Jars,* and several very good appendices and articles. Unfortunately it is out of print at the moment and likely to be expensive.

H.P. Lovecraft ranked James among the four "Modern Masters" (along with Algernon Blackwood, Arthur Machen, and Lord Dunsany) in his seminal essay, "Supernatural Horror in Literature." Of James he wrote, "…gifted with an almost diabolic power of calling horror by gentle steps from the midst of prosaic daily life, is the scholarly Montague Rhodes James, Provost of Eton College, antiquary of note, and recognized authority on medieval manuscripts and cathedral history. Dr. James, long fond of telling spectral tales at Christmastide, has become by slow degrees a literary weird fictionist of the very first rank; and has developed a distinctive style and method likely to serve as models for an enduring line of disciples."

This last observation proved prophetic. James did indeed develop a whole school of disciples, jokingly referred to by connoisseurs as "The James Gang," many of whose works you can find in print from Ash-Tree Press. His influence has also extended more generally, to writers like Ramsey Campbell, who cites him as a favorite, and to the late Charles Grant and *his* entire school of "quiet" horror, as typified by his own work and his celebrated *Shadows* anthologies, all of which have their roots in James.

James's fiction represented a distinct aesthetic of the ghost story. The typical James story is about an English scholar on holiday, visiting some remote district, who investigates a quaint church or ruin, acquires an ancient artifact (such as a manuscript, or, in one famous instance, a whistle), or otherwise manages to stir up *something,* either the spirit of a dead person, or some elemental force, which would be best left alone. Supernatural manifestations are usually, except sometimes at the climax, barely glimpsed, though their *presence* is strongly felt. There is something against a window which might be a seagull's wing, or might not be. A character slides his hand under a pillow and realizes he's placed it in a *mouth.* The hero of "Canon Alberic's Scrapbook," studying that precious medieval tome (which he has acquired for an impossibly low sum from a gentleman entirely too eager to get rid of it), seated in his half-darkened room, suddenly realizes that the thing on the table beside him is not a dust-mop or a crumpled rag, but an inhuman, hairy *claw.*

James had very exact ideas about how a ghost story should work and what it should be. He wrote several essays on the subject, most notably "Some Remarks on Ghost Stories" (1929). Unsurprisingly, his "rules" for the ideal ghost story most accurately describe his own work. This is always the case. Critical "theories" tend to be retrospective and descriptive, quite unlike scientific ones. The "evidence" they are based on comes from what has already been written. When the theory is produced by an actual practitioner, it tends to explain that writer's work. Whether it applies more generally is problematic. Raymond Chandler's "The Simple Art of Murder" will tell you a great deal about how to write a Raymond Chandler mystery story, but not a lot about, say, A. Conan Doyle. Hemingway on the realistic novel will tell you much about Hemingway and his methods. Lovecraft letters and essays on cosmic horror will illuminate Lovecraft, whose approach and aesthetics were similar to James in some ways, but profoundly different in others. Tolkien's "On Fairy Stories" reveals Tolkien's inner workings, but not necessarily anything that applies to the fantasy fiction of, say, China Mieville. Other writers can take away some useful bits, but critical theories are never hard-and-fast formulas, much less the literary equivalent of paint-by-numbers.

James knew this. Using a typical, elegantly-turned phrase, he remarked that he was listing "characteristics observed to accompany success." A few of his standards, we can, today, dismiss outright. It was entirely appropriate for an Eton provost who began telling ghost stories to the Chitchat Club in 1893 to conclude that sex had no place in the ghost story. Today, standards have changed. The supernatural story with eroticism out in the open has been a distinct type since the days of Clark Ashton Smith and early C.L. Moore, not to mention such masterpieces as Fritz Leiber's "The Girl with the Hungry Eyes." Maybe the flurry of *Hot Blood* type anthologies carried the possibilities a bit too far at times, but the erotic horror story is here to stay.

Nevertheless, we should still pay attention to James. He is wiser than he immediately lets on. He was perhaps too modest to claim any philosophical importance for ghost stories. Their purpose, he wrote, was to amuse, "with the sole object of inspiring a pleasing terror in the reader," adding, "If they do so, well; but, if not, let us regulate them to the top shelf and say no more about it."

Within his chosen limitations, James definitely knew his stuff. To achieve "pleasing terror," he insisted, the ghost or spectral manifestation had to be, first and foremost, malevolent. The next thing required was "reticence." He strongly disapproved of the unsubtle, the gross, and the crude, condemning more than once Christine Campbell Thompson's *Not At Night* series of anthologies, which were actually British, though he believed them to be American because much of the contents was drawn from early issues of *Weird Tales*. "Of course, all writers of ghost stories do desire to make their readers' flesh creep," he wrote, "but these are shameless in their attempts. They are unbelievably crude and sudden, and they wallow in corruption."

If James ever read any Lovecraft, it was, "The Horror at Red Hook," not a fortunate choice, and far from Lovecraft's best. The irony is that Lovecraft would have agreed with most of James's disparaging comments, even about his own work.

It would be simplistic to suggest that James was merely being a prude. The candid truth of the matter is that he was a lot more sophisticated and subtle than the pulp writers he encountered in the *Not at Night* books, but this does not mean his stories were polite and delicate to the point of vitiation. A good James story, as someone put it once, could scare a week-old corpse. His work contains images, very difficult to dismiss from the memory, such as the doomed victim hideously bouncing up and down in bed in an inexplicable manner in "The Ash-Tree" as a result of (we later learn) being bitten to death by enormous spiders spawned from the grave of a witch. It's likewise hard to forget that perfect phrase in "The Haunted Doll's House," in which, glimpsed from afar, a hairy, toad-like thing causes the deaths of two small children: "It was busy about the truckle-beds, but not for long."

James further advised that *setting* was an immensely important aspect of a ghost story, since the number of things a ghost can actually do (seek revenge, demand justice, reveal hidden secrets) is rather limited. Being as he was an expert in cathedrals and church architecture and an enthusiastic tourist to some of the more out-of-the-way parts of England and the neighboring countries, his stories tend to be set in carefully-described remote villages, half-forgotten country churches, or in similarly obscure parts of France, or in the case of the famous "Count Magnus," Sweden. In this, he has something in common with Lovecraft. Both believed that the setting should be made as convincing as possible, with deft use of prosaic details, to maintain plausibility once the fantastic element begins to intrude.

Intrusion is a key element. All James's stories are about something frightening and fantastic gradually breaking into the everyday world—although in James, as opposed to Lovecraft, it is not a matter of cosmic horrors from beyond the Earth, but something that is better left undisturbed, a potent remnant of the past that won't stay dead.

In order to keep up that prosaic sense of reality, James recommended that the story should not be set very far in the past, maybe a couple of generations back, but not so far as to seem fantastic and remote. "Anything, we feel, might have happened in the fifteenth century," he wrote in "Some Remarks on Ghost Stories," adding that "The seer of ghosts must talk something like me, and be dressed, if not in my fashion, yet not too much like a man in a pageant, if he is to enlist my sympathy."

Some of you may be impatiently compiling a list of classic stories that break every last one of the James "rules." It *is* possible to set a good ghost or supernatural story in the remote historical past. More familiar settings may still work better. It would be easier to set a ghostly story in the Rome of the Caesars than in Ur of the Chaldees, but the latter *could be done.* It would be possible to set such a story among cave men in the Ice Age. It is certainly possible, as everyone from Robert E. Howard to Tolkien proved, to place one in an entirely fabulous landscape. Clark Ashton Smith did them both one better and set such stories in the remote future, on the Earth's last continent of Zothique, or even on other planets. As I've already mentioned, the supernatural horror story with a substantial erotic element is now commonplace.

Not every such story needs to be *reticent* either. We may also observe the success of stories which are *loud* and completely up-front, not creeping slowly into the reader's sensibilities but socking him powerfully between the eyes on page one. Regardless of what one thinks of the short-lived Splatterpunk movement, it's undeniable that Harlan Ellison wrote such stories for decades before anybody proclaimed a movement. David Schow, Joe R. Lansdale, Clive Barker, and numerous others have also done so. They wouldn't have met M.R. James's approval, but theirs are still powerful stories, often put together with considerable artistry.

I return to the observation that when a practitioner ventures into critical theory, he ends up describing his own work. Certainly James describes *a* method for writing a very effective ghost story. He himself put it into practice brilliantly. His followers did it with varying degrees of brilliance or non-brilliance. The reason that, more than a hundred years on, his stories are still potent and that an actor like Robert Lloyd Parry can make first-rate theatrical performances out of them is because the Jamesian method, rule-book, formula, or whatever you want to call it, *still works*. Readers will continue to enjoy these stories for a long time to come. Writers will continue to learn from them. James continues to haunt us. His terrors remain pleasing. They do not have to be relegated to the upper shelf. We will continue to say a good deal about them.

PETER SCHLEMIHL AND OTHER CLASSICS THAT NOBODY READS

In the famous introduction to his *Seven Famous Novels* (1934), H.G. Wells explains his early imaginative stories, differentiating them from the serious speculations of Jules Verne: "They belong to a class of writing which includes the *Golden Ass* of Apuleius, the *True History* of Lucian, *Peter Schlemil* [Wells spells it without the "h"] and the story of *Frankenstein*. It includes too some admirable inventions by Mr. David Garnett, *Lady into Fox* for instance. They are all fantasies; they do not project a serious possibility…"

It would be decades before Brian Aldiss famously identified *Frankenstein* as the foundation novel of science fiction, and I am not sure Wells ever accepted himself as one of the fathers of the field either.

But that is not, to my mind, the most interesting thing about this. You will note that in the course of citing famous classics, as if they are the familiar heritage of all mankind, Wells mentions what is to most people an unknown title. *Peter Schlemihl* (or *Schlemil)*? What is that? Well, I think any American knows a few words of Yiddish, and having married a lady of the Chosen People myself, I certainly have had it explained to me that, "A schlemihl [pathetic loser] spills the soup. The [even more pathetic] nebbish cleans it up." A consultation in *The New Joys of Yiddish* by Leo Rosten and revised by Lawrence Bush reveals that the word has various spellings, and that the schlemihl spills the soup down the neck of the hapless shlimazl before the nebekh (their spelling) cleans it up—which does not seem immediately germane to anything, but definition #7 of "schlemihl" is interesting:

> Anyone who makes a foolish bargain or wagers a foolish bet. This usage is wide in Europe; it probably comes from Chamisso's tale "Peter Schlemihl's Wunderbare Geschichte," a fable in which the protagonist sold his shadow and, like Faust, sold his soul to Satan.

(p. 344)

Here again we have the story which H.G. Wells mentions in the same breath as Apuleius, Lucian, and *Frankenstein* and Leo Rosten actually thinks became part of the spoken language in Europe. So, what is "The Wonderful Story of Peter Schlemihl"? The curious reader, the adventurous reader, the reader likely to go beyond a very casual interest in fantastic literature, wants to know. I was in a book discussion of Wells's "The Island of Dr. Moreau" recently, in which I read aloud that passage from the introduction to *Seven Famous Novels*, and nobody there had any idea what "Peter Schlemihl" was, or showed any interest. A couple people asked if it was a joke.

I think not. Sometimes it is a proud and lonely thing to be an investigative reader, though not a difficult one, because a quick look in any literary reference work or Wikipedia tells us that "Peter Schlemihl" is a classic of German romanticism, a novella by Adelbert von Chamisso (1781-1838). Chamisso was of an aristocratic family, born in France, but after the French Revolution his parents fled to Germany, where young Adelbert got a good education and served as a page to the queen of Prussia. He had a brief career in the Prussian army, returned to France for a visit after his parents had gone back, once Napoleon recalled the émigrés. He was in Germany again when war broke out and Prussia rose against France, and found himself despised as an enemy alien, after he had been similarly regarded by the French. Unhappy in his career and circumstances, he applied himself to the study of German literature and, interestingly enough, to science. He became a noted botanist and in 1815 was probably quite relieved to sail around the world as part of an expedition trying to find the Northwest Passage, which may not have been as scientifically momentous as Darwin's voyage a few years later, but he made numerous observations, collected specimens, and returned to Berlin where he earned a Ph.D., received an appointment to the Botanic Gardens, and pursued natural history. But he hadn't given up on literature either, and wrote poetry, various romances, memoirs, and the like.

Chamisso, incidentally, was not Jewish. Why he gave his hero a Yiddish last name is not entirely clear, but we can only guess that some Yiddish words were at least as familiar to 19th century Germans as they are to 21st century Americans.

"Peter Schlemihl" was apparently written in 1813 and published in 1814. Because Chamisso was an associate of Friedrich de la Motte Fouque, the author of the famous *Undine*, the first English translation of "Schlemihl" was mistakenly attributed to Fouque.

I had a copy of "Peter Schlemihl" all along. Mine is a very large, ornately decorated and illustrated volume called *The Marvelous History of the Shadowless Man, and The Cold Heart,* by A. Von Chamisso and Wilhelm Hauff, published in Boston by the Dana Estes Company. No date, but the introduction by Dr. A.S. Rappoport, who does not say he is the translator but probably is, is dated 1913. Abebooks.com listings tend to list this book as 1914. Several other editions reprint the work as *The Shadowless Man* or some variant thereof.

Faced with a roomful of people who just did not seem at all intrigued by what appeared to be a reference (in Wells) to a world-class classic that nobody had ever heard of, as soon as I could afterwards, I got down the book and read it.

Guess what? It's good. This is a novella (88 pages, rather large type) which can still be read with pleasure. There is a rule here, I think, or at least something any reader should take under advisement: if something ever became a classic, even a forgotten classic, there was probably a reason.

The story opens with a strange old man who carries, interestingly enough, a botanical sample case, handing Chamisso a manuscript. This manuscript is Peter Schlemihl's own account of how he got off a boat with an introduction to a very rich man, Mr. Thomas John (possibly intended to be an Englishman?) and proceeded to that gentleman's house, where a garden party was in progress. No one among the upper-class company pays any attention to our hero, but he notices a "tall, elderly, meagre-looking man" in "an old-fashioned coat of gray sarsnet" (a fine cloth) who has the curious ability of producing out of his pocket whatever is desired, starting with a plaster for a lady who pricked her finger on a thorn, but moving on to a large telescope and quite a bit more which should not be able to fit into one man's pocket, including a tent, a Turkish carpet, refreshments, and even two horses. The most curious thing of all is that no one else seems to be aware of where these objects came from, or that they haven't always been there.

We are clearly in the presence of the supernatural. The reader may be justified in the assumption that the man in the gray coat is the Devil, although this is not explicitly stated. The Devil's wiles are more subtle than you might expect. He offers Peter a Faustian bargain, the possession of a bottomless purse, in exchange, not for his soul, but for his *shadow*. Foolish Peter, in an act that gave the word "schlemihl" a new meaning, agrees. Almost at once he sees his error, because without a shadow he is uncanny. He is stoned by street children, shunned by society, and can only venture out on the darkest nights or present himself in very carefully lighted rooms. He is now, of course, inordinately rich, and acquires a faithful servant (in addition to a wicked servant who later betrays him), but he would be very glad to have his shadow back. Alas, the man in the gray coat said he was going away for a year. So a year passes, during which Peter, travels from place to place as a man of mystery (rather like Faust), has various adventures and loses his sweetheart. Then he meets the Devil again, who makes him a second offer: his soul for the return of his shadow. But ultimately Peter is still a friend of God and refuses. (Wikipedia, not Rosten, supplies the datum—a factoid?—that originally the name Schlemihl meant "Friend of God," the equivalent of the Greek Theophilus.)

There is a genuinely unnerving moment when Peter asks if the rich man, Mr. Thomas Johns, has sold his soul to the Devil. But the Devil explains that he already owns such a one, and pulls the wretch partway out of his pocket.

Now having thrown away the bottomless purse, and still without a shadow, Peter can only wander, but luck is suddenly with him. When his boots wear out, he obtains a new pair, which prove to be the proverbial Seven League Boots, so that he can range about the world in them, crossing continents in a few strides. He devotes himself to Chamisso's other passion besides literature, botany, and is reconciled with a life in the wilderness, attuned to nature and to his own remaining goodness. (He didn't sell his *soul* to the Devil after all. Rosten is wrong. He hadn't read the story recently when he wrote, or perhaps at all.)

So what does it mean? Allegorical interpretations have been attempted. People pestered Chamisso for the rest of his life. He doesn't seem to have had any "meaning" in mind, but just written "Peter Schlemihl" as an amusing story, which it is. In the edition I have the language is a little archaic, as we would expect for a translation of an early 19th century fairy tale. The modern reader might object that the second part of the story, involving the Seven League Boots, seems to come out of nowhere, but of course in Chamisso's day "fantasy" was not a commercial genre and there weren't any "rules" about how such a story should be plotted.

Certainly "Peter Schlemihl" had widespread impact. Wikipedia gives us a long list of "later retellings." Peter wandered into an E.T.A. Hoffman story and from there into Offenbach's opera, *Tales of Hoffman*. Wittgenstein and Karl Marx both make allusions to Chamisso's story. The character is referenced in Leopold von Sacher-Masoch's *Venus in Furs*. There was even a television adaptation on American television in 1953 as an episode of *Favorite Story* with a very pre-Dr. McCoy DeForest Kelley in the title role. And so on. Or maybe *und so weiter*. I might also mention that for all Lord Dunsany's 1926 novel *The Charwoman's Shadow* deals with magic and the consequences of losing one's shadow, the two works otherwise do not have much in common. Was Dunsany familiar with Chamisso? Yes, almost certainly. He, like Wells, doubtless regarded it as a standard part of the world's classic literature.

The 1914 Estes & Co. volume is filled out with "The Cold Heart" by Wilhelm Hauff, who was another early 19th century German fantasist, apparently much more prolific than Chamisso, for all he died of typhoid at age 25 in 1827. E.F. Bleiler, in his *The Guide to Supernatural Fiction*, says that Hauff's tales are among the finest literary fairy tales in all of world literature. This one is thematically related to "Peter Schlemihl," in that it is also about a foolish, quasi-Faustian bargain. Peter Munk, a charcoal-burner of the Black Forest is dissatisfied with his lot. He makes a deal with a forest spirit, Master Glassmanikin, for three wishes, which, of course, he spends foolishly. He then encounters a far more sinister spirit, Dutch Martin, who offers him infinite amounts of gold in exchange for his heart. When Peter agrees, Dutch Martin replaces his heart with a stone, pointing out the advantages of a stone heart, i.e. that he will never experience fear, sorrow, remorse, etc. But of course this robs him of his humanity, and eventually he has to cooperate with Glassmanikin again to regain his living heart but give up his riches. He ends up better off where he was, as a humble charcoal burner. In this we see a story-arc very similar to the kind of philosophical/comic romance James Branch Cabell wrote a hundred years later. Jurgen, you will recall, regained his youth and ranged throughout the Earth and cosmos, but ended up where he started.

Well, now we know what that mysterious reference in the introduction to *Seven Famous Novels* of H.G. Wells is about, but the further question is raised: are these stories by Chamisso and Hauff genuinely forgotten, ex-classics? There are such things as ex-classics. I used to argue this one with professors in graduate school. Homer and Shakespeare may be pretty secure, but otherwise, if you have spent perhaps more time in used-book stores and libraries than in classrooms, you know that there are lots of books which have fallen out of the Canon. Charles Reade's *The Cloister and the Hearth* used to be ranked with Tolstoy. It isn't anymore. Winston Churchill's *The Crisis* (a novel about the American Civil War) used to be so famous that when Winston Churchill, the Briton, began to write, he had to sign his name Winston S. Churchill to distinguish himself from the other fellow, who is hardly remembered now, for all *The Crisis*, along with a huge number of other ex-classics can be found listed in the catalogues of old *Classics Illustrated* comic books. You can also find ex-classics listed in the back of very old Modern Library books.

I am not convinced that "Peter Schlemihl" is an ex-classic. It may be more a matter of the provincialism of American fantasy readers that they haven't heard of it. It's still in print in both German and English. There have been many, many editions over the past two centuries. Franz Rottensteiner in his *The Fantasy Book* (1978) refers to it as "immortal," as he sums up 19th century German romanticism quickly in the course of a discussion of E.T.A. Hoffman, whom he ranks with Poe and Gogol as the three finest fantasists, ever. (So, have you read Hoffman? Have you read Gogol?) This is a tip-of-the-iceberg situation. Someone needs to come out with an anthology of German romantic fantasy. It is clear that Germany in the early 19th century produced a great deal of fantasy and horror fiction (think of Poe's remark that "horror is not of Germany, but of the soul"). We can point to Chamisso, Hauff, Ludvig Tieck, Hoffman, de la Motte Fouque, and several others. This was also the period in which the Grimm brothers were collecting and publishing folktales, so it is not surprising that the approach in most of these fantasies is folkloristic. Literary writers respond to new material, as the surrounding culture absorbs it. A hundred years before this, imaginative writers were producing Oriental tales under the influence of translations of the *Arabian Nights*, which were then becoming available. This spawned a genre which persisted through the 18th century until about the time it was memorably parodied and absorbed into the Gothic by William Beckford in *Vathek* (1786).

The thing to keep in mind, then, is that fantasy wasn't invented by Tolkien, or Robert E. Howard, or Lord Dunsany, or L. Frank Baum, or even Poe. It is a norm in literature, which keeps turning up again and again throughout the centuries. It still seems to me that Apuleius's *The Golden Ass* may be the oldest extant example, but there is no reason to believe it was the first.

And yes, if you keep finding references to something that many people over many decades seem to think is worthwhile, it is usually rewarding to check it out.

CONSULTED:

Adelbert von Chamisso and Wilhelm Hauff. *The Marvelous History of the Shadowless Man and The Cold Heart*. Boston: Dana Estes & Company. 1914 (?)

Leo Rosten (revised by Lawrence Bush). *The New Joys of Yiddish*. New York: Crown Publishers, 2001.

Franz Rottensteiner. *The Fantasy Book*. New York: Collier Books, 1978.

H.G. Wells. *Seven Famous Novels*. New York: Alfred A. Knopf, 1934.

DISCOVERING JAMES HOGG

(Even if Lovecraft didn't)

"So why hasn't Lovecraft heard of him?" my friend Lee Weinstein asked, when I attempted to extol the virtues of *The Private Memoirs and Confessions of a Justified Sinner* by James Hogg, which E.F. Bleiler cites in his *The Guide to Supernatural Fiction* as "perhaps the finest supernatural novel of its century" (p. 252).

The Pulitzer Prize winning journalist and literary appreciator Michael Dirda says something rather similar when he writes in *Classics for Pleasure*:

> Among connoisseurs of dark fantasy, no nineteenth-century novel is more greatly admired than James Hogg's *The Private Memoirs and Confessions of a Justified Sinner* (1824). This masterpiece is a stunning amalgam of the weird tale, the mystery story, and the madman's confession, as well as a biting satire on religious fanaticism…"
>
> (p. 188)

Indeed, Dirda remarked to me last at a Capclave that "It's like 'Dr. Jekyll and Mr. Hyde,' only *better.*"

So I am not entirely on shaky ground here. I can cite authorities other than myself. Nevertheless, Lee's question is an intelligent one. Lovecraft mentions Hogg in passing, once, in "Supernatural Horror in Literature," but only as a poet. The short, easy answer is that the book had not been rediscovered in Lovecraft's time, and certainly was not part of the canon of the world's standard literature (today it is reprinted in The Oxford World Classics). Lovecraft made a very thorough survey, and established a good deal of the canon of supernatural horror fiction. A great number of books are remembered or even reprinted entirely because of what Lovecraft wrote about them. Who would ever have heard of *The Shadowy Thing* by H.B. Drake or *The Place Called Dagon* by Herbert Gorman if not for HPL's endorsement? But even Jove nods and the Old Gent missed a few.

That is the short answer. There is no mention of *Justified Sinner* in the five volumes of the Arkham House *Selected Letters*, but we need to keep in mind that the contents of those books are just the tip of the epistolary iceberg and often severely abridged. If we look a little further, into *Mysteries of Time and Spirit, The Letters of H.P. Lovecraft and Donald Wandrei* (ed. S.T. Joshi and David E. Schultz, 2002) we find a tantalizing near-miss.

On page 205, in a letter dated February 15, 1928, Lovecraft is writing to Wandrei, telling how he is reading John Buchan's *Witch Wood* and hoping to get to *The Place Called Dagon* and Lord Dunsany's *The Blessing of Pan*, and how Frank Belknap Long has just loaned him, "that James Hogg book you said you didn't care for." On page 207 Wandrei writes back (Feb 24) to ask HPL what he thinks of the Hogg book, admitting he owes Long "an apology" because he had apparently only read a small bit of *Justified Sinner*, and now "my opinion has practically reversed now that I have read it," although he is not nearly as enthusiastic as Long was about it the previous summer.

On page 209 (Feb 29) Lovecraft writes back to Wandrei, Lovecraft expresses relief that Wandrei has revised his opinion before he (Lovecraft) attempted to read "the debated volume," since "it is always more comfortable to approach a pleasure which qualified connoisseurs recommend, than to tackle one anent which expert opinion is divided." He promises a detailed response. But the rest is silence. Is it possible that he had a copy in his hands and never got around to reading it? He does complain in these letters that his revision work, from which he made his wretchedly meager living, was overwhelming. ("Revistory servitude has bowed me to the dust of illiteracy…")

We may never know the answer. If the fate of the writer is to put messages in bottles, toss them into the sea of futurity and hope for the best, it's entirely possible that Lovecraft found Hogg's bottle and didn't open it. However, just a few years before, someone else *had*, and the rediscovery of James Hogg began by a much more circuitous route.

In 1924, the French writer André Gide was living in Algiers. A friend sent him three English language books, one of which happened to be "a recent edition" of *The Private Memoirs and Confessions of a Justified Sinner*, with the result that he:

> …plunged with a stupefaction and admiration that increased on every page. I made enquiries of all the English and Americans I came across in Algiers—some of them remarkably cultivated. Not one of them knew the book. On my return to France I renewed my inquiries—with the same result. How explain that a work so singular and so enlightening, so especially fitted to arouse passionate interest both in those who are attracted by religious and moral questions, and, for quite other reasons, in psychologists and artists, and above all the surrealists

who are particularly drawn to the demoniac in every shape—how explain that such a work could have failed to become famous?

The above is from Gide's introduction (p. ix) of the Cresset Press edition *Justified Sinner* (1947), from which the book's modern recognition dates. Lovecraft may have missed this one, but ten years after his death, it was rediscovered anyway, in the mainstream. The book has been in print ever since. If the Cresset dustjacket flap is to be believed, prior to that it had been reprinted only once in the previous hundred years, which must account for the edition Gide received from his friend.

* * * *

My own discovery of this remarkable book, which Bleiler, Dirda, Gide, Frank Belknap Long, Donald Wandrei (perhaps grudgingly), and I all commend to your attention, came in stages. It was for me, as I suspect it is for a lot of readers, one of those classics one has vaguely heard about, but has never quite gotten around to reading. Certainly it is well represented in the critical literature of fantastic fiction—something that didn't much exist in Lovecraft's time. You can find a long entry on James Hogg in *The Viking Penguin Encyclopedia of Horror and the Supernatural*, for instance.

From standard reference sources, even Wikipedia, you may rapidly discover that James Hogg (1771-1834),who was known in his day as the Ettrick Shepherd—a phrase Lovecraft uses in reference to him—was a Scottish poet, a protégé of Sir Walter Scott, who is regarded as third fiddle in Scottish poetry, ranking right behind Robert Burns and Scott himself. He really was a shepherd, from the township of Ettrick near Edinburgh, who was illiterate until his late teens and almost entirely self-educated. Later in life he actually published books on the care of sheep, and went back to farming for a while, but first he became a poet. The preconceptions of the Romantic Era had an available niche for a rustic, who wrote quaintly and pleasantly about Arcadian subjects, a kind of natural man who wrote purely what was in his heart. As such, Hogg was a success, and quite acceptable in Edinburgh literary circles, for all he was a peasant and most of the rest were aristocrats. He became associated with *Blackwood's Magazine,* the leading Scottish literary journal of the day.

But he was a far more complex writer than just a shepherd-poet. He didn't entirely stick to the script, even from the outset. His long poem, *Pilgrims to the Sun* (1816), imagines interplanetary voyages. When he turned novelist and began to write in a blunt, direct manner that may have been a little out of step and ahead of his time, a lot of doors seem to have been slammed in his face. His work was not understood, even ridiculed, by critics who set out to demolish him. He persisted, and even edited a magazine, *The Spy*, for a time, but for all he published about forty books, he ended up back on the farm, and his work, certainly outside of Scotland, sank into obscurity.

The first stage of my own discovery of Hogg came in used-book stores. I found a copy of *Winter Evening Tales Collected among the Cottagers in the South of Scotland* (Silas Andrus & Son, 1853). Having first learned the name from Peter Haining's *Scottish Tales of Terror* a.k.a. *Clans of Darkness,* which contains a Hogg tale, I knew what this book was, and I got it very cheaply because the bookseller hadn't noticed that this was one of those two-in-one reprints where the pagination starts all over again after a second title page in the middle, so it was priced down as "volume one only."

You have to collect Hogg in stray 19th century books. His work seems to have been assembled into a variety of sets, in a variable number of volumes, all of which seem to have been edited and abridged differently. You often find them on the "fine binding" shelf in used-book stores, because most of the 19th century editions were bound in leather, which means copies today are usually either falling apart or nicely rebound. Lately I came upon a massive, bug-crusher of a tome of *The Works of the Ettrick Shepherd* in a new edition, "revised at the instance of the author's family" by the Rev. Thomas Thomson, published in 1869. This is clearly intended to be definitive, but despite 712 pages of prose in tiny type, it is only a selection, reprinting some, but not all of the contents of *Winter Evening Tales*. I've got two more stray volumes out of an indeterminate number from a broken set of *Hogg's Tales and Sketches* (William Nimmo, London & Edinburgh, 1878) which contain material not in any of the others. I still don't have all of Hogg's work by any means. Douglas Gifford, in his introduction to the Folio Society edition of *Justified Sinner* describes Hogg's first novel, *The Three Perils of Man* (1822) as "an authentic folk-fantasy which rivals anything later in the tradition of George MacDonald, C.S. Lewis, Tolkien, and Mervyn Peake. The great, shadowy and almost mythical figure of the prince of European necromancers, Sir Michael Scott, broods at the heart of a story of real medieval clashes between English and Scottish border princes and knights, and comic, earthy peasants, set against unreal, but superbly realized supernatural journeys, malignant zombie-seneschals, and battles between Magic and Science depicted on a cosmic scale." This sounds like something that belonged in the Ballantine Adult Fantasy Series, but I can't be sure. It is a text I have not been able to obtain.

Somewhere in the course of all this, I decided I should actually read something by Hogg, if only to justify the investments. I just needed to sample his prose, to make sure he was readable, so I picked something very short, "The Dreadful Story of Macpherson" in *Winter Evening Tales*. Yes, the writing is quite decent. The story itself is too fragmentary to be impressive. Major Macpherson, who has been cruel in the past, and has enemies among the peasantry, goes with some other gentlemen on a hunting excursion into the Scottish mountains. They spend the night in a *bothy* or lodge, but their merrymaking is interrupted by a mysterious young man who confronts Macpherson. There is some kind of urgent and perhaps angry exchange, but the others do not hear what is said. Afterwards, Macpherson seems afraid, but will not divulge anything. A week later, he insists on another outing, despite bad weather. His companions don't want to go, but he insists he will go alone if he must. They set out, and are not heard from for several days, after which searchers discover the entire expedition dead, their bodies hideously mutilated. No explanation is offered. To a modern reader, it seems like a tantalizing fragment, a prologue to a longer work that Hogg did not write, and that somebody else, even to this day, still could. The real story seems to be what wasn't told.

However, it did establish that Hogg is a perfectly readable writer. If occasionally he indulges in Scottish dialect, I can only reply that there's probably nothing "ye canna ken," with or without a glossary. Hogg seemed to be aware that he was writing for a more general audience and usually kept that sort of thing under control.

There was nothing left to do but take the plunge and actually read *Justified Sinner.*

But first, a word of caution. This novel is sometimes reprinted in those miscellaneous old sets, under such variant titles as *The Confessions of a Fanatic* or *The Suicide's Grave*. Read a modern edition. The early ones are may be unreliable and often abridgements. I read the Folio Society edition.

I was impressed. The book was every bit as good as Bleiler, Dirda, Gide, and the rest said it was. The *best* supernatural novel of the 19th century? I am not entirely sure. I confess I still have a considerable fondness for *Dracula* and have not read *Melmoth the Wanderer*, so there could be some room for qualification, but if you want to put it among the top ten for its century, yes, certainly, without a doubt. Among the top five, very likely. The top *three?* Maybe so.

One thing we should admit from the outset is that it *is* a supernatural novel. Much 20th century mainstream criticism had real problems with the concept of the fantastic, and tried to rationalize it away. This tendency seems more evident on the dustjacket flap of the Cresset Press edition than in Gide's introduction, though there is a hint of it there, too. For all the novel might be a "psychological thriller" (which it undoubtedly is) which anticipated Freudianism by the better part of a century, and for all it may be (as Gide suggests) fully as masterful and subtle as Henry James's "The Turn of the Screw," it is more like a version of the James story in which *other people* besides the governess can clearly see the ghosts, but in which this *solves nothing* of its central mystery.

The Private Memoirs and Confessions of a Justified Sinner begins, circa 1700, at the wedding of the Laird of Dalcastle. He is a jolly, Falstaffian soul, who ogles and dances with every lady in the hall. He gets more than a bit tipsy in the celebrations. This is just as well, because his dour, horribly mismatched bride is a crazed Calvinist fanatic of the worst sort, who only takes pleasure from discussing religion with her mentor, the Rev. Wringham, who may be just as crazed as she is, if possibly less sincere. All around her she sees sin and damnation. There is no possibility in her eyes that her husband could be a member of the Elect. He must be headed straight for Hell. This, as you may well imagine, is not the basis for a happy marriage.

For all Hogg is surprisingly frank for an early 19th century novelist on sexual matters, we are left to imagine that on the wedding night the new Lady Dalcastle refused her husband but he forced her. A son results. Shortly thereafter the couple separates, living in different parts of the manor, despite which Lady Dalcastle gives birth to a *second* son, whom, we are led to believe, is actually the preacher's bastard, although this is never quite certain. Lady Dalcastle and her younger son (whom her husband refuses to acknowledge) are removed to Glasgow. To add insult to injury, the Laird takes a mistress.

The two boys are thus raised apart. The first, George Colwan, is an outgoing, jolly fellow like his father. The other, raised as Robert Wringham, is a nasty, self-righteous young scoundrel, who grows up despising just about everyone around him, most especially the Laird and George Colwan. Robert eliminates rivals at school by telling lies about them, and convinces himself that this was the Lord's work in discomfiting the wicked.

This ability to rationalize anything he does is the key to Robert's character and to the Rev. Wringham's teachings. Wringham is an extreme believer in predestination, in fact a heretic, an "antinomian" of the sort found at the fringes of Calvinist theology, who believed that since Christ's blood, shed for mankind, is of infinite goodness, all the salvation that is ever going to occur was accomplished by that single act. The Elect, or "justified" are saved, their names written indelibly in the Book of Life. Human deeds are irrelevant. A logical conclusion of this is that *anything* a member of the Elect does is therefore righteous and good, since he is, after all, on the side of God. This, disconcertingly, can involve slander, at which Robert excels in school, or even murder.

In early manhood, Robert, who has been tormented by doubts all his life, is finally reassured by the Reverend that he, Robert, is definitely one of the Elect. He becomes convinced that it is his mission in life to smite the wicked, to be the sword and flail of the Lord.

At this point, the logic of Robert and his mentor becomes hard to follow, even as, in real life, the logic of religious whackos can be. If everything is predetermined, and nothing a "justified" person does can possibly deflect him from Heaven, why is it necessary to live a righteous life? Why not rob, steal, murder, chase ladies, bugger sheep, and get drunk every night, since *nothing* can change the outcome? Why is it necessary to denounce sinners? They can no more save themselves than they can lead a member of the genuine Elect astray. Why can't everybody just party?

But Robert, unsurprisingly, doesn't see it that way. He uses his religion to justify his hatred and envy. He is dispossessed, living in near poverty with his mother and the Reverend Wringham, while George Colwan lives in high style in Dalcastle. Robert begins to stalk George, causing a series of angry and embarrassing encounters. When he finally murders him, stabbing him in the back while he has been goaded into a duel with another man, it is no great surprise. The old laird having died of a broken heart soon after, Robert and his mother now inherit the estate. He intends to use his newfound wealth to do God's work, of course.

Detective work follows on the part of the old laird's mistress (who had loved George like a son) and a prostitute, along with a client, who witnessed the murder. After enough evidence is gathered, a warrant goes out for the arrest of Robert Wringham, who, having lost everything, disappears.

This could be a moderately interesting, early detective story with only hints of more-than-realistic strangeness (as when Robert seems to appear as an apparition in the sky as he stalks George on Arthur's Seat, the great height above Edinburgh), but we are at this point only about 40% of the way through the book. Hogg employs a daring, *Rashamon*-like narrative technique, very definitely ahead of his time, and tells the story again, with an *unreliable narrator*. Things get much stranger, fast. Very likely, if Donald Wandrei originally didn't finish the book, it is because he did not read this far.

The case-study of "The Editor's Narrative" ends. We now are given the transcript of a manuscript, which is Robert Wringham's "Confession."

Unsurprisingly, Robert tells things a bit differently. It seems that on the very day on which Robert learned he was a member of the Elect he met a "friend" who calls himself Gil-Martin, with whom Robert is in perfect theological agreement. Gil-Martin is so much his "other self" that he may well be a doppelganger, though he has other disconcerting characteristics. His face seems to change to resemble that of the person he is with. He can apparently change his shape enough to impersonate others. The strength of his arguments bring out the worst in Robert, leading him to murder an elderly, respected clergyman who had advised Robert to stay away from Gil-Martin. Walking brazenly away from the crime scene, smoking pistols in hand, Gil-Martin is able to assume the semblance of somebody else, who is accused of the crime. When they subsequently murder George Colwan, another man is likewise accused of the crime, but the witnesses watching from a window clearly see that man, a fellow named Drummond, with whom George has lately quarreled, walk through the square below and depart even as Robert and Gil-Martin arrive to stage the duel and kill George. But by this point, Gil-Martin has assumed the countenance of Drummond, and in that form knocks on a tavern door to lure George out to his death. Unsurprisingly, Drummond is convicted of the crime.

The central question of this novel is simply this: Who and what is Gil-Martin? Robert at first thinks he is really Peter the Great, Czar of Russia, who was traveling about Europe incognito at that time. There are strong suggestions that Gil-Martin is actually the Devil. When asked if he has parents, he says he has only one, whom he doesn't acknowledge. When asked if his "subjects" are Christians, he replies that the Christian ones are the most useful to him.

If Gil-Martin is the Devil, this is perhaps the finest characterization of Satan in all of literature. He is a thoroughly psychological fiend, the personification of evil desires, who leads Robert astray with theological argument, using religion to justify (both in a Calvinist and non-Calvinist sense) any act, however outrageous, and he makes his arguments supremely compelling because his conclusions always turn out to be exactly what Robert, in his darkest heart of hearts, wants to hear. Before long he's convinced Robert that even Lady Dalcastle isn't righteous enough, and that Reverend Wringham's extreme teachings *don't go far enough.* Robert, Gil-Martin insists, will go very far indeed in the course of his great mission. It becomes obvious to Robert that he must murder his brother and gain control of the Dalcastle fortune, not because he lusts after wealth, but because he needs these resources to further his ends. Being a member of the Elect, his deeds cannot possibly be wrong. He is "justified."

The key plot point is that other people are able to see Gil-Martin. The witnesses after the murder of the clergyman clearly see him, even though he is wearing someone else's face. The two women who gather the evidence, the laird's mistress and the prostitute, both encounter Gil-Martin, overhear him speaking with Robert, and then are confronted by him.

So Gil-Martin clearly has an objective "reality," unlike the ghosts in "The Turn of the Screw." But this, as I said before, solves nothing.

Gil-Martin is pretty obviously not Peter the Great. If he is not the Devil, he might be some kind of projection from Robert's mind, but one given physical reality by the strength of Robert's hatred and desires. Gil-Martin offers an extremely sinister suggestion to Robert toward the end:

> "I am wedded to you so closely, that I feel as if I were the same person. Our essences are one, our bodies and spirits being united, so, that I am drawn to you as by magnetism, and wherever you are, there must my presence be with you."
>
> (p. 200 of the Folio Society edition)

Is it possible, then, that the unacknowledged "single parent" Gil-Martin alluded to earlier was not God, but Robert?

Robert's mind is clearly deteriorating. He is having blackouts. He doesn't remember the murder clearly. Gil-Martin's account of it doesn't quite gibe with what the witnesses reported in "The Editor's Narrative." Robert, now in possession of Dalcastle, begins to experience what we would today call "missing time." Whole weeks of his life are unaccounted for. He finds himself accused of all manner of wicked behavior, including the stalking, seduction, and ultimately the murder of a young lady whom he swears, perhaps truthfully, he has never seen. Is Gil-Martin, very much like Mr. Hyde, beginning to take over? Is he wandering around the countryside, in the guise of Robert, committing crimes?

Ruined, a fugitive, Robert attempts to escape his now dreaded and overwhelming "other self." But he can't. Gil-Martin is always there, or reported near at hand. Robert begins to see monsters chasing after him. Is he going mad? Very likely. Are the monsters "really" there? Yes, as much as Gil-Martin is.

Ultimately this is a puzzle that does not unlock itself. Robert commits suicide. The "Confession," which had broken down from a continuous narrative into a series of hastily scribbled diary entries, ends.

The "editor" breaks in, contemplating what we have just read:

> What can this work be? Surely, you will say, it must be an allegory; or (as the writer calls it) a religious PARABLE, showing the dreadful danger of self-righteousness? I cannot tell. Attend to the sequel: which is a thing so extraordinary, so unprecedented, and so far out of the common course of human events, that if there were not hundreds of

living witnesses to attest to the truth of it, I would not bid any rational being believe it.

(p. 209 of Folio edition)

A very clever in-joke follows. We are given a letter that apparently really was submitted to *Blackwood's Magazine* to publicize the book. Mr. Hogg tells the readers how, a century after the death of Robert Wringham, his body has been dug up, miraculously well-preserved. (The modern reader should keep in mind that the first edition of *Justified Sinner* was published anonymously, so the 1824 reader would not necessarily know that Hogg was the author.) The "editor" then goes out to the countryside to view the reported wonder. He meets none other than James Hogg, who is too busy doing a deal in sheep to take much interest; but it turns out that the location of the grave given in "Hogg's" letter is wrong. Furthermore, most of the details don't match. In the Hogg letter, the excavators and souvenir-hunters find the remains of the humble shepherd's clothing that Robert was wearing (as a disguise, while he was on the run) at the time of his death. But the editor describes the remains of the much richer clothing, complete with the odd turban-like headpiece that Gil-Martin wore. The editor discovers the manuscript of the "Confession" in the grave, takes it home, dries it out, and thus was able to present it to us. (The main part is actually a galley-proof, as Robert had intended to print his story for the edification of the Elect, before things got out of hand. His desperate scribblings of his last days come at the end, on a couple of blank pages.)

Even in death there are contradictions. How many graves? Is Robert buried there, or Gil-Martin? Are they, in death, one and the same? The editor cannot resolve it. Was Robert tempted by the Devil? Is his "Confession" an allegory? Was he "a religious maniac" who began writing an allegorical tract but "arrived at the height of madness that he believed himself the very object whom he had been all along describing"? An intriguing notion that, almost post-modern: Did Robert ultimately become a fictional character of his own creation? Or was he destroyed by one? In any case, by his suicide, "in order to escape an ideal tormentor," he "committed that act for which, according to the tenets he embraced, there was no remission, and which consigned his memory and his name to everlasting detestation."

* * * *

This *is* a genuinely great work. We can see the seeds of everything we admire in the best modern horror here, in this rather short 1824 novel. A generation before Poe, here was a writer who made the transition from Gothic castles and clanking chains into the terrors of the mind. He didn't see any need to dispense with the supernatural altogether—to make his fantastic elements mere delusions of a crazy protagonist—any more than, to reach great psychological depths, more than a century later, Fritz Leiber needed to. *Justified Sinner* gazes upon the darkness within, prefiguring Poe's famous remark that "Terror is not of Germany, but of the soul." It springs from our own *desire* for evil, which, if we are deluded enough, we can convince ourselves is good. Isn't that the way of the world? Aren't the great monsters always convinced that they are heroes? If some powerful, charismatic person *always tells us what we want to hear*, isn't that the swiftest path to destruction?

As a literary technician, Hogg is a powerful, straightforward writer. His narrative is vigorous and swiftly-paced. Readers who are afraid that all "old-fashioned" novels are made tedious with long descriptions have obviously not read this one. There is one transition which comes a little suddenly. That is the only "glitch" in the writing I noticed.

More importantly, he understands the difference between murkiness and ambiguity. This is not a *confusing* novel. Every detail is easy to follow. But when you have all the details laid out in front of you, the mystery does not go away. The story is so powerful precisely because it leaves this unsolved object of contemplation resonating in the reader's mind long after the book is put back on the shelf.

The Private Memoirs and Confessions of a Justified Sinner is by all reports Hogg's masterpiece. Whereas he was formerly ridiculed by hostile critics, once the greatness of this book became apparent, some people tried to claim that he, a mere shepherd, could not have written something this good. Modern textual studies of the surviving manuscript make it clear that he did.

How influential has this book been? It is hard to imagine that Robert Louis Stevenson, being a Scot and interested in Scottish legendary and supernatural matters, did not read it. Hogg in his Ettrick Shepherd guise was still fashionable in Stevenson's day, at least in his youth. Stevenson (born 1850) would have been 19 when that *Collected Works* volume I cite came out. But since Hogg is still in the process of rediscovery, perhaps the more apt question is how influential is this book *going to be?*

This is a writer who needs to be explored more thoroughly. I've since read two other of his stories. "George Dobson's Expedition to Hell" is about an Edinburgh cabbie who drives a customer to Hell. He himself is not allowed to leave until he signs a bond that he will return the following noon. He wakes up. Is it a dream? Maybe so, but he dies at the appointed hour. This has the essayistic start common to early 19th century short fiction, but it's an effective story. "The Brownie of the Black Haggs" is about a mysterious servant, who has the body of a child but the face of a 100-year-old man, who is persecuted by a laird's evil wife. Yet everything she does rebounds upon her, despite which she is as obsessively bound to the other as Robert Wringham is to Gil-Martin. Hatred drives her to her death. This is the story Haining anthologized, but it actually isn't a good place to start reading Hogg, if only because too much of it is told through dialogue, in thick Scottish dialect. The place to start reading Hogg, of course, is *Justified Sinner.* Explore outward from there.

Even if most Hogg's of other supernatural stories are not as good as his one great novel, he certainly wrote interesting material. A selection of the best in a modern edition would be well worth publishing.

Yes, it seems very clear. Lovecraft missed something.

WORKS CITED:

Bleiler, E.F. *The Guide to Supernatural Fiction.* Kent, OH: Kent State University Press, 1983.

Dirda, Michael. *Classics for Pleasure.* New York: Harcourt, 2007

Haining, Peter (ed.) *The Clans of Darkness, Scottish Stories of Fantasy and Horror.* London: Gollancz, 1971.

Hogg, James. *The Private Memoirs and Confessions of a Justified Sinner.* London: The Cresset Press, 1945. Introduction by Andre Gide.

_____. same. London: The Folio Society, 1978. Introduction by Douglas Gifford.

_____. *Winter Evening Tales* (2 volumes in 1). Hartford, CT: Silas Andrus & Son, 1853.

_____. *The Works of the Ettrick Shepherd* (2 vols.). ed., Rev. Thomas Thomson. London: Blackie and Son, 1869.

H.P. Lovecraft and Donald Wandrei. *Mysteries of Time and Spirit.* Ed. S.T. Joshi and David E. Schultz. San Francisco & Portland: Night Shade Books, 2002.

HALF-WAY BETWEEN LUCIAN OF SAMOSATA AND LARRY NIVEN: EARLY 19TH CENTURY SCIENCE FICTION COMEDIES

Even the venue is intriguing. The first volume *The Library of Fiction or Family Story-Teller* is published in London by Chapman and Hall, 1836. The anonymous editors make mention in the introduction of the great favor the public has shown to this series when it was issued in "monthly parts," which implies that *The Library of Fiction or Family Story-Teller* must have originally been either a pamphlet series or a fiction magazine. It is hard to get details. I can only tell you that I have a second volume, from the same publisher, dated 1837. Early 19th century popular fiction is poorly documented, largely unindexed, and generally unexplored. Abebooks.com tells me that print-on-demand editions of this book exist, so you don't have to worry about crumbling leather bindings or virtually non-existent monthly issues. I am still unable to discover who the editors are, though many listings offer the name of Charles Dickens because the first volume contains the first publication "The Tuggs's at Ramsgate" which is part of *Sketches by Boz*.

At first glance, the content is what you'd expect for an anthology. There are social stories, comedies, character sketches, historical fiction, etc. The fantasy fan goes looking for gothic or ghost stories. There are some promising titles: "The Castle of Cleves, or The White Hand," "The Alchymist," and even "The Sibyl's Stone" by "the author of *The Gentleman in Black,*" a known late gothic novel by James Dalton which has been reprinted recently.

But what you don't expect to find in a book like this is actual science fiction.

"Tale of a Chemist" is by the ever popular and prolific Anonymous. As is typical for the period not all of the contents of *The Library of Fiction* is bylined.

This one is not. A credit is given to *Knight's Quarterly Magazine*, which, I learn from Wikipedia, was founded in 1823 and lasted six issues. Assuming that it really was a quarterly, the first publication of our story would be 1823 or 1824.

The writer is presumably British. The setting, however, is Moscow, and the story tells of a Russian chemist who discovered the formula for gravity ("It is little more than a combination of carbon, oxygen, hydrogen, and azote"—this last being an obsolete term for nitrogen) and learned how to remove the "gravity" from his body, at which point he is devoid of weight. This leads to an embarrassing episode in which he leaps into the air from behind the Cathedral of the Seven Towers (presumably St. Basil's in Red Square) and finds himself stuck in the middle of the air in full view of crowds, who are first amazed, then bored, then contemptuous. A marksman takes a shot at him. Our hero might have been stranded, gravity-less, forever, had not a storm blown him against the cathedral, enabling him to climb down.

Undaunted by this misadventure, the chemist dreams of greater things. First, he develops a pocket-sized "gravity pump" which can draw the gravity out of his body, or put it back. Thus he can control ascent and descent.

Then he proposes to shoot himself to the planet Venus. This is to be achieved by what sounds like a circus cannon. He stands in a long tube, and a spring flings him forth ... but, alas, he becomes terrified of the possibility that, sans weight, the slightest breeze could deflect him from his course and cause him to miss, dooming him to soar through cosmic space forever.

So it is only in a frenzy of terror that he *imagines* conditions on Venus. For a story written circa 1823, they are quite interesting. Venus is inhabited by "colors," by which the author seems to mean what we would call gaseous or plasma beings:

> I saw innumerable forms of bright hues moving to and fro; they had neither shape nor substance, but their outline was in perpetual change, now swelling to a circle, sinking to an oval, and passing through every variety of curve; emitting the most glittering coruscations, and assuming every diversity of tint.... But there was order in their motions and I could discover that they were rational beings, holding intercourse by faculties we neither have nor can conceive; for, at one time I saw a number collect about a pale feeble light whose coruscations grew less frequent, and the vividness of its colors faded. At last it seemed to die away and melt into the surface of the planet, from the very sameness of color; and then the forms that stood about were for some time feeble and agitated, and at last dispersed. This, I thought, is the death of an inhabitant of the planet Venus. I watched two bright colors that seemed to dance about each other, which floated in the most winning curves, and sparkled as they passed.... There is love here, I thought, even in this insubstantial clime. A little after I saw vast troops of hues collect and flash violently; but their flashes were not the soft and gentle

colors I had just seen, but sharp and dazzling, like forked lightning. Vast quantities faded into nothing, and there remained but a few on the spot, brighter, indeed, than they had arrived: but I thought those few brilliant shapes a poor compensation for the numbers that had perished. Even in the planet Venus, I said, there is death, and love, and war; and those among beings impalpable, and destitute of our earthly frailties.

(pp. 78-79.)

It is hard to think of any extraterrestrial life form that alien anywhere else in 19th century science fiction. Most other-planetarians of the era are more or less human. It is true that H.P. Lovecraft topped this, with "The Colour Out of Space," in which he depicted a gaseous being with no anthropomorphic qualities at all, but that wasn't until 1927.

Now, having survived this visionary trauma and offered more speculations about the dangers of gravity-free interplanetary travel (no problem with breathing, since without gravity one does not have earthly appetites, but you could slide right by a planet and miss it entirely, if there isn't a convenient tree to grab onto), our hero is still in Russia, now afraid that he will be prosecuted as a sorcerer. He resolves to flee and offers his services to a sea captain who is going to India to bombard a British fortress. (Why is not clear. This is much too early for the Crimean War.) On the voyage the hero demonstrates his invention for the amusement of the crew, removing enough gravity from himself so he can leap over masts, but when he offers to reconnoiter the British fortress, he makes a ghastly mistake and overshoots the target entirely. Why? Because he had performed all his prior feats at higher latitudes. On the equator he forgot to take into account the centrifugal force of the Earth's spin, removed too much gravity from himself and thus went soaring out of sight, eventually managing to make his way back to Russia after a series of Munchausen-like adventures. But even then, he has not learned his lesson, and tells us that he has been laboriously extracting gravity from the Earth itself, in order to move the planet closer to the sun: "How far I have succeeded may be guessed from the recent errors in almanacs about eclipses, and from the late mild winters." (p.84)

Global warming! Now we know the truth.

Years ago, I found another such item, in *The Knickerbocker Monthly Magazine* for July 1853. "The Planet," subtitled, "How I Was Induced to Leave the Earth and Become One, Mss. Found in the Portfolio of a Lunatic" is likewise the work of Anonymous, albeit a quite different member of that creative tribe. The story is set in a satirical version of the year 2076. People travel about by balloons, ranging from ranging from "dark, piratical looking crafts" to "neat business-carriages." The Mormons and the Nebraska infantry are still skirmishing. There is a republic in Constantinople. There being too many John Smiths in the world, Congress has decreed that all future Smiths shall be named after stars or constellations, hence Aldebaran Smith, Arcturus Smith, "even one scaly specimen named Libra." The president of Ireland is planning to drive a tunnel through the Mountains of the Moon in Africa in order to "facilitate the Caffre trade," which might leave the modern reader a little uneasy when you realize that "Caffre" is a variant of "Kaffir," an insulting term for a black African. Irish slave trade? Sometimes you just have to gloss over an offhand remark like that in a story this old. The author sees the Civil War coming and is definitely pro-Union. He remarks on a memorial "commemorating the bravery of some patriot who fell fighting for the integrity of the Union."

The main thrust of the story is that the Earth is starting to shrink. The narrator's neighbor asks him if he has moved the fence between their properties, when he obviously has not, because there are no fresh post holes. But *both* properties have gotten smaller. Soon it is clear that the entire world is shrinking, collapsing upon its porous cavities like a sponge squeezed by an enormous hand. Mankind is doomed. There are satirical digs at the Millerites, predecessors of the 7th Day Adventists, notorious for causing national hysteria by announcing Judgment Day several times in the 1840's.

Streets become narrower. Oceans recede. Populations fall into lassitude and despair. Things get grim:

> Soon men could no longer move; the weakest could not support themselves upright; then the strongest sank powerless; till, finally, all were held bound immovable to the earth. I have reason to believe that most were unconscious of this terrible death, for a merciful Providence had taken away the light of reason, and the world for days had been a world of maniacs. Yet, to see the poor idiots turn smiling faces up to the sun and stars, and with insane laughter make merry with dissolution, was appalling!
>
> (Pp.13-14)

Somehow the narrator is not crushed, but swoons for an indefinite period, then awakens to find a world in which the days grow shorter and shorter as the diminishing Earth's spin accelerates. The atmosphere has become thick and difficult to breathe. The oceans are now smooth and hard as crystal. By the time the Atlantic has shrunk to "the width of a ferry," it is an easy matter to stroll to formerly far-away lands:

> I was in England. But where were London and the vast cities of the Thames? I was in Austria. Where was "cannon-girt Vienna?" I was in Russia. Where were the gorgeous cities of the Cossack Empire? Further

eastward, I reached what were once the wide plains of Bactriana, near which I knew had been the Garden of Eden. Here had been the cradle of the human race. "Here," I exclaimed, "it is fit that the LAST MAN should find his grave." My journeying on Earth was ended. I wandered no more; but there, in dogged indifference, awaited my fate.

(p. 15)

His fate, once the Earth has shrunk to the size of a boulder, is to lose his grip on it and go into orbit around the sun, thus becoming the planet of the story's title. ("Here the manuscript ends, or rather runs into insane ravings about freedom and the bliss of the planetary state.")

But the above-quoted passage does echo something else. This springs to mind:

> Neither joy nor hope are my pilots—restless despair and fierce desire of change lead me on. I long to grapple with danger, to be excited by fear.... I shall read fair augury in the rainbow—menace in the cloud—some record dear to my heart in everything. Thus around the shores of deserted earth, while the sun is high, and the moon waxes and wanes, angels, spirits of the dead, and the ever-open eye of the Supreme, will behind the tiny bark, freighted with Verney—the LAST MAN.

That's from the last page of Mary Shelley's *The Last Man* (page 342 in the Bison Books edition). Similar? Has our *Knickerbocker* author given Shelley a wink in his reducto-ad-absurdum end of the world tale? Let's not jump to conclusions, but it is distinctly possible. There was a pirated edition of *The Last Man* published in Philadelphia in 1833. Our author could well have read that.

While not jumping to conclusions, I do want to spin out a hypothesis. We notice that "The Planet" in particular bears a certain resemblance to Edgar Allan Poe's "Mellonta Tauta" (1849), although, frankly, both of these Anonymous tales are considerably more entertaining. It is not a major Poe work, not really a story at all, more of a rambling discourse in the futuristic setting, which is at its most interesting in its last few pages when it anticipates the "archeology of the present" genre (*The Last American, Digging the Weans, The Motel of the Mysteries*) speculating on how a future civilization would excavate the author's present and get things hilariously wrong. But still—balloon ships, a satirical future. I suggest that the Poe is related to these others not through influence, but by being a member of the same literary genus.

How many more stories are there like this? More research is clearly necessary. They could turn up anywhere, in early 19th century magazines or books. My hypothesis is as follows: that there existed in the early to middle 19th century a distinct genre, a recognized convention, of absurdist science fiction. Here I have closely examined two specimens, which may put me in the position of a paleontologist trying to reconstruct a new species from one vertebra and a tooth.

But consider: the absurdly fantastic tale is as old as literature. It can be dated back to, at least, Aristophanes' "The Birds." Lucian of Samosata's "A True History" (which is, ironically, anything but true) features a ship carried to the moon by a whirlwind, the discovery that the stars are shining drops of dew on a cosmic spider web, and even an adventure in a sea of milk where there are islands of cheese and whole nations of men living between the teeth of enormous sea monsters. In the 18th century Voltaire wrote several stories about interplanetary visitors, who come to Earth to observe mankind's follies.

But none of those stories make any real use of science. Yes, in Lucian's day some people did believe that the Moon and the planets were worlds, but they did not believe the stars were dewdrops. The difference is that in a story like "Tale of a Chemist," while the author is still joking around, but he is using the materials of science. Chemistry. Elements. Centrifugal force. That he fails to distinguish between mass and gravity (aside from the notion that gravity—or mass—is substance that can be extracted) hardly matters. In "The Planet," the author is again playing with real scientific concepts: gravity, density, inertia, and celestial mechanics.

When Shelley's *The Last Man* came out in 1826, it was trashed by the critics as morbid nonsense. Mankind wiped out? Impossible! But in "The Planet" the whole thing is reduced to a joke, which doubtless made it more palatable.

Likewise, an interplanetary adventure featuring Venusian gas-beings, if taken straight, would probably have been incomprehensible in 1823-24. But as the frenzied delusions of a not totally sane narrator, the idea could get across.

These stories are thus halfway between Lucian's absurdities and the modern hard science story of the Larry Niven sort. Whether it was ever the authors' intentions or not, the function of these stories—and this will make a lot more sense if we can discover more of them   was to put completely far-out ideas into the popular consciousness. The joking nature of these stories did not require the reader to take the ideas seriously, but the ideas were there nonetheless. Speculation sugar-coated with farce can still be speculation, at least in subtext. By the end of the 19th century or the early 20th, there were lots of stories about anti-gravity, future skies filled with airships, trips to Venus, the end of the world, or even gaseous alien entities and they weren't necessarily funny. As the public became more aware of the advance of science, these notions became more familiar and seemed less ridiculous.

But no more cheese islands floating in milk oceans, though. That's not scientific.

WORKS CITED:

Anonymous. "Tale of a Chemist." *The Library of Fiction, or, the Family Story-Teller.* Vol 1. London: Chapman and Hall, 1836. Pp. 74-84.

Anonymous. "The Planet." *The Knickerbocker or New York Monthly Magazine.* New Series, Vol 25, No 1, July 1853. Pp. 8-16.

Shelley, Mary. *The Last Man.* University of Nebraska Press, 1965.

* * * *

Postscript. Imagine my chagrin, when, after my exciting independent discovery of "Tale of a Chemist" in a fascinating 19th century volume, and the composition of this article, I learned that someone had beaten me to it by 64 years. August Derleth anthologized this story in *Far Boundaries* (Pelligrini and Cudahy, 1951), which leaves me rather in the position of the *second* person gazing down on the Pacific from a peak in Darien. Derleth seems to have found the story in the same place I did, although the lengthy subtitle he quotes does not match my copy. He gives the date as 1843. I suspect he had a later edition, possibly an American one. Derleth gives the editor's name as Robert Bell—the jury may still be out on that one—but since he does not seem aware of the *Knight's Quarterly Magazine* printing of 1823-24, his speculation that Bell is the actual author of the tale is almost certainly incorrect. Since none of this invalidates my hypothesis about the nature and function of such stories in 19th century literature, the preceding article still stands.—DS

THE LIGHTER SIDE OF DEATH: ROBERT BLOCH AS A HUMORIST

Anyone who ever knew Robert Bloch or saw him in public can attest that he was a very, very funny man, whose droll, macabre wit could rise to any occasion, even the moment at the First World Fantasy Convention in 1975 when Bloch had just told the banquet audience how tired he was of being accredited with the shower scene in *Psycho* (which was Hitchcock's idea), whereupon the mayor of Providence, Rhode Island, where the convention was being held, came in and commended Guest of Honor Bloch for the shower scene in *Psycho*....

At the same banquet, when he was given the first World Fantasy Award for Lifetime Achievement, he exclaimed with genuine emotion, "I haven't had this much fun since the rats ate my baby sister!"

"I have the heart of a little boy," he was fond of saying. "I keep it in a jar on my desk."

"Bloch was a superb" was a byword at such events for decades, where he was always in demand as a speaker.

He could be very funny in private, too. One of his colleagues once told me a story about how he and Bloch were in an elevator and, realizing that there were "normal" people present, launched into a totally deadpan, ghoulish conversation on household methods for disposing of corpses.

Bloch's humor was the humor of the era of his youth, of the fading days of vaudeville, the tail-end of the silent film era, and of Hollywood screwball comedies, the Marx Brothers, and W.C. Fields. His interest in humor and in stage performances were in evidence from the beginning. His first letters to H.P. Lovecraft have not been published (and possibly do not still exist), but we can deduce their content by Lovecraft's responses to them found in *H.P. Lovecraft: Letters to Robert Bloch,* such as the following, written in 1934, to Bloch when he was seventeen:

> Congratulations on your minstrel success! You certainly appear to have constituted about nine-tenths of the performance...a 12-man cast in yourself! I can imagine the effect of your costume and rendition—plus, no doubt, the widely imitated rubber cigar!

(p. 48)

While Bloch's first professional sales were stories of blood-curdling terror, he was also trying to write humor from the very outset of his career. Collaborating with a highschool friend, Harold Gauer, he composed a surrealistic novel, *In the Land of the Sky-Blue Ointment*. "*I suppose* it was a novel," Bloch wrote later in his autobiography, *Once Around the Bloch*. "…It dealt with a group of characters cast up on a remote tropical island presided over by a rich and eccentric scientist, Dr. Nork, and visited by a variety of somewhat unusual guests: a bulimic photographer, a magician named Black Art, pious proponents of the Anti-Amusement League, the members of an opposing group called the Sexual Congress, a church official named Bishop Shapiro, and a scroungy author, one Lefty Feep. Gauer had appropriated the latter name from some long-forgotten magazine source." (p.88)

Bloch and Gauer wrote alternating sections of *In the Land of The Sky-Blue Ointment*. Years later, he was to mine his own contributions for stories, including "The Strange Island of Dr. Nork" (*Weird Tales*, March 1949) and "The Traveling Salesman" (*Playboy,* Feb 1957.)

The name "Lefty Feep" is enormously important in any consideration of Bloch as a humorist.

Nevertheless, he broke into print first as a horror writer, as a student of Lovecraft's. Lovecraft had corresponded with Bloch graciously and brilliantly in the last three years of his (HPL's) life. He had read and critiqued many early Bloch stories, and recommended them to fellow correspondents, making Bloch a full member of the legendary "Lovecraft Circle."

Even in his early horror stories, there is an element of play, most evident in "The Shambler from the Stars" (*Weird Tales,* September 1935), in which Bloch causes a thinly-disguised Lovecraft to be devoured by a cosmic monstrosity. This might seem an overly-bold move by a novice writer, but Lovecraft took it with exceedingly good grace and retaliated by finishing off a young weird-fictionist named "Robert Blake" in his "The Haunter of the Dark" (*Weird Tales,* December 1936). Years later, out of a combination of humor, nostalgia, and deep respect for his dead mentor, Bloch rounded out the sequence into a trilogy with "The Shadow from the Steeple" (*Weird Tales* September, 1950). All three of these are ostensibly horror stories, with the in-joke aspect just under the surface.

Nevertheless, Bloch at some point had to get the Lovecraft monkey (or possibly something less describable) off his back. His stories of the mid-1930s were full of long paragraphs and sesquipedalian sentences which mimicked Lovecraft's manner fairly well, and made Bloch's work fit seamlessly into the *Weird Tales* without ever standing out as anything distinctly his own.

The break came in 1938, when an ambitious young fan named Ray Palmer took over the editorship of the world's first and oldest science fiction magazine, *Amazing Stories,* which had fallen on hard times. Palmer immediately threw out the entire inventory he had inherited from his predecessor, feeling (rightly) that it had been part of the magazine's problem, and now had to scramble for material to fill issues. One of the writers he turned to was Robert Bloch.

Writing science fiction for *Amazing* forced Bloch to write things he'd never had to in the Lovecraftian stories, such as extensive, conversational dialogue, as opposed to Lovecraftian monologues, and snappy action. One of his early science fiction stories, "The Strange Flight of Richard Clayton" (March 1939) about a man artificially aged by the psychological effects of space travel, remains a classic. Some of the others of this period, if not so classic, still moved Bloch in a new direction.

Palmer's *Amazing Stories* was a success. Before long it spawned a companion, *Fantastic Adventures,* to which Bloch was to become a regular contributor. *Fantastic Adventures,* true to its title, published a great deal of adventure fiction right on the borderline between science fiction and fantasy, including some of the late works of Edgar Rice Burroughs, but it also had a substantial component of rather lowbrow, screwball humor, and stories with titles like "Freddie Funk's Flippant Fairies" (by Leroy Yerxa, September 1948) and "The Strange Voyage of Hector Squinch" (by David Wright O'Brien, August 1940).

Re-enter Lefty Feep. Bloch took the name Gauer had appropriated from wherever and applied it to a new character, a "reformed" racketeer and racetrack tout straight out of Damon Runyon, a tall, thin man who wears enormously brimmed hats and outrageous suits. "Even a blind man would have found Feep at once," we are told. "If he couldn't see the suit, its color was so loud he'd hear it."

Lefty talks in a wise-cracking, often rhyming jive as he periodically encounters the author-narrator (Bloch himself) in a greasy-spoon restaurant called Jack's Shack and regales him with some outrageous yarn. The style of these stories is more easily quoted than described. Here is from the opening of "The Pied Piper Fights the Gestapo," as collected in *Lost in Time and Space with Lefty Feep*:

> Feep was waving his arms at Jack as I approached. He turned and gave me a nod of recognition, then continued to place his order.
> "Make please with the cheese," he demanded. "But snappy."
> "You want some snappy cheese?" Jack inquired.
> "I do not care what kind of teeth the cheese is using," Feep asserted. "Just so there is plenty of it. Let it be long and strong. Let it be

mean and green. Let it be old with mould. But bring me lots of plenty in a fast hurry."

(p. 83)

There are many more extreme examples. At one point Bloch describes Feep as "a one man assault on the English language." The narrative technique of all the Feep stories is that of the vaudeville comedian, a fast patter containing so many jokes that if not all of them work, enough of them still do to have the desired effect.

In the first Feep outing, "Time Wounds All Heels," Jack also confides to Bloch that Lefty is "the biggest liar in seven states," but before Bloch can get an answer to the next logical question, "Which seven?" Feep has launched into a Rip Van Winkle sort of tale, about how he encountered the annual picnic of The Diminutive Society of the Catskill Mountains, is invited to drink and bowl, and wakes up twenty years later—in 1962—a future of flying cars and towering cities, in which, as a result of the food shortages after World War II, everyone lives on vitamin pills. Lefty thwarts a pill-hijacking racket, then manages to be sent back to his own time.

In later stories, he likewise defeats Axis agents, is often at odds with a gangster named Gorilla Gabface, and encounters assorted supernatural beings and magical wonders. He learns the secret of King Midas's touch, much to his grief. In what is probably the strongest story in the series, "The Weird Doom of Floyd Scrilch" (a title which clearly parodies Bloch's Lovecraftian past), he makes the acquaintance of the statistically "average man" for whom all advertisements work with 100% efficiency, which can be a problem as he is likewise unable to resist them. When the average man glimpses an ad that says "Use your own basement to raise giant frogs," tragedy ensues. Black Art, the magician *from In the Land of Sky-Blue Ointments* turns up again in "Son of a Witch."

There were ultimately twenty-three Lefty Feep stories published in *Fantastic Adventures* between 1942 and 1950, although the main sequence of them stopped with "Tree's a Crowd" (July 1946), in which Lefty gets turned into a tree while involved with a breakfast-food manufacturer and trying to escape alimony demands from three ex-wives. Ghastly puns abound. ("Speaking as a tree surgeon, I must admit the problem stumps me.") There is a good deal of satire about the advertising industry. Bloch, and Lefty, are in fine form. That probably should have been the end of Feep, but one last adventure, aptly entitled "The End of Your Rope," was requested by Palmer's successor, Howard Browne, and duly published in the July 1950 issue. It involves mystical hijinks with the Hindu rope trick and some spies, but is much weaker than the rest of the series. The absurd, punning language which made the earlier stories so magical is gone. Bloch had, by his own admission, lost interest in the character, and in any case, times had changed, and Lefty was already a bit of an anachronism. One last 1958 effort, published in a fanzine, "The Return of Lefty Feep," is not really a story, but a humorous convention report, written for the science-fiction fan in-crowd, and never intended for a broader readership.

The stories remained unreprinted for decades until, in 1987, the publisher Creatures At Large issued what was to be the first of three volumes collecting the entire series. The first volume was beautifully done, with the stories interwoven with comments by Bloch (mostly taken from an interview), and capped off with a *new* Lefty Feep story, "A Snitch in Time," telling how Bloch, in the present, is astonished to meet an absolutely unchanged Lefty Feep, right out of the zoot-suit era, on the streets of New York. It's a case of time-travel again. Feep has been sent forward to obtain various items from the future. For a while he decides he likes the late 1980s and proceeds to make his way in Hollywood, yet ultimately decides that with the decay in taste and social standards, the past was better, and returns to the 1940s. Bloch, the narrator, agrees and accompanies him.

Unfortunately the other two volumes were never published, and the rest of the series is only available in old (but thankfully neither uncommon nor expensive) copies of *Fantastic Adventures*.

For all the Lefty Feep stories may sound and even read like inspired, lunatic slapdash, an outpouring of ridiculous riffs, Bloch made it clear from interviews that they were not. He plotted his comedies carefully, having worked out the punchlines ahead of time. This was also true, although even less evident in another major sequence of comic fantasies that he produced about the same time, which with broad generalization and less than total accuracy can be described as being of the "Thorne Smith type."

It is perhaps necessary to explain to today's readers that Thorne Smith, the author of *The Night Life of the Gods, The Stray Lamb, Topper, Turnabout,* etc. was immensely popular from the 1930s until well into 1950s. He still has readers today, though is only sporadically in print.

Smith's humor has a lot in common with what we see in such movies of the period as *The Thin Man* and sequels. His are "sophisticated," boozy comedies which reflect the attitudes of the American public right after the repeal of Prohibition. Many bizarre things happen to people, often upper-class people, under the influence of alcohol. Characters virtually swim in martinis and highballs. Drunkenness itself is regarded as funny. Nobody has ever heard of alcoholism. Hangovers are one more joke. Nobody throws up, and if they pass out, they do so decorously or at least amusingly. Smith then added supernatural elements into the mix. *The Night Life of the Gods* is about the Olympian deities coming to Earth and enjoying a spree on New York's Broadway. Inebriate and risqué situations follow.

But, as David J. Schow remarked in an introduction to a volume of *The Lost Bloch,* where Smith stuck with high-class characters and a Marx Brothers type humor, Bloch more often wrote about ordinary working stiffs, and his approach was a little closer to the Three Stooges.

There is a great deal of Thorne Smith influence evident in the fiction published in John W. Campbell's *Unknown* magazine, later entitled *Unknown Worlds.* Campbell was a brilliant science fiction editor, who, in the course of just a few years created science fiction's "Golden Age" in *Astounding Science Fiction,* having become the editor of that magazine about the time Ray Palmer took over *Amazing.* His approach was considerably more highbrow than Palmer's, enough so that Palmer admitted that he aimed *Amazing* and *Fantastic Adventures* deliberately *below* the audience that Campbell was reaching for.

About the same time Palmer started *Fantastic Adventures*, Campbell started *Unknown.* This was a brilliant publication, which published many of the classics of mid-20th century fantasy, including L. Sprague de Camp and Fletcher Pratt's *The Incomplete Enchanter* and Fritz Leiber's *Conjure Wife.* But *Unknown* also had a place for the Thorne Smith type story, for all Bloch did not get up to stride with this sort of material until it was almost too late. He had sold one story to *Unknown* quite early. "The Cloak" (May 1939) is a darkly comic tale about a man who makes the mistake of wearing a genuine vampire's cloak and gradually turns vampiric, but the first substantial humor piece Bloch had in the magazine was also his last.

"A Good Knight's Work" (November 1942) is about a modern-day, impoverished chicken farmer who finds himself confronted with a genuine armored knight, sent forward in time from Camelot to retrieve the table on which the Holy Grail rested. Misadventures, many of them quite boozy, ensue. The knight helps the farmer defeat some extortionate gangsters. The farmer helps the knight complete his quest. At the climax, suits of armor in the local museum (all of which, coincidentally, belonged to various Round Table knights) are suddenly inhabited by their former owners and came to the rescue. All of this is told as fast-moving, slapstick farce.

The sequel, "The Eager Dragon," appeared in *Weird Tales* for January 1943. Now *Unknown* lasted until the October 1943 issue, but it is entirely possible that its inventory was full before Bloch submitted "The Eager Dragon." *Weird Tales* was a bimonthly. Since the dates on magazines are off-sale dates, the January 1943 issue would have appeared in November 1942. The lead-time for material going into that issue must have been at least a couple more months, so either John Campbell knew, sometime in mid-1942, that *Unknown* was going to fold with the October 1943 issue, or else for some reason he rejected "The Eager Dragon."

In any case, the story appeared in *Weird Tales* only two months after its predecessor appeared in *Unknown.* It is very much more of the same. Merlin, in gratitude for assistance rendered, leaves our hero a gift—a genuine dragon egg, which causes more comic mayhem when it hatches and proves impossible to feed and keep under control.

The narrative voice of both of these stories is about halfway between the Damon Runyon mode and that of Thorne Smith: Very fast-paced, present-tense narration, more booze, fewer puns.

Meanwhile Bloch had sold another set of such stories to *Weird Tales.* "Nursemaid to Nightmares" (November 1942) and "Black Barter" (September 1943), which were twice reprinted combined into one (as "Mr. Margate's Mermaid" in *Imaginative Tales* for March 1955 and under the collective title "Nursemaid to Nightmares" in the 1969 book, *Dragons and Nightmares.*) These concern an out-of-work writer who takes a job with an eccentric millionaire whose hobby is collecting mythological creatures. Thus the house-guests at his vast mansion include a defanged vampire, a werewolf that has to be walked on a leash, a centaur, a mermaid, and so on.

Weird Tales did not prove to be a long-time market for this type of fiction either. Perhaps the low word-rates it offered by the end of the 1940s were insufficient to attract any writer, including Bloch, who could sell the same sort of story to *Fantastic Adventures,* which was still going strong and paid better.

"The Devil with You!" at about 36,000 words is close to novel-length, but has never been published as a book. It first appeared in *Fantastic Adventures* for August 1950, was reprinted as "Black Magic Holiday" in *Imaginative Tales* #3 (1954) and has been included in Volume One of *The Lost Bloch.* It is very much in the Thorne Smith vein, awash in alcohol, virtually plotless, but filled with mildly risqué incidents and dialogue that would have been right for Mae West:

> "Hello, Annabel," Hicks cried, genially. "What took you so long?"
> "Just stopped on the way for a drink and a chaser."
> "Ten minutes for just a drink?"
> "No, but it took me a while to get rid of the chaser. He was very persistent."
>
> (p.36)

The "hero" of this escapade is another writer, one Bill Dawson, very young, naive about the world, who decides for once to take his vacation somewhere other than the public library. Off he goes to the Big City, New York. He rents a room, but soon finds two strange men in his bed. They are hotel deadbeats, who have been slipping from room to room ahead of the management, to avoid paying their bills. The manager arrives. Everybody gets drunk. They shoot craps for not just the hotel bill but ownership of the hotel itself and, way too easily, our hero wins. The manager is only too eager to get rid of the place because of the magicians' convention that is beginning the next day. Before long Bill, the former manager, the two deadbeats, and a couple tipsy ladies are in a haunted room where the bed comes alive and goes galloping down the stairs with all of them aboard. The bed is alive because a magician slept in that room during last year's convention, muttered spells in his sleep, and brought the furniture to life. Craziness piles on craziness. A vampire and a werewolf check in. Out of the audience, an amateur magician offers to saw a lady in half, and does, whereupon he is chased through the hotel by her angry lower half which won't stop kicking him. He is considerably less sure about how to put her back together. And so on, until the assorted wizard and warlock conventioneers sink an elevator shaft to Hell in order to bring up Beelzebub as their guest of honor.

The Devil is also a major player in "Hell's Angel" (in *The Lost Bloch* Volume Three). This is a story which was written around a cover by the great fantasy artist Hannes Bok, for *Imagination* (June 1951), and as such is a remarkable performance, at 23,000 words, where most stories written around covers tend to be little more than squibs.

The painting shows a man in the cockpit of a spaceship, looking out through a glass bubble at an angel, scantily clad, but with harp and halo. She looks distressed. He looks somewhat maniacally pleased with himself. We know the story was written around the cover because the narrative actually says at one point that the spaceship looks like something designed by Hannes Bok.

The story is about a young man, out of work and hard up for cash like a lot of Bloch protagonists. He isn't a writer, however, but is trained in public relations. In desperation he calls up the Devil, offering, not his soul, but his services. The Devil is at first uninterested, but then accepts and sends the young man on a mission to Heaven in a magical spaceship such as we see on the magazine cover. The job is to kidnap an angel. The young man succeeds, but meanwhile he has become fond of the angel (whose name is Angela), a sweet, naive young thing who was only on Earth for a short while before she died and became an angel. She plays the harp nicely, but isn't very clever otherwise.

Our hero refuses to turn her over to the Devil, but the Devil reassures them that he doesn't wish to harm the angel. He wants to *copy* her form exactly. Satan's fiendish plan is to market a line of "robots" which are actually imitation angels, possessed by demons. Before long every rich person in the world will have such a demon as a confidant, and Satan will rule. When the hero foils this plot, he and the angel are carried off to Hell, accompanied by his cat-like familiar, Brimstone. Brimstone destroys the strings of the angel's harp, but the hero and the angel escape, Orpheus-style, because he has managed to restring the harp—at Brimstone's expense—with catgut.

Imagination was a companion to *Imaginative Tales*. Both were edited by William Hamling, a long-time associate of Ray Palmer. *Imaginative Tales*, particularly in its first years, was very much a successor to *Fantastic Adventures*, which had folded in 1953. Hence the heavy use of Bloch material, including reprints. The magazine also featured a series of quite deliberate Thorne Smith imitations by Charles Myers about a ghost named "Toffee," designed to cash in on the Topper series, based on Smith, which was on television at the time.

This was a market which would have supported Bloch's supernatural slapstick as long as he cared to write it. He did offer other contributions, such as "The Miracle of Ronald Weems" (*Imaginative Tales* #5, 1955), but as the 1950s progressed Bloch was making his way into the book field with a whole series of crime and suspense novels including the famous *Psycho* (1959). He was beginning to work in Hollywood, writing for television and movies. Very likely, it was simply a matter of money and career demands that drew Bloch away from fantastic comedy.

Bloch continued to write a lot of short fiction for magazines, mostly crime and science fiction, since the supernatural horror market shrank to near vanishing in the 1950s, but the days of the long, crazy novellas were over. They had gone the way of Lefty Feep.

After that, though there was a great deal of black irony in Bloch's horror fiction, he wrote less overt comedy. One of his most famous ghastly-joke endings actually occurred quite early, in a story called "Catnip," published in *Weird Tales* for March 1948. This is very much in the vein E.C. Comics would make famous a few years later. An obnoxious, nasty-mouthed boy causes a neighborhood witch to be burnt to death. When the witch's feline familiar has actually gotten into his mouth and removed his organ of speech, leaving him bloodily gurgling, the boy's mother, noticing he has not replied to her summons, asks, "What's the matter? Has the cat got your tongue—?" The reader shudders and laughs at the same time, but it is an uneasy laughter.

Bloch summed up his ideas about comedy in an interview with

Douglas Winter included in Volume Three of *The Lost Bloch*:

> Comedy to me, as I have often remarked, is akin to horror in that both are opposite sides of the same coin…since both deal with the grotesque and unexpected, but in such a fashion as to provoke two entirely different reactions. The so-called "sick" joke, which was popular about a dozen years ago, is, in effect a synthesis of the two and illustrates what I am trying to say. But comedy is based on fantasy; comedy *is* fantasy usually. It's exaggeration. I am not talking now about the comedy of manners, of the highly stylized verbal wit of the French and British playwrights in this and previous centuries; I am talking about physical comedy, the comedy that is based upon an extrapolation of reality. The farce, with its comings and goings and slammings of doors and hidings under beds and extreme overreaction to commonplace events, all the way up to the whimsicality and fantasy of physical punishment that hurts no one that you will find in most of the silent features.… You can cite literally hundreds of examples with Chaplin and Keaton and Lloyd and Langdon and the Marx Brothers. Virtually every major comic deals in fantasy, pure and sometimes not so simple. But we don't generally regard it as fantasy because it's designed or promote laughter rather than tension or fear. Again, the element of catharsis is common to both. Once that tension is relaxed in the so-called serious fantasy or is exploded by the resolution of a comic incident with laughter, we have obtained a catharsis."
>
> (pp. 269-70)

Bloch was also a lifelong aficionado of silent movies. We can also see the roots of his fantastic comedies in the works of the comedians cited above, particularly Buster Keaton, one of Bloch's heroes since childhood and a friend in later years. Like silent film comedies, Bloch's literary comedies are period artifacts. It is a mistake to try to update them, and it was a mistake even for Bloch to attempt this when he gathered "A Good Knight's Work," "The Eager Dragon," "Nursemaid for Nightmares," and "Black Barter" into the collection *Dragons and Nightmares*. The stories are so much of their time, in language and attitudes, that a dropped-in reference to Chairman Mao or Jane Fonda is just jarring. Hopefully, the next time these are reprinted, the editor will follow the original magazine texts.

Bloch's comic fantasies, from Lefty Feep through such works as "The Devil with You!" are what they are. They served a specific purpose in the development of Bloch as a writer. First, they broke him away from the Lovecraftian model—as far away as it was possible to go. Then they enabled him to achieve a new synthesis of humor and horror which gave so much of his mature work its unique flavor.

It is worth mentioning, too, about those early stories, particularly the

Lefty Feeps, that they are still funny.

WORKS CITED:

Robert Bloch. *Dragons and Nightmares.* Mirage Press, 1969.

_____.*The Lost Bloch.* Three volumes. Edited by David J. Schow. Subterranean Press, 1999-2002.

_____. *Lost in Time and Space with Lefty Feep, Volume 1* Creatures At Large, 1987. (Note: subsequent volumes have not appeared.)

_____. *Once Around the Bloch, an Unauthorized Autobiography.*

H.P. Lovecraft. *Letters to Robert Bloch.* Edited by David E. Schultz and S.T. Joshi. Necronomicon Press, 1993.

THE LEFTY FEEP SERIES:

(all in *Fantastic Adventures* except the last two)

"Time Wounds All Heels." April 1942. In *Lost in Time and Space with Lefty Feep.*

"Gather Round the Flowing Bowler." May 1942. In *Lost in Time and Space with Lefty Feep.*

"The Pied Piper Fights the Gestapo." June 1942. In *Lost in Time and Space with Lefty Feep.*

"The Weird Doom of Floyd Scrilch." July 1942. In *Lost in Time and Space with Lefty Feep.*

"The Little Man Who Wasn't All There." August 1942. In *Lost in Time and Space with Lefty Feep.*

"Son of a Witch." September 1942. In *Lost in Time and Space with Lefty Feep.*

"Jerk the Giant Killer." October 1942. In *Lost in Time and Space with Lefty Feep.*

"The Golden Opportunity of Lefty Feep." November 1942. In *Lost in Time and Space with Lefty Feep.*

"Lefty Feep and the Sleepy Time Girl." December 1942.

"Lefty Feep Catches Hell." January 1943.

"Nothing Happens to Lefty Feep." February 1943.

"The Ghost of a Chance." March 1943.

"Lefty Feep and the Racing Robot." April 1943.

"The Goon from Rangoon." May 1943.

"Genie with the Light Brown Hair." June 1943.
"Stuporman." July 1943.
"You Can't Kid Lefty Feep." August 1943.
"Lefty Feep's Arabian Nightmare." February 1944.
"Lefty Feep Does Time." April 1944.
"Lefty Feep Gets Henpecked." April 1945.
"Tree's a Crowd." July 1946.
"The End of Your Rope." July 1950.

"The Return of Lefty Feep." *Shangri L'Affaires* November 1958. In *Out of My Head* by Robert Bloch, NESFA Press, 1986.

"A Snitch in Time." Original to *Lost in Time and Space with Lefty Feep,* 1987.

READING THE WORLD'S OLDEST NOVEL: SOME FURTHER THOUGHTS ABOUT GENRE

We all know the familiar cant. I've expounded it myself on numerous occasions: that Fantasy is the oldest of all forms of literature, the trunk of the primeval story-tree from which all else, including such johnny-come-latelies as "mainstream" (realistic stories of contemporary life without fantastic content) and even science fiction are but branches. There can be a touch of holier-than-thou when fantasy writers go on like that, the subtext being that *my* genre is older and deeper and more noble an undertaking than yours.

But there may be reasons to reconsider. I think this argument is a product of the Ballantine Adult Fantasy Series as edited by Lin Carter, 1969-73, in which *every* fantasy work was presented as a unique masterwork of individual, eccentric genius, and, yes indeed, a lot of them genuinely were. Sure, there *are* books like that, but the Age of Darkness and Del Rey followed, and we learned soon enough that fantasy can be formulaic trash like anything else. I remember how shocked I was at Dean Koontz's cynical suggestion in *Writing Popular Fiction* (1972) that the active ingredient of *The Lord of the Rings* could be isolated and one could turn out further trilogies for the same audience like hamburgers. How absolutely spot-on he was, we learned about a year later when *The Sword of Shannara* appeared.

There are reasons to reconsider the fantasy genre's claim to hoary antiquity, too. This becomes clear to me, after reading the world's oldest surviving novel, *Callirhoe* by Chariton of Aphrodisias, about which, as we say, more anon.

Let's be honest. The real root and trunk of the story tree is *mythic* narrative, the sort we see in the early books of the Bible, in Homer, or *The Epic of Gilgamesh*. This is not the same as *fantasy* in any generic sense, because it lacks that agreement between the writer and the reader which is explicitly stated by Lucian of Samosata:

I am writing about things I neither saw nor heard of from another soul, things which don't exist and couldn't possibly exist. So all readers beware: don't believe any of it.[6]

Genesis or the *Iliad* are not like that. They were very serious works indeed for the cultures that created them, writings which defined who the audience was and what their relation to the moral and cosmic order of the universe might be. They certainly inspired, and were intended to inspire, literal belief. Recall that the trumped-up charge against Socrates was that he had encouraged the young to doubt the existence of the Olympian gods. There were even Homeric fundamentalists in those days, who insisted that if Homer said the Indian Ocean was landlocked, then, by Zeus, it must be landlocked. Yes, mythic narratives contain numerous supernatural episodes and things we now regard to be impossible, but in a mythic narrative, these are *not* acknowledged to be made-up.

Fantasy comes later. Lucian was writing satirical fantasy. His "A True Story" or "A True History" is sometimes claimed as proto-science fiction, but it's actually a whopper to top all whoppers, very much in the style of Baron Munchausen, a parody of travelers' tales, and very much a satirical fantasy. His contemporary or near-contemporary, Apuleius, was also writing fantasy in *The Golden Ass* (2nd half of the 2nd century AD), which might be described as the later Roman Empire's equivalent of a really good Terry Pratchett novel, though in the last chapter all the racy, magical adventures are shoved aside and the tone turns pious, as the hopelessly entangled protagonist turns to the goddess Isis for relief and is redeemed. (Maybe we should think of this as a Roman Terry Pratchett novel with the last chapter by a Roman C.S. Lewis.)

And now a word about the oldest novel in the world. There is still scholarly debate on the subject, but the best guesses are that *Callirhoe* by Chariton of Aphrodisias dates between about 50 BC and AD 50., which means that this was something that contemporaries of Caesar or maybe contemporaries of the emperor Claudius read concealed inside the scroll of something more edifying. It was written in Greek, but is now available in a lively translation by G.P. Goold in the Loeb Classical Library series, so anybody can now read this oldest surviving example of ancient light fiction.

The plot is something on the order of *The Perils of Pauline*. Callirhoe, the most beautiful woman in the world, is married in Syracuse to the comparably handsome Chaereas. But, alas, a jealous, unsuccessful

---

[6] Lucian of Samosata, "A True Story." *Selected Satires of Lucian* edited and translated by Lionel Casson. Chicago: Aldine Publishing, 1962. p. 15.

suitor, Iago-like, convinces Chaereas that Callirhoe is unfaithful. He, in a fit of rage, kicks her while she is pregnant and she falls down, apparently dead. (*How* did this resonate a few years later when Nero kicked Poppea to death?) She is buried in a tomb, whereupon, shades of Juliet, she awakens to bemoan the horror of her predicament. Enter grave-robbers, led by the pirate Theron, who, discovering her alive, carry her off. By this time Chaereas seems such a whiny twit that we find ourselves rooting for Theron.

Alas, again, Theron takes Callirhoe to Miletus (in Asia Minor) where he sells her as a slave to Leonas, steward of the wealthy Dionysius. Dionysius immediately glimpses Callirhoe's ravishing beauty and falls hopelessly in love with her. But he's too decent to just take advantage of her. Crisis arises when Callirhoe is found to be pregnant. She is persuaded to marry Dionysius in time to convince him that the child is his.

Meanwhile that colorful rogue Theron, whom we'd hope might turn out to be the real hero of this story, is captured, confesses everything at his trial, and is crucified. Learning that Callirhoe is alive, Chaereas and a companion set out for Miletus. Some plot complications later, their ship is seized as piratical by the authorities and the two are sold as slaves to Mithridates, governor of Caria (also in Asia Minor). Callirhoe has been given a deliberately distorted account of these events and believes Chaereas to be dead. To convince her of this, Dionysius holds a funeral for Chaereas and even builds a tomb for him. Callirhoe gives birth.

Mithridates attends the funeral, beauty ravishes again, and *he* falls hopelessly in love with Callirhoe. Mithridates learns the identity of his slave and induces him to write a letter to Callirhoe. This letter falls into the hands of Dionysius who then accuses Mithridates of designs on his wife. Everybody is hauled off to the court of the Persian king, Artaxerxes, for trial, at the dramatic climax of which Mithridates exonerates himself by producing Chaereas alive.

This leaves the problem of who is Callirhoe's legal husband. Beauty works its mischief one more time and the king falls madly in love with Callirhoe too, to the displeasure of his queen, Statira.

At this juncture Egypt revolts against Persian rule and the king goes off to war. Chaereas escapes and leads a band of Greek mercenaries to fight on the Egyptian side, performing incredible feats of valor, which very much echo those of Alexander the Great. He captures the Persian queen and her ladies, including (though he does not know it), Callirhoe. Dionysius, meanwhile, has fought bravely on the Persian side so that the king has decided in his favor, declaring Callirhoe to be the legal wife of Dionysius.

The war ends on a compromise. Chaereas discovers that Callirhoe is in his custody and the couple are reunited. Queen Statira, who has been treated honorably, is sent back to Persia. Callirhoe writes a letter to Dionysius, expressing regrets, and relinquishing "their" son to him. With this little white lie, all is resolved and Chaereas and Callirhoe go back to Syracuse to give thanks at the temple of Aphrodite. At last, Callirhoe's beauty is no longer a curse and she lives happily ever after.

The first thing I'd like you to notice about this is that it is a genuine novel. If we define a novel as a prose narrative of some length, about a single subject, following a conflict between a set of characters to a conclusion, this is a novel. It is not a chronicle, historical or otherwise, or a cycle of stories like Malory's *Le Morte D'Arthur.* It is *one* story, with a beginning, middle, and end. Being the oldest extant novel in the world, it isn't surprising that it has one of the world's oldest plots. Boy meets girl. Boy loses girl. Boy seeks girl and in the process is transformed into a manly hero actually worthy of her.

Never mind what you were told in school about the novel being invented by Defoe or Richardson or somebody else in 18th Century England. No, the novel was invented in post-classical Greece, probably in the Hellenistic Age, the time between Alexander and the beginning of the Roman Empire. This was a sophisticated, cosmopolitan era of considerable prosperity, relative peace, large urban populations, and enough literacy that written, prose fiction could reach beyond the courts of kings or the circles of the very wealthy. There was such a thing as popular fiction, and a considerable culture of novel-writing continuing uninterrupted into Roman imperial times, so that the Latin novelists (of whom we have only a fragment of Petronius, and *The Golden Ass* of Apuleius complete) were aware of the Greek ones and perhaps responding to them. Such works were popular in the Greek-speaking part of the Empire well into Byzantine times, though it is difficult to reconstruct the literary scene from such fragmentary evidence. Imagine what it would be like reconstructing the literature of our time some millennia later if the religious Right had taken over and destroyed nearly everything except, say, fragments of Gore Vidal's *Myra Breckenridge,* one really good Terry Pratchett novel, and four or five bodice-rippers. That is rather what happened to the ancient world. For bodice-rippers, read "Greek romances," of which *Callirhoe* is the oldest surviving example of its genre, though by no means the first.

Now keep the words "romance" and "genre" in mind.

The next thing I want you to notice about *Callirhoe* is that it is *not* a fantasy. It has no fantastic content, not even incidental bits which most people of the ancient world might have seen as realistic: spells, prophecies, apparitions, etc. While the goddess Aphrodite might be said to have guided events from a distance, since the driving force of this narrative is love, she does not appear or intervene.

So much for the claim that fantasy is the oldest genre of fiction. This is a *romance*. More than that, it is a historical romance, set roughly 400 years prior to the time of the book's composition. King Artaxerxes is the same who figures in Xenophon's *Anabasis*. His brother Cyrus revolted against him in 404 BC. Plutarch mentions his queen, Statira. That many of the details are wrong is hardly disqualifying. Since when have historical romances gotten all the facts right or been required to? Regardless, *Callirhoe* is more the remote ancestor of *Gone with the Wind* than it is of *The Lord of the Rings*.

Incidentally, if some of the elements in the story seem positively Shakespearean, that is because they are. Shakespeare indeed chipped off a few bits from this very ancient part of the story-tree. His genius was in making such outrageous situations as were routine in such stories psychologically plausible. His *Pericles, Prince of Tyre* is based on a lost Greek romance called *Apollonius, Prince of Tyre,* which was transmitted through the medieval *Gesta Romanorum* to Chaucer's contemporary John Gower, from whom Shakespeare swiped it.

The important thing to remember about *Callirhoe* is that it is a work of *genre*. If we define a *generic* work as one which arises, not solely out of the author's individual inspiration, but out of pre-existing expectations of form and subject-matter, then this is definitely a work of genre, the same way that a mystery novel is a work of genre (there will be a crime; somebody solves it) or the revenge tragedy (of which *Hamlet* is the supreme example) is a genre. Or science fiction for that matter. Or modern fantasy, for all that we can argue about whether fantasy *is* a single genre or contains many.

The *oldest* genre is romance. Sorry about that, but 'tis true. The other surviving examples of the ancient Greek romance are *Leucippe and Clitophon* by Achilles Tatius, *An Ephesian Tale* by Xenophon of Ephesus (not the author of the *Anabasis*), *Daphnis and Chloe* by Longus, and the *Aethiopica* of Heliodorus, all of which are later, and which develop, exaggerate, or slavishly imitate the same story-pattern found in Chariton's novel: hero and heroine separated, pirates, adventures, each thinking the other dead, and a final reunion. There are further examples known from Byzantine synopses, and in the later Byzantine Empire, in the Comnenan period (12th century) there was even a revival of what were by then consciously archaic Greek romances of the sort that Chariton would have more or less recognized.

There is nothing wrong or demeaning or inferior about genre fiction. A genre occurs when a *type* of story becomes popular and people want more of the same, another book which will entertain them the way the last one did, only maybe better. The result can be a work of hackwork or of genius. That's up to the writer and depends on his or her innate ability.

But if you want to know what the public wants, it is this: interesting characters, at least some of them likeable, getting into all sorts of troubles, with captures, escapes, the tension of separated lovers longing and questing for one another, and, as a satisfactory resolution, a happy ending. (At one point Chariton actually breaks into his narrative to reassure us that there will be one.)[7] Sure, this may be dressed up in any number of ways, with fantastic or science fiction or historical elements, perhaps, but as Michael Dirda suggested in one of his books of literary appreciation, most novels are devices for generating anxiety in the reader.[8] That's exactly what Chariton was up to. He knew what would get 'em every time, and what he did still works to this day. Of course we can't have *all* anxiety-generating novels being about beautiful lovers stolen away by pirates, etc. etc. That would get pretty stale after a while, as, by middle Byzantine times, it probably did. That is why we have more than one genre. Authors had to invent other methods of achieving the same effect. But traces of that most ancient of story elements, that first of genres, the separation romance, can be seen in almost all subsequent fiction, in medieval romance, in most modern novels, and yes, in modern fantasy. Lord Dunsany's *The King of Elfland's Daughter* is very clearly a descendent of Chariton's *Callirhoe,* although what was added *later* to the mix was the fantasy element.

WORK CITED:

Chariton of Aphrodisias, *Callirhoe*. Edited and translated by G.P. Goold. Cambridge MA: Harvard University Press (Loeb Classical Library), 1995.

Koontz, Dean R. *Writing Popular Fiction*. Cincinnati, OH: Writer's Digest Books, 1972.

---

[7] The tragic ending, a.k.a. the tear-jerker, while well known in drama at this time, had apparently not crossed over into the novel yet.

[8] Michael Dirda, *Book by Book*. NY: Henry Holt & Company, 2005, p.119.

TEXTS, AUTHORS, AND THE ENDURING MYSTERY OF EDGAR ALLAN POE

There are writers whose image or legend is inextricably tied to their fiction. Does anybody read Hemingway's without some reference to the macho, posturing, great-white-hunter, careerist behind those stories? The truth of the image is another matter entirely. It is what comes to mind when we read Hemingway. Think, too, of Mark Twain, Philip K. Dick, H.P. Lovecraft, Robert E. Howard, Jack London, and any number of others for whom biographical details, or even (as in Twain or London's case, or Hemingway's for that matter) a professionally manufactured public image will always color our perceptions of their texts.

Writing is so much more than just words on paper. Some schools to the contrary, biographical criticism isn't going to go away. The ancients never gave up trying to figure out who Homer was, and had to invent the Blind Poet. I think that what drives the crackpots crazy about Shakespeare is that, for all we know *more* about him than about any other Elizabethan commoner, it just isn't possible to tease a clear idea of who he was out of either the outline of his life or out of his work. Of course if the same level of scrutiny were applied to any *other* playwright of the period, extraordinary results would follow. Maybe poor Will was actually the most unpoetic soul alive and the entire population of England, other than Shakespeare, contributed to the plays. Think of it: Shakespeare the Fake asks if his horse is ready and the stable-boy says, "To be or not to be." So Shakespeare says, "Yeah, I can use that," and jots it down. The bar-maid suggests "'tis nobler to endure the outrageous fortune" of not having a drink rather than having one without being able to pay for it, and Shakespeare says, "Great!"

Or, more modestly, we might find out that the Earl of Oxford really wrote the plays of Thomas Dekker. There is no logical connection between deception and genius. Why should the impostor-poet also be the best? But since there is no glory in such a discovery, it will be ignored. It's the same reason science cranks always go after Einstein, as the big target. But I digress. The imagination runs riot.

Then there's Edgar Allan Poe. His image haunts his own work, the brooding, doomed, sorrowing, tragic, dark romantic poet. The visual iconography comes from one or two late photographs, which are indeed suitably gloomy. The legend was given a boost first by Griswold, then by Baudelaire. Indeed, the acceptance of Poe has often depended on attitudes toward his perceived life. He was never quite respectable to the Victorians, because…gasp, horrors…he not only married his child cousin, which was weird enough, but he…*drank*, and all but died in the gutter. Griswold's memoir of Poe was malicious and included actual forgeries of his letters. Baudelaire, inadvertently, further blackened the reputation of the man he hoped to glorify. To Baudelaire, if Poe was a drunk and possibly an opium addict (definitely not so) whose life ended in wretchedness, that only made him more romantic. It made a better story.

The problem is that much of the standard Poe story may simply be untrue. The irony is that the truth may be an even *better* story than the legend. It is ironic, too, that the inventor of the detective story died a mysterious death fully worthy of the talents of his own C. Auguste Dupin, or even of that later parvenu, Sherlock Holmes. Most readers know some of the details.

After the death by tuberculosis of his child-bride, Virginia, Poe desperately struggled to put his life back together, trying to regain the security of family. He started courting several women at once, two-timing, even three-timing, so it might well have been whispered. He was famous, but his personal reputation was deteriorating. He may or may not have showed up at Sarah Whitman's house drunk and gotten thrown out, with or without the assistance of the police. That at least was the rumor. Their possible engagement was definitely off. He was also rumored to have fathered an illegitimate child by the poetess Fanny Osgood in 1846. (The child was definitely real. But who was the father? There were no DNA tests in those days. This would have been even more shocking because Virginia wasn't quite dead yet.)

Certainly Poe tended to favor poetesses and rich widows. In any case, by the middle of 1849, he thought he'd finally gotten things together, winning (or regaining) the heart of Sarah Elmira Royster Shelton (usually called Elmira), his childhood sweetheart, whom he'd tried to marry as a teenager. She was now a particularly rich widow. She still loved him. They became engaged, apparently on the condition that he give up drinking. He very publically joined the Temperance Society, making sure it was reported in the newspapers, starting with *The Banner of Temperance* for August 31. He even sent the signed pledge card to his mother-in-law, Mrs. Clemm. Then, taking leave of Elmira in Richmond on September 27th, he travelled north to take care of some literary business and disappeared from the historical record for almost a week until he was found in Baltimore, very drunk and ill, minus his luggage, wearing clothes obviously not his own. He was taken to a hospital, where he died on October 7th before he could give any coherent account of himself. To people who disapproved of him, the conclusion was obvious enough. One last drunken debauch had proven fatal. But to subsequent generations of readers and admirers, the result has been an enduring mystery. Theories and fictions abound, the cause of death attributed to everything from election-day violence to rabies. Fritz Leiber once wrote a fine supernatural version called "Richmond, Late September, 1849."

John Evangelist Walsh's *Midnight Dreary, The Mysterious Death of Edgar Allan Poe* (Rutgers University Press, 1999) is not new, but something I recently found in a used book store. I commend it to your attention. In the spirit of Dupin, Walsh attempts to assemble the clues and solve the mystery. What *did* happen during the missing days? Poe's luggage eventually was found. It continued no clues among its contents, but was its location itself a clue? What of the incident of the "borrowed" sword-cane, which Poe managed to lose before he may have needed it? Much more dramatic is the recollection on the part of a writer friend in Philadelphia, George Lippard, that the last time he saw Poe alive the poet arrived "on a hot summer day" at Lippard's office, ill-clad, missing a shoe, without luggage, desperate for money. Poe remained at Lippard's office and sent Lippard around to various friends and publishers to solicit money for his (Poe's) relief. The next day, in a more rational frame of mind, Poe was terribly grateful, took the money and left. Another Philadelphian, John Sartain, also had an encounter with a very disturbed, shabbily-clad, desperate Poe, whom Sartain variously described as possibly suicidal and in fear for his life. Much of Poe's talk seemed quite mad, about visions and such, but he also claimed that due to his unusually acute hearing (think of Roderick Usher) as he was on the train to New York, he overheard men plotting to kill him. He gave them the slip in New Jersey and doubled back to Philadelphia. He needed to disguise himself. He wanted to shave off his moustache. Sartain either didn't have a razor or didn't trust Poe in this state with anything sharp, and so took him into the bathroom and snipped his moustache off with a pair of scissors. Why were the men plotting to kill him? "Revenge." For what? "Woman trouble." A gentleman of that era would not ask more.

All of this is enormously suggestive. Some of it doesn't quite add up. Walsh spins out a fairly persuasive tale which goes as follows: not only did Elmira's children plead with her not to marry Poe, but her three brothers (James, Alexander, and George) were determined that this shady, drunken, womanizing, adventurer was *not* going to get his hands on Elmira's money. Poe may have been a celebrity, but he was still perpetually short of cash, and to some people his perennial campaign to raise subscriptions for the magazine he hoped to start, *The Stylus*, may have seemed like one more scam. Maybe Elmira's heart was aflutter, but the brothers took a far colder view. They followed Poe north, confronting him in a Philadelphia hotel, telling him firmly that he was *not* going to marry their sister and must proceed on to New York and never come back. Otherwise, they would do their worst. Somehow, Poe escaped. He was rattled when he encountered Sartain because this had just happened. Meanwhile he had gone to a second-hand clothing store and switched clothing *as a disguise.* For the same reason he needed to get rid of his moustache. He remained in Lippard's office and sent Lippard around to gather money rather than going himself because he was *in hiding.* His ravings and delusions were not entirely ravings and delusions. He really *was* being pursued by the Royster brothers. Meanwhile, he concluded that his only hope was to get to Elmira first. He turned south again. He stopped to recover his luggage where he'd left it (and it was later found) at a depot in Baltimore. But trains didn't connect. He had to spend the night, left his luggage at the depot, and checked into a hotel. The Roysters followed, broke into his room, overpowered him, and poured a bottle of whiskey down his throat. He may or may not have suffered a serious blow to the head in the process. The rest is almost history. He was found a day or so later, very drunk, and in great distress, sans luggage, in ill-fitting clothing not his own. Possibly he had passed out in the street and spent the night in the open, in the rain. What the Royster brothers had attempted to do, of course, was make it look like he'd broken his pledge and gone on another alcoholic binge, which would have ruined his chances with Elmira. What they didn't plan on, but possibly didn't trouble themselves overmuch about, was that his health was already delicate and he died from the mistreatment.

The pieces all come together—almost. The missing days are accounted for—three in Philadelphia, two with Sartain, one with Lippard, another in Baltimore waiting for the train, then maybe yet another staggering drunk and sick in a back alley. The luggage is accounted for, as is the strange clothing which everybody agreed was not his own. The drunkenness, the despair…it all fits. Except that both Sartain and Lippard recalled that they had both last seen Poe in the *summer*, not late September, which is undeniably, quite a bit of a stretch, and the weakest part of the argument. Walsh would have us believe that both men were wrong or sufficiently vague about the dates that it could be September. It could have been a hot day in September, and summer does technically extend until September 20th. July would not fit at all. At that point, Poe passed through Philadelphia on his way south, bound for Richmond to see Elmira, and he was in good spirits. Furthermore, Sartain may have in recollection conflated two strange encounters (one in which Poe seemed suicidal, another in which he was in fear for his life) into one.

This is all entirely possible, but for me at least a red flag goes up when someone has to *stretch* the evidence to fit the theory. I am reminded of the Jack-the-Ripper theorist I encountered as a tour guide in London in 1990, who explained that everything fit if only you accepted that the suspect's impossibly difficult Polish name was garbled by the authorities. That sounded pretty good too, but it was just one more Jack-the-Ripper solution. Many more followed. The case is by no means closed.

So, too, I am afraid with Poe. With that evidence-stretching, we do not quite achieve closure. Very likely we never will.

I can say that it makes a very good story. It would make one hell of a fine movie, very dramatic, with love, revenge, villainy, pursuit, horror, despair. It would certainly be a lot closer to the truth than the recent Shakespearean secret-history film, *Anonymous*. The film would, I think, have to deal with one loose end Walsh leaves dangling. *Did Elmira know what her brothers had done?* They had destroyed her chance at happiness. She spent the rest of her life as a recluse, refusing to talk about Poe for many years, then denying that she and Edgar had ever been engaged, but finally admitting that they had shortly before her death. Did she live out her life in bitterness and despair, or in fear, a captive of her unscrupulous brothers? That particular ticking bomb would have to go off somehow, to make the drama complete.

Call it one more stretch. Was Edgar Poe, a father of science fiction, you will recall, only the second science fiction writer on record (the other one is Homer Eon Flint) ever to be murdered? It only adds to his inescapable legend.

PEOPLE: IT'S WHAT'S FOR DINNER
(ALL ABOUT SAWNEY BEAN)

Does the name Sawney Bean mean anything to you, Gentle Reader? If so, it surely conjures up images of the darkest depths of human depravity and degeneracy, next to which Lovecraft's "decayed" New England Whateleys and Marshes are paragons of civic probity, although the Martense family in "The Lurking Fear" is a bit closer to the mark: inbred, dwarfish, half-human cannibals dwelling in caves and tunnels underneath an ancient mansion in the Catskills.

Indeed, cannibalism is the crux of the matter, because Sawney Bean (or Beane) and his extended family were the most famous cannibals in the history of Scotland. This is not to suggest that people eating people is a particularly common phenomenon in the north of Britain, and we will refrain from prying questions about what precisely is *in* that wonderful haggis they serve there, but Sawney Bean is something else again.

"The following account, though as well attested as any historical fact can be, is almost as incredible, for the monstrous and unparalleled barbarities that it relates," begins the "standard" version of the story, which tells how, some centuries ago, one Sawney Bean, the "idle" and generally ne'er-do-well son of a Scottish laborer, removed himself from respectable society in the company of a lady similarly inclined, and took up residence in caves in Galloway, where the happy couple was fruitful, multiplied astonishingly, and supported themselves entirely by highway robbery and cannibalism. So successful were they at this that they continued undetected for twenty-five years, as numerous travelers disappeared, several innocent innkeepers were hanged on suspicion of murder, and *no one* encountered the Bean family and did other than "stay for dinner," even as the prolific clan increased incestuously unto a third generation. At last, a man and a wife, riding on the same horse on the way home from a fair, were attacked by the cannibals. The woman was dragged off the horse, butchered, her blood drunk "with great gusto" and her entrails were ripped in front of her husband's eyes. He fought bravely "with sword and pistol," knowing his fate would be the same, until a party of thirty more people returning from the same fair suddenly arrived on the scene. For the first time, someone had encountered the Bean clan and survived. Soon the king of Scotland himself, with four hundred armed retainers scoured the countryside, discovered the Beans' cave complex with its vast stores of smoked and pickled human remains, and after a stout fight, all the cannibals were hauled off to Glasgow for edifyingly gory executions without any need for a trial. Not one of them repented, all screaming hideous curses to the end.

Such families of murderous rural cannibals have become a horror archetype, a staple of the field. Among the novels on the subject are *The Flesh Eaters* by L.A. Morse (1979) and Guy N. Smith's *The Cannibals* (1986). Jack Ketchum's first book, *The Off Season* (1980) transplants the story to the Maine coast. Among film adaptations or films somewhat inspired by the story are Wes Craven's *The Hills Have Eyes* (1977, with a 2006 remake), *Evil Breed: The Legend of Samhain* (2003), *Hillside Cannibals* (2006), *Hotel Caledonia* (2008), which sets the story in the present day, and (although a less literal adaptation), *The Texas Chainsaw Massacre* (1974, remade 2006).

So "well attested" and documented is the tale of the Bean clan that it turns up in any number of "true crime" books, including Jay Nash's *Encyclopedia of Crime* and *Almanac of World Crime*, C.E. Maine's *The World's Strangest Crimes,* and William Roughhead's *Rogues Walk Here.*

There is only one problem: not a word of this story is true.

I owe this insight to my friend and colleague Lee Weinstein, the editor of several books, a sometime fiction writer who had one wrenchingly splendid story, "The Box," in *Whispers* way back when, and an authority on such classic writers as William Hope Hodgson and Robert W. Chambers.

When I repeated the basic Bean story to him and insisted "it's very well documented," he said, "Oh really? Show me."

Lee is a librarian by profession and a researcher *par excellence*, who was once engaged by the editors of *Shocked and Amazed* to document the existence of "Le Petomane," an eccentric French performance artist whose, ahem, "talent" cannot be described delicately. (Look it up. That's why God made the Internet.) He also worked for a *National Enquirer* writer carefully documenting each reported instance of human physiological oddities, cyclopses, "mermaids," two-headed babies, that sort of thing. He was the one who introduced me to Philadelphia's Mütter Museum, with its world-class collection of bizarre medical specimens. Sawney Bean seemed right up his alley.

I have to confess that Lee did more of the research than I did, but I take credit for goading him on, and what we found out is quite instructive in showing how such stories assemble themselves and how you can take them apart again.

We began with the obvious question: *Which* king of Scotland? Various accounts cite a King James, sometimes James the First, but here we are already in difficulties, because this could mean either James the First *of Scotland* who ruled only part of the country between 1406 and 1437 (and did not control Galloway, where the Bean caves are "still to be seen" to this day; so he would not have been able to take an army there) or perhaps James the Sixth of Scotland who became James the First of England in 1603, Shakespeare's patron, for whom the Bard wrote *Macbeth.*

We've already got a spread of about 160 years here.

The next question was this: Why didn't Shakespeare or one of his contemporaries mention Sawney Bean? We followed this up with: Why isn't the "documentation" *even better?* The life of James VI a.k.a. James I, the first Stuart king of Great Britain, is exceptionally well chronicled. You would think that if he had participated in something as shocking as an armed raid on a clan of cannibals, and had personally presided over all those dismemberments and burnings afterwards, which were carried out in fully public view in Glasgow (Edinburgh by some accounts), this would have, in effect, made the evening news. People would talk about it. Writers would mention it. It would become proverbial. There would be lurid ballads written, and maybe an even more lurid play on the order of Thomas Kyd's *The Spanish Tragedy,* the 16th century equivalent of a slasher flick.

But there is silence. Almost.

We found a very old "Historie of Scotland" by Robert Lindsay of Pitscottie (circa 1532-1578) which reports strange portents marking the death of James the Second (1460) including a "blazing star," the birth of a hermaphrodite, and, incidentally, "a certaine theefe" who lurked in "a den in Angus called Fenisden," where he and his family robbed and ate passers-by, until finally caught, whereupon all the family was burnt at the stake. One daughter was spared, she being only a year old at the time, but by the time she was twelve she displayed similar appetites and met the same fate.

The story is repeated in Raphael Holinshed's *Chronicles of England, Scotland, and Ireland* (1577). This is the same Holinshed that Shakespeare used as a source for several of his plays.

This looked like paydirt, but it was not definitive. The Lindsay/Holinshed version does not mention Sawney Bean by name, nor does it contain the heroic husband and the disemboweled lady on her way home from the fair. Holinshed was not noted for extreme accuracy, which is one reason why many Shakespeare history plays only slightly resemble the actual reality of the events they depict. There is also, clearly, an oral tradition at work here. Note, too, that the daughter who was spared only to reveal her evil nature has been dropped from later versions.

All this was very tantalizing, but it did not prove the case. That was where, in the course of our researches, the matter rested. The standard version of the Sawney Bean story, the one quoted above, "as well attested as any historical fact can be," seems to have appeared in the English sensational press about 1730 under the byline of Captain Charles Johnson, which some scholars think to be a pseudonym of Daniel Defoe, the author of *Robinson Crusoe*.

The early 1700s were a golden age of sleazy journalism in England, a time of quickie pamphlets and broadsides which were the equivalent of today's supermarket tabloids. There lots of mentions of Sawney Bean from that period. But just because something is in print doesn't make it true, then or now. The Johnson version found its way into John Nicholson's *Historical and Traditional Tales Connected with the South of Scotland* (1843), from which it was included in the widely reprinted and very common landmark anthology *The Omnibus of Crime* (1934) edited by none other than Dorothy L. Sayers of Lord Peter Whimsey fame. Most mystery or horror fans have this book in their libraries.

The Newgate Calendar, another popular 18th century compendium perhaps comparable to *The Encylopedia of Crime* or *Serial Killers from A to Z* tells us that Sawney Bean's original first name was Andrew and that he was born in East Lothian in the 16th century.

There was still something wrong with this picture. The story could not be *quite* connected back to its alleged source. The literature of the 17th century *is* curiously silent on the matter. That the story seems to shift around both in time and in place (in some versions Galloway becomes Galway, in Ireland) is a sure sign of what would today be called an "urban legend," i.e. a folktale, improved with the telling, whispered from person to person until its source has been forgotten.

Or it might even be a slander against Scotsmen. Remember that the early 18th century was the time of the Jacobite uprisings (Bonnie Prince Charlie and all that) and that the English of the day tended to view Scots as dangerous and barbaric. So, why not cannibalistic too? Isn't it to be expected of wild men in kilts who come screaming out of the fog-shrouded highlands to lop your head off with their enormous claymores?

Finally, Lee and I discovered that all our work had been done for us and that Ronald Holmes had written an entire book on *The Legend of Sawney Beane* (Frederick Muller, Ltd, 1975). This covers everything, the legend, Sawney Bean in literature, documentation such as there is any, the question of which king of Scotland, Galloway vs. Galway, folk beliefs on ogres, prehistorical cannibalism, and much more. Holmes even brings up an objection we hadn't thought of, which is that if you do the math and figure out how old Sawney Bean and his wife must have been and how long it would take Mrs. Bean to give birth to the attested eight sons and six daughters and for *them* to produce eighteen grandsons and fourteen granddaughters (not counting stillbirths and early childhood mortalities caused by the filthy conditions inside the cave), Papa Bean must have been presiding over a cannibal nursery. Most of the Beans would have been children.

Nutritionists have also calculated that, in order to support that many people for that long by cannibalism alone, the Beans would have had to have eaten the entire population of southern Scotland.

Sure enough, the name "Sawney" was once a derogatory term for a Scotsman. Very likely then the story was made up, or at least developed, to exploit English fears of the "wild Scots" in the popular mind circa 1730. From there it spread out. Once the political context was forgotten, the Scots somehow came to embrace the story as a colorful piece of *their* folklore. When I took a ghost tour of Edinburgh in 1995, the guide solemnly repeated the whole, ghastly tale. It was not a place to express doubts. That would have spoiled the fun.

So, one of the standard horror icons came out of, almost, nowhere. There might have been a basis in oral tradition, but there is none in history. The spectacular parts of the tale, the involvement of the Scottish king with his army and the mass, public executions of the Bean clan, cannot be found in history at all. But the power of the image remains. One lesson we drew from this is that "true crime" books tend to repeat "facts" from other "true crime" books and should not necessarily be taken any more seriously than the average UFO book. Another is that when the story is good enough and ghastly enough, mere facts (or the lack thereof) do not much matter.

We have not heard the last of Sawney Bean.

THE COMPLETE POETRY AND TRANSLATIONS OF CLARK ASHTON SMITH

New York: Hippocampus Press, 2012. Volume One: *The Abyss Triumphant*. Volume Two: *The Wine of Summer*. Volume Three: *The Flowers of Evil and Others*. Edited by S.T. Joshi and David E. Schultz. $75.00, Tpb. The first two volumes are paginated consecutively, 808 pp. Volume Three, 444 pages.

* * * *

The way to review something as massive as *The Complete Poetry and Translations* by Clark Ashton Smith is to just stop and force yourself to do it. There are hundreds of poems here, many of them previously unpublished, not even counting the translations from French and Spanish poetry, and it would take years to truly master all of them. You could find yourself dipping in and discovering something new indefinitely, and never get around to writing the review.

First, let me say that this paperback edition is an event of considerable importance. Inasmuch as Clark Ashton Smith, the noted *Weird Tales* author and colleague of H.P. Lovecraft can be accounted a major American poet, it is impossible to exaggerate *how* important this edition is. It makes Smith's poetic oeuvre available *for the first time, ever.* Before this, in 2002, Hippocampus (and the same editors) brought out a much smaller collection of the best fantastic poems of Smith, called *The Last Oblivion* (hopefully not a prophetic title), which, on a smaller scale, made Smith's poetry available to the general reader *for the first time.*

For once we can't blame the benighted academics, or mainstream prejudice, or anything but scarcity of the texts for Smith's lack of general recognition. After a small flurry of publications and a certain amount of critical acclaim in in the first years of the 20th century, he was reduced to self-publication by the 1920s and he fell into complete obscurity thereafter. Later, his poetry was published in a couple of slim volumes by Arkham House (*The Dark Chateau, Spells and Philtres*), and a much thicker *Selected Poems* from Arkham (1970), but these only reached a very specialized audience, and the books went out of print quickly and copies soon cost fantastic sums on the used-book market. A handful of pamphlets and micro-editions published by Roy Squires reached an even smaller audience of collectors.

That was it. Everything was out of print, very rare, and very expensive. The noted poet and fantasist Fred Chappell once told me in an interview that, no, he had not been much influenced by the poetry of Clark Ashton Smith because, alas, he had missed *Selected Poems* when it came out and had been unable to afford it or any of the others thereafter. (To give you an idea of contemporary prices, a quick search on Abebooks.com reveals *The Star-Treader and Other Poems,* 1912, Smith's first book, for a mere $1750.00. *The Hill of Dionysus*, 1962, goes for $1500.00. *Spells and Philtres,* 1958, $1200.00. You get the idea. While collectability may have nothing to do with literary merit, prices like that lead to a sheer unavailability of reading copies, which can be a significant factor limiting a writer's impact.)

So we must be deeply grateful to Joshi and Schultz for the job they have done. They have assembled everything, with extensive scholarly notes. The third volume, consisting of translations, gives the original French and Spanish texts (including the entirety of Baudelaire's *Flowers of Evil*) on facing pages to the Smith versions. (In addition to Baudelaire, Smith translates a great variety of French decadents, symbolists, and aesthetes, including Theophile Gautier, Gerard de Nerval, Victor Hugo, Paul Verlaine, etc. This is all the more astonishing when you consider that he taught himself French, and Spanish, entirely from books, without ever speaking those languages with anyone.)

We couldn't ask for a better edition. I will admit the one thing I could ask for is a glossary of the rare and unusual words, about which more anon. *The Last Oblivion* had such a glossary. It is still useful. For the *first time*, I say again, the poetical corpus of Klarkash Ton (as Lovecraft playfully dubbed him) is made available. University libraries need this set. Seventy-five dollars may still seem a bit steep, but there literally is no alternative. I do think, though, that Hippocampus would do Smith a service by reprinting *The Last Oblivion* (which sold for $15.00) and keeping it in print permanently, as an introductory volume for people not ready to take the plunge into buying the big set.

This then, is only the beginning for Smith as a poet. I mentioned not blaming benighted academics. Do not be surprised if, to this day, the name Clark Ashton Smith draws only blank stares in college Literature departments. He is outside the Canon. For most scholars, his work, along with that of some of his predecessors and all of his successors, is unexplored territory. A point I used to argue in graduate school was that outside the official canon there are other canons, whole separate traditions which may have fallen into obscurity through the odd zigs and zags of critical fashion. In this case it's nobody's fault. Smith's work was never widely enough available for academia or the critical establishment to discover it.

How about for readers? If you're a Baby Boomer, very likely you discovered Smith through Lovecraft (who is the gateway drug for so many others) and read his *Weird Tales* fiction first. His poetry, you only heard about. Maybe you found a couple of examples in old issues of *Weird Tales,* or his celebrated poem "The Hashish-Eater" reprinted in a Lin Carter anthology. Maybe you were quick and bought a *Selected Poems* when the getting was good, at which point you were left struggling with it for the next forty years. Smith is that sort of writer. Problematic and fascinating at the same time. He won't let go, any more than Lovecraft will.

Clark Ashton Smith is certainly a poet of very considerable merit, a real, serious poet, someone who regarded poetry as his main career and mode of expression, light-years beyond the sort of folks who just wrote verse fillers for pulp magazines, and even well ahead of many of his genuinely gifted *Weird Tales* colleagues, Lovecraft, Robert E. Howard, Donald Wandrei, and a few others.

At the same time, Smith is a difficult poet. There is nothing wrong with that. Difficulty does not preclude greatness. Examples from Edmund Spenser to Ezra Pound readily come to mind. But even his difficulty presents difficulties. There will be, first of all, a considerable amount of culture shock when he makes contact with mainstream academia. I recall the time thirty years or so in the past, when I showed his work to a poet/playwright I knew, saying, "Some people think this is a major poet." My friend read a few lines, then stopped and said, "That's a shame." For someone trained on modern poetry, it was just too strange.

Smith's roots are in Milton, Poe, Baudelaire, maybe Swinburne, in the French Symbolist school (about which most Anglophone readers know very little). His work is usually rhymed, or else in blank (not free) verse. He is completely out of step with the direction English language poetry took in the 20th century, from Pound and Eliot on through William Carlos Williams, Allen Ginsburg, and onward. He used, not plain language, but elevated language, deliberately Latinate, and defended this choice for both prose and verse, as when he wrote to a correspondent in 1950:

> As to my own employment of an ornate style, using many words of classic origin and exotic color, I can only say that it is designed to produce effects of language and rhythm which could not possibly be achieved by a vocabulary restricted to what is known as "basic

English." …An atmosphere of remoteness, vastness, mystery and exoticism is more naturally evoked by a style with an admixture of Latinity, lending itself to more varied and sonorous rhythms, as well as to subtler shades, tints and nuances of meaning—all of which, of course, are wasted or worse than wasted on the average reader, even if presumably literate.

(*Selected Letters of Clark Ashton Smith*, p. 365.)

But, as they say, moderation in all things. Legend has it Smith educated himself by reading the unabridged dictionary cover to cover. Certainly he had little formal schooling, but was enormously self-educated, often along eccentric lines. His vocabulary was *odd*. He wasn't showing off when he wrote "arboraceous fuel" instead of "firewood" (a choice which made a young Isaac Asimov give up on his tales). That was just the way the language worked for Smith, and it certainly came more from book-learning than from conversation. In his poems, this can be an irritant, as in "Antony and Cleopatra," an exquisite, erotic poem in which we find the two famous lovers in bed, experiencing that post-coital "drowsy joy that is not ecstasy," and then we read:

> Dawn shall rise,
> *A hueless nenuphar in heavenly pools ...*
>
> *The Abyss Triumphant,* p. 57)

A hueless *what?* Maybe you imagine a nenuphar as an eldritch, lurking frog-like creature the color of pale, dead flesh, but if you use the handy glossary in *The Last Oblivion* you learn that a nenuphar is merely a water-lily. Couldn't Smith have written "water-lily," without even damage to his meter?

And then, "The Hashish-Eater" is full of things like "volcanoes lava-langued" and "And quench his dome with greenish tetter" and "sapphires fine as orris-seed" and "cliff-like brows of plunging scolopendras," and so on and so on. Now, we have to grant an author his vocabulary, and not expect him to dumb things down to "basic English." We can even accept the need to learn a bit of the author's personal jargon, particularly from a poet (think of Yeats with his "perne in gyre"), but arguably too much is too much, and for most readers of Smith ("even if literate," as he would doubtless sneer) the effect is merely to produce *lacunae*—gaps in the text—which the reader just skips over on first reading. Yes, these are real words, not made-up gibberish, but the best one can hope to do is to look them up later, then come back to the poem as if preparing a translation, and eventually work out what the poet means. The only solution I can see, which the editors did not pursue, would be to have, as in a college textbook of Shakespeare or Chaucer, notes in the margins of every page, line by line, so this sort of thing can be taken in at a glance, rather than turned into a research project. Otherwise all possible spontaneity is lost, and the best of Smith's poems have considerable spontaneity to them. They need to be read in a kind of emotional rush, as does this one, one of my own favorites, "Resurrection," which begins:

> *Sorceress and sorcerer,*
> *Risen from the sepulcher,*
> *From the deep, unhallowed ground,*
> *We have found and we have bound*
> *Each the other, as before,*
> *With the fatal spells of yore,*
> *With Sabbatic sign, and word*
> *That Thessalian moons have heard.*
> *Sorcerer and sorceress,*
> *Hold we still our heathenness—*
> *Loving without sin or shame—*
> *As in years of stake and flame.*
> *Share we now the witches' madness,*
> *Wake the Hecatean gladness,*
> *Call the demon named Delight*
> *From his lair of burning night.*
> (*The Wine of Summer,* p. 447-448)

Notice that this poem contains no "rare words" and is all the stronger for it. It demands little more rudimentary classical knowledge. If you don't know who Hecate is or what a sabbat is, you as a reader of fantastic literature, should find out right away. Thessaly is a region of Greece, famously witch-haunted.

I am not alone in preferring Smith's medium-length or shorter poems to his very long ones. Fred Chappell articulates this point of view in some detail in an essay in Scott Connors's admirable Smith symposium, *The Freedom of Fantastic Things,* and goes so far as to suggest that the fame (such as it has, mostly from the enthusiastic praise by Lovecraft) of "The Hashish-Eater" may ultimately hamper a truer appreciation of Smith's actual merits. "The Hashish-Eater, or, The Apocalypse of Evil," is one of Smith's cosmic poems, almost 600 lines, filled with stars, monsters, and alien landscapes, and every possible excess of description. It begins magnificently, with lines every Smith devotee has doubtless memorized:

> *Bow down: I am the emperor of dreams;*
> *I crown me with the million-colored sun*
> *Of secret worlds incredible, and take*

> *Their trailing skies for vestment when I soar,*
> *Throned on the mounting zenith and illume*
> *The spaceward-flown horizon infinite.*
>   (*The Abyss Triumphant*, p. 207)

But I, blasphemously, wonder how many readers have actually *finished* "The Hashish-Eater." Description piled upon description palls after a while. This is not to say that Smith's long poems, like this one, or the stately "The Star-Treader" are bad works of art. But they take some getting used to. They are not the place to begin. It may take, indeed, years, before you work your way up to them. Start instead with "Satan Unrepentant" or "Nero" which, as Chappell argues, are considerably more restrained, better organized than such a massive gush as "The Hashish-Eater." Chappell particularly recommends, "In Saturn" (14 lines).

Smith is, as I have said, far more than a magazine-filler poet. His best work is romantic, elegant, and darkly beautiful. It has a considerable erotic element, something notably lacking, in say, the verse of his pal Lovecraft. His work is also, unsurprising for a poet so inspired by Poe and Baudelaire, intensely macabre, filled with images of death and desolation and ruminations on the folly of human striving. He is a poet who stares into the abyss. This is not likely to gain him wide-spread recognition in mundane circles. Donald Sidney-Fryer (in the interview I did with him in NYRSF) once described Smith as "the specter at the feast." His work is certainly not written to cheer you up.

Smith showed considerable range, writing long cosmic poems, sonnets, and haiku, even producing an entire play in blank verse, set in Zothique, the Earth's last continent of the far future, with the intriguing title of "The Dead Will Cuckold You." (As drama, probably not all that workable. It is hard to imagine actors delivering Smith's lines the way they might deliver Shakespeare's, or even Christopher Fry's, as something that sounds like actual speech, for all it is in verse. This is surely meant to be read, not performed.) His work was all else, immensely imaginative, intended, as was all his work, to transport the reader beyond everyday concerns, "beyond the human aquarium," as he once put it. He is the kind of poet whose works you should keep on your shelves, to dip into every once in a while. Each time you do, you will discover gems.

CITED:

Fred Chappell. "Communicable Mysteries, The Last True Symbolist." In *The Freedom of Fantastic Things: Selected Criticism on Clark*

Ashton Smith edited by Scott Connors. New York: Hippocampus Press, 2006.

Selected Letters of Clark Ashton Smith edited by David E. Schultz and Scott Connors. Sauk City, WI: Arkham House, 2003.

ALL THE WONDERS WE SEEK

by Felix Marti-Ibanez
Clarkson N. Potter, Inc., 1963

* * * *

This is a remarkably little-known book, neither it nor its author being listed in most of the standard reference works of fantastic literature. Nevertheless, Marti-Ibanez came close to being "discovered" as a fantasy writer at least three times. Two of the stories in this collection appeared in *Weird Tales* in 1953 and 1954, two more in *The Magazine of Fantasy and Science Fiction* in 1962 and 1963, and in the 1980s Terri Windling began to mine the book for her anthologies.

It's not that Dr. Marti-Ibanez (1912-1972) would have felt any need to be discovered. He led a full and even adventurous life. He was a Spanish physician, specializing in psychiatry. He was appointed General Director of Public Health and Social Services by the Spanish Republican government in the 1930s, representing Spain at World Peace conferences. Fleeing the Franco regime, he settled in New York in 1939. He wrote novels, stories, essays, and founded MD Publications and the medical news magazine *MD*, for which he wrote numerous articles, not necessarily on medical subjects, but on things he thought might interest doctors. His books of essays make excellent reading today, ranging over art, literature, writing, travel, philosophy, and science. He was widely-read in both Spanish and English classical literature, and also in popular writing. His favorite book and lifetime companion was *Don Quixote,* but he also read Poe, Chesterton, and even Raymond Chandler, and Dennis Wheatley. As for his life, he wrote in a self-interview in *The Mirror of Souls and Other Essays* (1971):

> Mine has been a wandering and restless life.... I have suffered the perils of the bloody Civil War in Spain—the fire of cannon and machine guns, the devastating attack of bombers, and the terrible menace of dumdum bullets, one of which ripped open my right arm and part of my scalp. I have crossed the icy Pyrenees on foot in the height of winter, my bare feet wrapped in rags.... Soon after the Second World War, warned just before entering the Russian zone at Marienborn that I

might be arrested by the Russians because I was a physician-journalist, I jumped off a moving train bound for Berlin. I lost my way in the Angkor jungle of Cambodia, have been within an ace of eating poisoned *mei* noodles in Singapore, have miraculously escaped an attack by a gang of Soho thugs in London, have crossed the Libyan Desert on a mule tracing the footsteps of the physician-architect Imhotep. I have explored dark, lonely areas in Istanbul, in Kyoto, in Panama, and in Bangkok.

(p. 294-95)

Somehow amid all this he found time to practice medicine, edit, publish, and write. *All The Wonders We Seek,* subtitled "Thirteen Tales of Surprise and Prodigy" could have made it onto the Magic Realism critical bandwagon ten years later, despite the author being a Spaniard resident in New York, not a South American. His work has much in common with that of, say, Gabriel Garcia Marquez. His stories are set in the Caribbean or in Central and South America—Cuba, Columbia, Ecuador, Guatemala, Peru, Paraguay, Brazil, Bolivia, El Salvador, Costa Rica—all described with such detail to suggest that the author has visited these places. We are given a distinctly Spanish perspective, the author expressing awed admiration for the ignorant and but idealistic *Conquistadors* who carried the Cross to the farthest corners of the Earth, despite incredible hardships. In "The Sleeping Bell," the narrator makes such an observation as he and a companion come across a lost mission deep in the Columbian jungle. Here, Christianity snuffed out paganism by using one of the local golden goddess idols for the clapper of the mission's bell. But, we learn, these statues were actually immortal women suffused with gold, and they can still come to life. If this had been published in 1900 it would be a Lost Race story. In the 1970s or later, it would be Magic Realism. It reads like folklore, though much (possibly all) could be the author's invention.

"Between Two Dreams" (*Weird Tales,* September 1953) tells of a young Costa Rican lawyer, about to be wed, who experiences serial dreams of a *Conquistador,* sorely wounded, being pursued up a mountainside by enemies, but helped by an Indian maiden. The dreams become increasingly vivid. The man 300 years in the past dreams of the "future," until the lawyer is not sure which is the dream and which is reality. He falls in love with the maiden in the dream. When the 17th century man is wounded by an arrow, the 20th century one has the wound. There is the eerie suggestion that the man of the past knows the 20th century man's fate.

The other *Weird Tales* story, "A Tomb in Malacor" (September 1954), is about a mining engineer who discovers that in a remote Guatemalan town he has led an entirely different life from the one he remembers, and that he is buried there.

In "The Buried Paradise" a Bolivian cave-explorer finds a vast cavern filled with fabulous Indian and Spanish treasure, and, rather implausibly, the means to live there, forever, in ease and comfort. When he wishes that his true love were with him, she appears. When he wishes he had a harem, and his lady-friend's cousins show up, he fears he has gone mad, only to discover later that he was wearing a magical amulet which actually made these things happen.

"Nina Sol" (*F&SF* May, 1963) involves a painter so obsessed with the sunny highlands of Peru that he is bewitched by a Sun Maiden.

"Amigo Heliotropo" is about a mysterious magician who joins a traveling circus in El Salvador. He may be a local saint, who had been sent to Earth to atone for a past sin by resisting the love of a woman. Meanwhile he has the power to make flowers (heliotropes) magically appear. This one, too, has the feeling of local legend.

Marti-Ibanez is at his best with this sort of eerie, colorful story of magic in remote places, written from the cultural viewpoint of an almost-insider. The author has a very different take on the history and antiquity of the Guatemala or Peru than a Yankee American would, even if it is not quite that of a native.

Marti-Ibanez sometimes ventures into comedy, even farce, with varying success. He can come off like a Spanish Thorne Smith, with bawdy humor that may not have aged all that well, though some of the madcap situations in "Senhor Zumbeira's Leg" (*F&SF* Dec 1962) are worthy of the Marx Brothers. Less extreme is "Threshold of the Door" in which a poet teaches a shopkeeper (an ex-magician has lost his imagination) how to walk into the "poetic" world, where everything is fanciful, exhilarating, and slightly absurd. It is a place of dreams. But the people who live there long for our mundane world.

The best stories are the ones, which indeed, as the title suggests, seek wonders. This is a book any serious connoisseur of the fantastic should have. It deserves to be reprinted, though in the meantime it is fortunately quite common used. There were at least two printings. Felix Marti-Ibanez did publish one other collection, *Waltz and Other Stories* (1965), which is much scarcer. Fantasy content unknown. I have located a copy but it isn't in my hands yet. If it proves to be of interest, I'll report on it in this column.

WHAT CAN BE SAVED FROM THE WRECKAGE? JAMES BRANCH CABELL IN THE TWENTY-FIRST CENTURY

by Michael Swanwick
Upper Montclair, NJ: Temporary Culture, 2007
$15.00 tpb, 54 pp.

* * * *

This is the best literary monograph I have read in a long time. It is not so much a survey of the works of James Branch Cabell but the story of how Cabell, "standing at the helm of the most successful literary career of any fantasist of the twentieth century" with "diligence, hard work, and a perverse brilliance of timing" "drove the great ship of his reputation straight and unerringly onto the rocks." All but forgotten at the time of his death in 1958, Cabell was not only a bestseller in the 1920s, but seriously mentioned as a possible Nobel laureate by Sinclair Lewis in his own Nobel Prize acceptance speech in 1930.

The chief tool for self-destruction, Swanwick argues, was the Storisende Edition, an 18-volume, definitive compilation of Cabell's works, published between 1927 and 1930. The problem was that Cabell cemented into this vast and imposing edifice a great deal of inferior material, claiming that all his characters were related, and that everything he had written up to that point, fantasy novels, mainstream novels, essays, short stories, and poetry were all parts of a single opus called *The Biography of the Life of Manuel*. Always a compulsive tinkerer, a man whose professed ideal was to "write beautifully of beautiful things," he revised his works once again for the Storisende Edition, which meant that readers who had bought the early Harper editions (which are illustrated by Howard Pyle), then went on to the Kalki editions from McBride in the 1920s (the revisions between the Harper and McBride editions were significant), possibly investing in some of the extremely attractive and doubtless expensive versions illustrated by Frank C. Papé, were now expected to buy many of the same books *all over again* because Cabell had tweaked a phrase somewhere or substituted a comma for a semi-colon.

Guess what? The Great Depression had just hit and people were not buying. Talk about great timing.

Worse yet, this vast literary mausoleum was soon seen an ordeal for the reader rather than a pleasure. Swanwick, who seems a bit shell-shocked himself after having waded through everything, quotes a critic of the day who said of Cabell, "We are bored with him at the outset, yet read from a sense of duty; our minds atrophy, our organs decay, our flesh shreds from our bones as we whip through him again...."

The final wreck of the Good Ship Cabell came in 1929 when the author announced (in the afterword to *The Way of Ecben*) that the world was done with James Branch Cabell. What he *meant* was that henceforth he would reinvent himself as *Branch* Cabell, but critics and the public were a little too eager to take him at his word. Again, the timing was perfect. Reading tastes were shifting radically. The 1930s were the high-water mark of modernist realism, when "literature" meant Hemingway or Steinbeck or Faulkner or Thomas Wolfe, not aristocratic Southern gentlemen who wrote witty, cynical, and elegantly anti-romantic fantasies about magical and sexual doings in an imaginary Middle Ages.

Alas, when Cabell reinvented himself, he could not come up with anything but more of the same, only, as Swanwick emphasizes, *not as good*, the nadir being reached in *Hamlet Had an Uncle* (1940), which was a kind of primal scream at an audience its author knew had abandoned him. The book was received (deservedly) with "near-universal loathing." When primates are threatened, we are told, they throw feces. Cabell produced *Hamlet Had an Uncle*.

What can be salvaged from the wreck? Basically, Swanwick argues, the fantasy novels might still float, the ones reprinted by Lin Carter in the Ballantine Adult Fantasy Series: *Figures of Earth, The Silver Stallion, The High Place, The Cream of the Jest,* and perhaps *Domnei;* plus *Jurgen*, which was not in the Ballantine series, because it was still in print from Avon at the time. These books still have the power to delight. Swanwick can tell you why. But more than that, his little treatise makes clear, in a way we've never quite seen it explained before, what happened to Cabell's career and why. It is a definitive autopsy report. Even the most devoted, lifelong Cabell fan will come away with new insights. Every present-day fantasist, particularly the writers of multi-volume bug-crusher epics which are Really Too Long To Begin If You Haven't Already, should read it with a certain trepidation and examination of conscience. There is greatness in five or six Cabell books. Some of the lesser ones are of varying degrees of interest. We should indeed still read Cabell. But at the same time, we are warned, "do not sail past the Shipwreck Coast of his career without a second glance."

THE WORD OF GOD, BY THOMAS M. DISCH

San Francisco, CA: Tachyon Publications, 2008
$14.95 trade paperback; 177 pp.

* * * *

>...he insisted on being treated as a god—sending for the most revered or artistically famous statues of the Greek deities (including that of Jupiter at Olympia), and having their heads replaced by his own.
>—Suetonius, *Caligula*, 22.

>I...assure my worshippers that they will be not called on to be lunatics or assassins on my account. The worst they may have to face is a little ostracism from the terminally humorless, the same people who... would keep nine-year-olds from going to Halloween parties costumed as witches and ghosts.
>—Disch, pp. 127-128

* * * *

So now he's done it. While there is a certain precedent for such things in history, and for all L. Ron Hubbard may have made certain secret revelations to his innermost circle of initiates, Thomas M. Disch is surely the first science fiction writer to publicly announce his own godhood and then expound upon it at book-length. While the publisher is perhaps inaccurate to describe the result as the author's "first novel in nine years," it is, one certainly hopes, a *fiction,* something the author acknowledges he has made up for artistic purposes, because just after the passage quoted above, Disch goes on to write:

>If such a person, finding this book in its hidey-hole down in your den, should get fussed and ask you outright whether you knew that I was Satan or the Antichrist or some other false god, all you need to say is, "For heaven's sake, you don't believe *anyone* supposes Tom Disch is God, do you? He's a satirist, and in the worst possible taste!"
>(p. 128)

Yet in his divine aspect, Disch reassures us that he is not even being particularly egotistical:

So in revealing myself to be a god, I am not claiming that much more than many others in the SF community. Admittedly, it may strike many at first as a bold claim, even immodest, but really it is a mainstream American ambition with many antecedents. Ann Lee, Ralph Waldo Emerson, Mary Baker Eddy, Joseph Smith, L. Ron Hubbard, Charlie Manson—they've all been there before me, links in one golden chain, steps in one vast celestial staircase, and all of them ready to invite their fellow countrymen to join them in the big tent of their mystic invention.

(p. 135)

Of course, the ways of gods are subtle, and if they seem to contradict themselves, any competent theologian can quickly wriggle out of the difficulty by explaining it in terms of "mystery" beyond human ken.

Thomas M. Disch is not a particularly jealous god, and seems more amiable that most. He is not given to smiting or causing plagues, nor is he the sort to send his followers off on crusades or to demand the sacrifice of suicide bombers. In fact, the most difficult pronouncement he makes is to forbid war altogether, even in self-defense. While he is aware that obedience might well thin out the ranks of his worshippers, he points out that other gods have made far more unreasonable demands, as in the instance of Abraham and Isaac. The god does not have to explain. The mortal must merely obey.

Once that's out of the way, Disch settles down to explain the truths of Heaven, Hell, and existence. The result is an odd combination of satirical essay, fiction, and memoir. This is not in itself an especially innovative form. Writers have been mixing narrative, essay, and satire for a long time, at least since the days of Petronius. Borges wrote stories in the form of a book review or an encyclopedia entry. Disch's *The Word of God* is even a little reminiscent (to me at least) of Lord Dunsany's *If I Were Dictator* (1934).

It must be admitted that Disch does this sort of thing well. The book is a whimsy, but a whimsy with sharp teeth and serious satirical purpose, about religious, literature, sexuality, and the art of being Thomas M. Disch. He pronounces on anything and everything. He quotes his own (quite good) poetry liberally. His recounting of his "miracle" which kept Virginia Kidd alive for several years is either very moving or exceptionally tasteless—one would probably have to be close to the principals to decide which.

Perhaps the most intriguing revelations here, of greatest interest to science-fiction readers, concern Disch's own birth, as the illegitimate son of Thomas Mann, and how Philip K. Dick escaped from hell, traveled back in time, occupied his own (Dick's) 10-year-old body in 1939 and not only attempted nefariously to prevent the conception and birth of Thomas M. Disch, but tried to change the timeline of history itself until it conformed more to the vision of the Axis-dominated world in *The Man in the High Castle.* Fortunately the world was saved via appropriate means: a *deus ex machina*, in fact.

How serious is Disch about any of this? Is he kidding an old (deceased) pal or somehow getting posthumous revenge on a rival? In many ways this whole book can be read as a parody of *Valis.*

Amusing? Good-natured? Mean-spirited? Cruel? You know how these deities can be. Inscrutable. It is for the rest of us merely to worship and wonder.

ON SF, BY THOMAS M. DISCH

University of Michigan Press, 2005
171 pp. $75.00 (hardcover), $24.95 (trade paper)

* * * *

So, why am I reviewing a book that is five years old, two years after the author's death? The answer is, first, that it is a book of exceptional interest, and, second, it's likely that a lot of Thomas Disch's admirers don't even know that it exists. I missed this one, too. It was published with *great* stealth, and surely the combination of zero promotion, high price, and poor distribution kept it out of the hands of most SF readers. When I did begin to hear rumors of a second Disch non-fiction book about SF, I could find no dealer carrying the title (or who knew what the title was). Very likely, it was suggested, I was confusing it with *Such Dreams Our Stuff Is Made of* (1998). Very likely I was. I eventually tracked a copy down on eBay, a jacketless first edition hardcover for $15.00. The seller listed it as a third printing, 2008. He was wrong. He evidently didn't know how to read a copyright page. Whether the hardcover was issued in jacket, I still do not know. I have not seen another copy. At $75, few copies can have been sold to other than libraries, and libraries don't care about dustjackets. Someone would do well to stock at least the paperback of this title at Readercon and similar gatherings. It can still be ordered from University of Michigan Press.

I think I got a very good buy on eBay, jacket or no, because I've had a very enjoyable time with this book. The first thing you notice about Disch as a writer of criticism is that he is a *good* writer, sharp and direct, entirely free of the sort of jargon or outright gobbledygook that some academics use to evade the need to master English. No post-modern deconstructionist, he.

Considering how Disch's life ended, how has our possible perception of *On SF* changed? Not much. That he devotes a couple of pieces to the "appalling life" of Edgar Allan Poe takes on a certain irony. Poe and Disch had certain things in common. Both excelled at short fiction and verse. Both wrote brilliant, knife-sharp criticism. Both were at times visibly angry at their own lack of widespread acceptance. (Writes Disch:

"Poverty rarely ennobles. Stifled ambition breeds envy and vindictiveness." p. 39) But the profound difference is that Poe was *corrupt* from the get-go, and Disch was, as far as I can tell, unfailingly honest—even when writing things he must have known were not true, about which more in a moment. One cannot imagine Disch shamelessly flattering someone he despised in hope of furthering his career, yet Poe would do just that. Disch always maintains at least the illusion of objectivity, even when, one suspects, he is nursing a grudge. (e.g. in "The Labor Day Group" suggesting that the awards in SF are controlled by a generational cabal to which he, alas, is not admitted.) Poe, in our litigious time, would have been sued for libel again and again for his endless *ad-hominem* attacks. Disch was too cool, too reserved to so lower himself, at least in print.

In any case, what we have to focus on when dealing with such writers as Robert E. Howard, H. Beam Piper, and Thomas M. Disch—or Poe for that matter, not technically a suicide, but pretty close—is not how they died but what they accomplished before they did. A great deal, is the answer, when it comes to Thomas Disch. A very great deal indeed.

On SF collects most of Disch's essays and reviews on the subject, some of which appeared in science fiction publications, others from sources as varied as *The Times Literary Supplement, The New York Times Book Review, The Washington Post Book World, The Atlantic Monthly, The Hudson Review,* and *The Nation.*

Disch might have been surprised, even offended, if someone pointed out how much his essays have much in common with John W. Campbell editorials, but it's true. You want to *argue* with this book. A Disch essay, like a Campbell one, was designed to start a fight, by taking an outrageous position, then forcing the reader to *think* his way out of it. The typical Disch essay is a kind of literary physical therapy of an extreme sort. He *hits* you with something. Then you are expected to stagger to your feet and deal with it.

In "The Embarrassments of Science Fiction" (1976), he went on at great length to count the ways that SF is best considered a branch of children's literature, noting its limitations in aesthetics, intellectual horizons, morality, emotional range, etc. Did Disch really believe that SF was mostly read by children? Did he, like a lot of people, confuse the age that the SF reader begins reading (early adolescence) with the age of the average SF consumer? No data have *ever* supported this contention, in fact quite the reverse, as the twenty-to-thirtysomethings on the early *Astounding* and *New Worlds* polls of half a century ago aged, and were very likely many of the *same people* who drove the SF boom of the 1980s and 1990s. At the same time as Disch was writing most of these essays, books by Asimov, Heinlein, Herbert, Farmer, Clarke, McCaffrey, etc.

were dominating the bestseller lists in *hardcover*, precisely because they were *not* being bought by or for children, but by Baby Boomers who had grown up reading those writers, and who could now afford hardcovers, which they bought all at once, thus turning, first, *Foundation's Edge,* and then much else into bestsellers. (Disch has choice words about *Foundation's Edge.* He is not among its admirers.) The gloomier among us suggest that science fiction is largely a Baby Boomer phenomenon, and that the field is failing as that particular demographic lump is edging toward retirement and will one day be gone, quite unlike the seemingly endless supply of old ladies who keep mystery publishing afloat. Meanwhile, the people who put on SF conventions bemoan the "graying of fandom" and wonder how they can make such events more attractive to the younger set—i.e. people *under forty*. Disch could not have been unaware of this.

Not children's literature at all. I don't think that Tom Disch believed, when he was writing *Camp Concentration, 334,* or *On Wings of Song* that he was addressing an audience of children. At times he makes comments that he and his fellow New Wave writers (back before they became ancient history, at least) were trying to write something more mature.

I think what we're supposed to take away from this essay is that Disch found most SF so limiting—so self-limited by the demands of timid publishers and an unadventurous audience—that it *might as well be* children's literature, for all it addresses the concerns of real literature. Not that it actually *is* written for 12-year-olds.

In other words, the Dischean critical method is a kind of satire: exaggeration intended to inspire reconsideration and reform.

How about this one? As Disch begins to explore the "embarrassments" of sex in science fiction, he comes to this famous conclusion about Robert A. Heinlein's *Starship Troopers:*

> The hero is a homosexual of a very identifiable breed. By his own self-caressing descriptions one recognizes the swaggering leather boy in his most flamboyant form. There is even a skull-and-crossbones earring on his left ear.
>
> …such sexual confusions make the politics of the book more dangerous by infusing them with the energies of repressed sexual desires. It may be that what turns you on is not the life of an infantryman, but his uniform. A friend of mine has assured me that he knows of several enlistments directly inspired by a reading of *Starship Troopers.* How much simpler would it have been for those lads to go and have their ears pierced.
>
> (pp. 13-14)

Now Disch was openly gay, at least later in life, although he did not write what he considered to be "gay literature." Possibly he knew more about "swaggering leather boys" than many of us do. We may have to remind younger readers that back in 1975 straight guys did *not* wear earrings. But did Disch really believe that Heinlein was *purposely* writing about a homosexual character, or was the aim of this exercise to show how the book's over-the-top macho posturings could lead the literal-minded (or more perceptive) reader down unintended paths? Again we have satire, exaggeration in order to highlight absurdity.

Likewise, did Disch really believe, as he often claimed, that SF readers are half-literate, blue-collar types without a hint of culture (despite what reader polls have shown us about their education levels), or was he saying that for what he perceived as their oafishness and resistance to any sort of artistic sophistication, they might as well be?

What I am suggesting is that Disch was too smart to be just plain wrong. He knew that SF fandom, and its readership generally, is packed with PhDs to an inordinate degree. But maybe he saw them as uncouth, lazy PhDs.

One of the reasons Disch is so entertaining as a critic is that he could often pull off this sort of thing with great charm and humor. There is no rule (except maybe in university journals) that good literary criticism can't be funny. For a satirist, this can be a real strength. Disch is at his very best when he goes off on imaginative riffs, as when he has a sudden visitation from Jesus, and he and the Lord discuss the various books Disch is supposed to be reviewing, including Philip K. Dick's *Valis*; or in his celebrated demolition of Whitley Strieber's *Communion* and its sequel, in which Disch proves that he can play this game too, and relates what a quite different set of aliens have revealed to *him*.

The Strieber/UFO theme is pursued at some length, through several essays. When he writes about skepticism, Disch moves beyond strictly literary ideas, but he uses the same satirical method, a pretend-obtuseness of a sort whereby he suggests that all claimants to the marvelous and miraculous, whether they be early Christians, Joseph Smith, Madame Blavatsky, UFO abductees, or whatever, are simply *lying*, the first few for the fame and money, others to gain empowerment by participating in an impressively Big Lie which is larger than themselves. This, he suggests in a piece called "UFOs and the Origins of Christianity," is the whole purpose of a church.

Of course such a single-minded explanation precludes numerous other possibilities, ranging from temporal-lobe epilepsy to sincere self-delusion, and at one point Disch lets his guard down describing his one meeting with Philip K. Dick, shortly after the *Valis* experience ("I believed that *he* believed he had been in touch with something supernatural." p. 92), but the satirical exaggeration seems just true enough that, as we are supposed to, we have to stop and consider. I will admit that I once attended a lecture by the prominent UFOlogist Stanton Friedman, and while the believer friends I was with did not come away with the same conclusion, *I* recognized the similarity to a church service immediately. Friedman made assertions but presented no proofs. He showed some photos of what could easily been faked documents. (The MJ-12 stuff—they were.) But the real purpose, and the theme he kept returning to, was the need to form a community of believers, who were not afraid of the "laughter curtain" which, we were told, was all that kept the majority of people everywhere from accepting the UFO faith. I have a Catholic background similar to Disch's. I went to church regularly longer than he did, well into my twenties. I knew religion when I saw it. Disch saw religion in the works of Whitley Strieber, but suggested that all visionaries, everywhere, are simply liars.

He then turns this idea back to literature in "Science Fiction as a Church." Did you ever think about SF as a religion? You will think about SF differently after you have.

The rest of the book is filled with surprising bits. You may not agree with much of it. He sees real potential in Stephen King, but finds it rarely realized. He trashes Barry Malzberg's *Engines of the Night* for being, self-serving, self-pitying, and too gloomy, which will surely cause some to reach for the familiar cliché of the pot and the kettle. He crucified Ray Bradbury in *The New York Times* with "A Tableful of Twinkies," in which he makes the dubious point that there is no difference in fuzzy prose and mawkishness between early Bradbury and late, and backs this up by quoting two inferior stories ("The Night" and "The Black Ferris") which, for decades, Bradbury had the good sense to leave *out* of his collections. But imagine Disch, in such a major venue, saying of one of America's most beloved storytellers, "He is an artist only in the sense that he is not a hydraulic engineer." I am sure that Disch chortled while writing *that* one.

Of course Disch never became beloved. He isn't likely to. This may be because of his refusal to pander to his audiences. He tended to write the difficult, unpleasant parts, rather than gloss over them. Michael Swanwick has suggested that the reason Disch was never as popular as, say, Samuel R. Delany, is that Delany is a hedonist, who suggests that anything and everything you may want to indulge in is just fine, whereas Disch is, at heart, a moralist, that voice in the back of your head saying, "No, no, *don't.*"

But Disch did command respect. By his own lights, he did not sell out or compromise. He wrote clearly and well, and with passion. That's why he is still worth reading.

THE DISCOVERY OF SARBAN

Mark Valentine. *Time, a Falconer, a Study of Sarban*. Carlton, Leyburn, North Yorkshire: Tartarus Press, 2010. 138 pp. HC. £25/$45.00

Sarban (John William Wall). *Discovery of Heretics, Unseen Writings*. Carlton, Leyburn, North Yorkshire: Tartarus Press, 2010. 382 pp.

2 volumes, issued together as a boxed set. No price given for the set, or for *Discovery of Heretics* by itself.

* * * *

There are writers who have very short careers and then fade. As soon as they're gone, no one cares. Then there are others who have very short careers, and become enigmas, leaving whole generations wondering *Who was THAT?*

Sarban was definitely one of the latter. The byline is an obvious pseudonym, a Persian word for a camel-driver who tells stories. This name appeared on three books in rapid succession, all published by Peter Davies: *Ringstones and Other Curious Tales* (1951), *The Sound of His Horn* (1952), and *The Doll Maker and Other Tales of the Uncanny* (1953). Then, silence. There was one "security leak" of sorts, when *Book Review Digest* for 1951 listed "Sarban," and added "See Wall, John W." But few people noticed that, and the author otherwise remained a complete mystery.

What mattered was that his works were not forgotten. The Peter Davies editions did not have much circulation, but when all three books were reprinted by Ballantine in 1960 and 1961 as part of one of the very first paperback horror lines, this not only reached a much wider audience, but made Sarban, within the horror field, at least, canonical. Unfortunately the Ballantine editions only contained the title novellas of his two collections. This made him a three-story author, but it was enough. *The Sound of His Horn* in particular became a small classic, much admired by Kingsley Amis among other critics. It is an alternate-history story, but like few others, more of a horrific dream-vision than a science fictional extrapolation of the sort Harry Turtledove writes so successfully today. In *The Sound of His Horn,* a British POW during World War II escapes, then slips through time a hundred years into the future, after the Nazis have won the war and sunk into feudal decadence. He finds himself on a rural estate where a Nazi lord reduces "inferior" persons to bestial status and hunts them for sport. All this is told with great power and subtlety, in the manner of an English ghost story, with elaborate framing. (Most of Sarban's stories are framed, with a narrator telling the story to someone else.) The author also shows, as critics noticed at the time, a strange and even disturbing imagination, with barely concealed (or not at all concealed) eroticism and much preoccupation with pursuit, dominance, and bondage. Among the hunters in the Nazi forest are semi-naked women surgically altered to make them into predatory cat-like creatures. It's almost as if Sarban had reached the boundaries of John Norman territory here, but, being far more humane, did not actually *embrace* the fantasies he has evoked. The story also includes a very competent, rather tomboyish heroine, with whom the protagonist has a brief love idyll before she sacrifices herself to help him escape. Indeed, as his later writings show, his ideas about gender-relations were anything but simplistic or one-sided.

The other two Ballantine books, or, even more so the Peter Davies collections from which they were derived, reveal Sarban to be a supernatural fictionist of considerable power, whose work, often dealing with strange worlds existing alongside our own and mysterious forces of nature, puts him on the same shelf with Algernon Blackwood, Arthur Machen, John Buchan, and Walter de la Mare. The influence of Kipling is also manifest, particularly in "A Christmas Story" (in *Ringstones*) which owes a lot to Kipling's "A Matter of Fact."

Nothing more appeared after these three books. One could deduce from the texts that the author was clearly an Englishman, fond of the countryside rather than big cities, and that he was intimately familiar with the Middle East. But who was he? Had he written anything else?

What Mark Valentine has done so admirably is answer all these questions. He has gained the cooperation of John Wall's daughter, examined his private papers, and given us as clear a picture as we are ever likely to get of the man who was Sarban.

John William Wall was born in Mexborough in Yorkshire in 1910. He lived until 1989. He came from a working-class background but nevertheless went to Cambridge, and spent his entire professional life in the British diplomatic service, being posted mostly to the Middle East. He was an expert in Middle Eastern languages. He had a competent but undistinguished career. Valentine several times makes the point that Wall was not really very sociable and therefore lacked the key diplomatic talent of schmoozing at endless embassy parties. His last posting was as Consulate General in Alexandria, about the time of the Suez Crisis in the

1950s, which made things quite difficult, but he did what was expected of him and then retired back to England. Meanwhile his personal life had been, outwardly, unexceptional. He married, fathered a daughter, and was eventually divorced.

But inwardly, John Wall became Sarban. Diplomats were discouraged from publishing while on active duty anyway, and he may have felt more freedom to express himself behind the pseudonym. He was never a professional writer. He submitted his work only to Peter Davies, and only at his wife's insistence. He was not, apparently, in touch with any sort of literary community, though he cannot be considered an "outsider" writer either, since he had absorbed the literary culture of his time, from Kipling to de la Mare, whom he acknowledged as a particular influence. He wrote to please himself. If sometimes his scene-setting and story-framing (as in the title novella "Ringstones") seemed a little leisurely, it was because he enjoyed visiting certain places in his fiction. When posted in Arabia or Persia, he longed for England. He had a very keen sense of nature and of the outdoors, even for places he had apparently *not* been. The above-mentioned "A Christmas Story" contains a vivid description of frozen tundra in the Russian Far East. The story is about an encounter with the last, dying mammoth. The setting must surely derive from descriptions he got from White Russian refugees he met during his diplomatic travels.

Why did he stop publishing? Did he write anything else? He once answered the first question with one word, "Laziness," but that is by no means the entire truth. Yes, he continued writing. *Discovery of Heretics* contains almost four hundred pages of previously unknown Sarban material, following up a previous Tartarus volume, *The Sacrifice and Other Stories* (2000), which contained four complete stories, all published therein for the first time.

Most of the items in *Discovery of Heretics* are fragments. That is the real answer to why Sarban's career came to a sudden end. He continued to write, at length, to please himself, but too many of his stories lost focus, and then he didn't finish them. Of course the volume we now have, courtesy of Mr. Valentine, is a first-rate piece of scholarship and of book-making, everything you could want in such a publication, but the contents are mostly of interest to specialists, more for what they reveal about the author than for their own intrinsic merit. Wisely, Tartarus has limited this to a print-run of 200 copies, which are issued in a slipcase with *Time, a Falconer* as a special, ultra-deluxe package. (*Time, A Falconer* is also sold separately.)

The writing in these unpublished pieces is often very good, but these are still mostly fragments and failures. One complete early story, "The

Father," is not weird or fantastic in any way, but quite moving, despite its obvious use of coincidence. A short play, Their "Blood Cannot Die," is set during the Spanish Civil War, all political bombast and heroic speeches, but no drama. There are fragments of three failed novels. The title item, "Discovery of Heretics," was actually completed, but declined when submitted to Peter Davies. "The Artemists" and "The Gynarchs" and another fragment, "Agorit," all deal with a theme Wall wrestled with but could never quite master, that of the relationship between the sexes, and of female-ruled societies. His was not, as Valentine explains at length, a simplistic vision of men dominating women or women dominating men. He saw the masculine in the feminine and the feminine in the masculine and was not afraid of this. His vision of a woman-ruled world, most elaborately detailed in the long novel *The Gynarchs*, is not a dystopia. But it is not a successful novel either. This is a work on a level of ambition with, say, Ursula Le Guin's *The Dispossessed* as a political/social thought experiment, but Wall stumbled where many writers of such novels do. He got lost in the detail. Ultimately even his wife told him that there simply wasn't enough *story* in the thing, and apparently Mark Valentine agrees, because he has presented only representative chapters, admitting that the whole work does not hold interest. While this is intriguing coming from the same mind that produced *The Sound of His Horn*, even if the entire work is published one day, it is not a book that is ever going to reach very many people.

"The Papers of Henry Sugden" suggests the core of his problem, if he saw it as a problem in his later writings. He was actually best at shorter lengths, the novella being his forté. He was also at his best with elaborate framing devices, approaching the supernatural through an aesthetic similar to that of M.R. James, i.e. requiring that the setting be somewhat distanced from the reader, but not impossibly so. His supernatural stories were the sort to be told around a winter's fire, reminiscences of long ago, and far away, not an immediate and visceral "I met the horror face-to-face!" but "You know, I met a fellow once who told me about something quite strange." "Henry Sugden," after considerable buildup begins to approach the weird, then stops. Another failure.

The conclusion we come to is that Valentine's biography is exemplary and excellent, but while the contents of *Discovery of Heretics* will add to our understanding of Sarban/Wall, they will not significantly expand his *oeuvre*. All the Sarban you really need to read is in *The Sound of His Horn* and his other collections.

ATOMIC MUTANT HILLBILLIES

The Hogben Chronicles by Henry Kuttner
edited by Pierce Watters and F. Paul Wilson
Introduction by Neil Gaiman
Baltimore, MD: Borderlands Press, 2013; $12.95 tpb, $25.00 unsigned hc, $50.00 signed/limited; 139 pp. + unpaginated appendix.

* * * *

What we have here is the definitive collection of the "Hogben" series by Henry Kuttner, consisting of five stories. The first, "The Old Army Game," from *Thrilling Adventures,* November 1941, has never been reprinted before and had become something of a rumored rarity, unknown to most readers. When you read it, you'll see why. It is not consistent with the others, and is only marginally fantastic. The other four, what we might call the main sequence, all appeared in *Thrilling Wonder Stories* between 1947 and 1949. Kuttner himself must have thought well of them, as three were included in his Ballantine collections, *Ahead of Time* and *Return to Otherness.* Two are in the 1975 Ballantine *The Best of Henry Kuttner.* (Three, in the earlier, British two-volume version.) So they have not been totally unavailable, and, given the enormous quantity of material Kuttner turned out for the pulps under a variety of pseudonyms, it is significant that these were singled out more than once for preservation.

The reason is, of course, as Gaiman explains in the forward and Wilson in an afterward, they're genuinely funny. Readers liked them and remembered them. So too did at least some of the critics. Damon Knight, in *In Search of Wonder,* speaks favorably of them and suggests that they deserve a volume of their own. Somewhere I read a critic or essayist of that era remarking that "even Kuttner wrote the Hogbens in a hungry season," which sounds like a bit of curmudgeonliness from James Blish a.k.a. William Atheling, but I have not been able to find the quote. In general, though, the series was well received, and a couple, particularly "Exit the Professor" and "Cold War" tended to be remembered.

Henry Kuttner's Hogben series may be quickly and not too inaccurately described as Zenna Henderson's *Pilgrimage: The Book of the*

People starring the Beverly Hillbillies and narrated by Jethro Clampett; only the weird folks are mutants, not extraterrestrials. They are *hillbillies*, too, not the sort of Southern Mountain people that Manly Wade Wellman used to write about. I can't imagine Manly would have liked these stories much, as he once told me in an interview that if you went up in the hills of Appalachia and called a man a hillbilly he would "think it his born duty to take the neck out of your body."[9] *Hillbillies* are caricatures, the product of movies and TV and comic strips like *Li'l Abner* rather than real life. But Kuttner used them inventively. Think of *Duck Dodgers in the 24th and a Half Century.* The humor works precisely because the supposedly serious Buck Rodgers tropes are acted out by the absurd Daffy Duck. Kuttner was doing something similar: stories with gee-whiz super-science and psionic mutants starring, not two-fisted Campbellian engineers, but a comic hillbilly family consisting of a naïve young hulk who can be mistaken for a bear; Pa, who can turn invisible; an uncle who flies when he's likkered up; Grandpa who mostly sleeps in the attic, but is telepathic and speaks Elizabethan; a telepathic Maw; and then there's the Baby, who is three hundred years old and kept in a tank in the basement:

> Can't believe a word them Haley boys say. Three haids! It ain't natcheral, is it? Anyhow, Little Sam's only got two haids, and never had no more since the day he was born.
>
> (p. 43)

All the Hogbens seem to be extremely long-lived. Saunk, the narrator, is only a "boy" and he doesn't think it worthwhile to remember old-time stuff, but he can vaguely recall Cromwell and Charles II. Grandpa knew Roger Bacon and may have gotten his powers when irradiated in a British tin mine in the days of the Druids. (But as Gaiman points out, these stories are not totally consistent. In others we are told the Hogbens originally came from Atlantis. They are nearly illiterate, but they are also scientific geniuses. They can produce death rays out of shotguns, or, in one instance, Saunk takes a child's sled, twists a few wires around it, and creates a time-machine for the purpose of sending a jug of cream into next week and back so it will sour quickly.

Humor in science fiction was not an unheard of thing in the science fiction magazines of the 1940s. There had even been a kind of lumbering, elephantine humor in the Gernsback publications of earlier decades.[10]

---

9   Darrell Schweitzer. *Speaking of Horror.* San Bernardino CA: The Borgo Press, 1994, p. 100.

10   And one genuinely funny story, "The Radiation of the Chinese

Weinbaum had written funny and been imitated widely. Nelson Bond wrote funny. So did Kuttner, even before he created the Hogbens.

A bit more context here: by 1947, the atomic bombings that ended World War II had already given science fiction the willies. The magazines were filled with stories of radiation-induced mutants, including the "Baldy" series by Kuttner (as Lewis Padgett) running in *Astounding*, later collected as *Mutant*. Wilmar Shiras's *Children of the* Atom began as a series of stories in 1948. There were lots of nuclear dooms, and post-holocaust worlds filled with monsters. Kuttner's lead novel in the April 1947 *Thrilling Wonder*, "Way of the Gods," is blurbed: "Spawn of atomic fission, this strange company of mutants exiled by humanity battles against enslavement in a foreign world dominated by the evil spirit of the Crystal Mountain!" That sounds a little bit like the X-Men to me, a super-powered pariah elite. But the most important point here is that when the Hogben stories were being published, Kuttner was parodying familiar ideas, which everybody else was taking *very* seriously.

Well, almost everybody. There was *another* hillbilly series running in *Thrilling Wonder* at the time, featuring a backwoods genius named Bud Gregory and written by "William Fitzgerald" a.k.a Will Jenkins, better known as Murray Leinster. (Kuttner and Jenkins/Leinster were among the most prolific *TWS* contributors in this period. Since the magazine, like most SF pulps, was a bimonthly, there were no serials, so the way to keep a steady paycheck coming was to establish oneself with a series, usually series by character. But if you wanted to sell more than six stories a year, that meant doubling and tripling up under pseudonyms.) The first three of the Gregory stories were fixed up as a novel called *Out of this World* in 1958.

The series began with "The Gregory Circle" in *TWS*, April 1947. It would be a mistake to assume, as Sam Moskowitz always seemed to, that just because Story A appeared before Story B, it must have influenced Story B. "Exit the Professor" appeared in the October 1947 issue. Was that enough time for Kuttner to have read the Jenkins/Fitzgerald story, be influenced by it, and get the result into print? Almost certainly not. In any case, Leinster's version is much less funny. In fact, it has tone problems. Bud Gregory, more or less a generic hillbilly, but less broadly caricatured than the Hogbens, is an intuitive scientific and mechanical genius, who can fix a car in a couple of hours where a normal mechanic would require four days, and he can whip out super-scientific whatsits that would revolutionize the world if he only had the ambition. But he's lazy. Real

---

Vegetable" by C. Sterling Gleason, Science Wonder Stories, December 1929, reprinted in Startling Stories Winter 1945.

lazy. Not interested in money either, or not much. (By contrast there's a Hogben who's so lazy that when he gets thirsty he doesn't get up from his snooze, but just opens his mouth and makes it rain over his face.)

Bud Gregory did somehow help some shady character with an atomic something-or-other, which not only killed the operator but left a gigantic atomic reaction going on and on, until radioactive dust is killing thousands of people, wiping out whole communities, and rendering large swaths of the countryside totally barren. A heroic scientist has to figure out what is going on, then badger Bud into doing something about it. The world is saved, but Bud doesn't seem too concerned about all those deaths, as if he is just an automaton, without emotions or conscience, neither a real human being nor an effective cartoon. The result doesn't really work as comedy, because of the scale of the death and destruction, and because Jenkins is better at epic descriptions of sweeping doom than he is at comedic wit. It is true that the Hogbens have killed people on occasion, but we forgive them. They wiped out the above-mentioned Haley clan because they threatened to reveal the secret of the precious two-headed infant, but that was self-defense, and generally Grandpa Hogben forbids killing.

That rare, first story, "The Old Army Game," hardly counts. Saunk is drafted into the army. He is a huge, innocent lunk, addicted to moonshine and not very bright. He foils some German spies because he thinks they're revenuers after his still. The Hogben series proper begins with "Exit the Professor," in which a nosy geneticist gets wind of the Hogbens and threatens to expose them, who have, very much like Henderson's "People," hidden their talents over the centuries to avoid being persecuted as witches. Hijinks ensue with a kind of ray-gun, which at one point gives everybody in town a burning toothache because it makes their gold fillings radioactive. Government investigations loom. In the end, since they can't kill him, the Hogbens have to shrink the professor down and store him in a bottle.

"Pile of Trouble" begins typically:

> We called Lemuel "Gimpy," on account of he had three legs. After he got his growth, about the time they fit the War Between the States, he was willing to keep his extra leg sort of tucked up behind him inside his britches, where it would be out of sight and people wouldn't talk. 'Course it made him look a little like one of them camel critters, but then Lemuel was never vain. It was lucky he was doublejointed, though…
>
> (p 64)

In this story we learn that Grandpa and Baby Sam need regular jolts of electricity to keep alive. So Saunk and Maw build a uranium pile in the henhouse. The results are considerably less dangerous than what Bud Gregory did, but the resultant trouble involves a crooked politician, a dam that hasn't had water behind it in a hundred years (and suddenly bursts when Saunk starts to control the weather), and some teleported truth serum which causes the politician to break out in uncharacteristic honesty. Another one of Lemuel's lazy habits is hypnotizing raccoons so they build a fire and cook themselves. Saunk never does figure out how he gets them skinned.

And so on. By the time the series ends in "Cold War," Saunk has used that sled/time machine to send the obnoxious, neanderthaloid Pugh clan back in time on a promise that they will propagate themselves forever. They do. They devolve (or maybe evolve; hard to say) into cold germs. The other story, "See You Later," tells how another trespassing clan accidentally got exterminated when they threatened the Hogben household and Baby screamed at them in ultrasonics. Then the vengeful father of the deceased demands recompense. He wants to materialize in front of every person in the world simultaneously and hit them over the head with a wrench, to pay back whoever stepped on his corn in a crowded New York subway thirty years earlier. He got the idea from some crazy pulp magazine story about flying hillbillies.

The basic fantasy here is that of the marvelous family. Think of Ray Bradbury's "weird family" series, "Homecoming," et al. Think of the Addams family. Think of the magical family in Neil Gaiman's *The Ocean at the End of the Lane* (whose literary descent from the Hogbens Gaiman readily acknowledges). Wouldn't we all like to have grown up in a household of friendly, supportive, wonder-working freaks who *don't have* to be like everybody else? I know when I was a kid I wished I could have lived at the Addams house. It would be fun to visit the Hogbens too, though you *would* have to be careful around Baby Sam.

These are fun stories. They do not take themselves seriously, as Jenkins' Bud Gregory series sometimes almost does. That's the reason the Hogbens continue to appeal, having lasted far beyond the context that produced them.

WEIRD TALES PAST: DECEMBER 1936

The December 1936 *Weird Tales* must have looked like an exceptionally good issue of a magazine in its prime. Yes, the letter column is filled with people expressing shock and regret at the recent death of Robert E. Howard, and there is even some discussion of whether or not the Conan stories should be continued by another writer, but the cover features one of Howard's best horror stories, "The Fire of Asshurbanipal." Also in this issue is the first new H.P. Lovecraft story in some time, "The Haunter of the Dark," with "The Thing on the Doorstep" announced for January. And there's work by a promising new generation of writers, Robert Bloch, Manly Wade Wellman, and Henry Kuttner, plus such established stalwarts as E. Hoffmann Price and Otis Adelbert Kline in collaboration, and August Derleth. John Russell Fearn, a British pulpster, also makes his *Weird Tales* debut.

If there's any sense of change in the issue, it seems a positive one. The artwork is getting better, with increased use of the popular work of Virgil Finlay inside and a splendid cover by J. Allen St. John, who was best known for illustrating the works of Edgar Rice Burroughs. St. John's work had a sense of the weird generally lacking in Margaret Brundage's perennial nude covers.

Of course no one but possibly Lovecraft himself knew that his return would prove ephemeral. Lovecraft would die of cancer on March 15, 1937. With him and Robert E. Howard gone, and Clark Ashton Smith curtailing his production, the golden age of *Weird Tales* was about to come to an end. This issue has a kind of Indian summer glow to it in retrospect.

When we actually go to read the stories, how do they hold up? Howard's hero, one of his footloose American adventurers swashbuckling his way through Asia in classic fashion, as an Afghan sidekick named Yar Ali, oddly addresses the American as "sahib," which is a term they used to use in British India, meaning "master." Yar Ali doesn't seem to be anybody's servant, but never mind. Pursued by murderous Arabs across vague geography, the duo find a lost city which may be something mentioned in the *Necronomicon*. There's a cursed jewel clutched by a skeleton, and an eldritch horror evoked when the Arabs touch the jewel. The

American only glimpses the Thing from *behind*. Had he seen it face-on, he is certain, he would have gone mad.... This is grand stuff in a slightly silly way, probably Howard's best combination of his own action-packed style and Lovecraftian material. Lovecraft had praised Howard for his ability to evoke ancient horrors, and here we see this talent at its height. And of course the classic in the issue is Lovecraft's own "The Haunter of the Dark," one of his real masterpieces, about which little needs be said. This story's origin is actually frivolous, as a good-natured riposte to Robert Bloch's earlier "The Shambler from the Stars," in which Bloch had killed off a character very much like Lovecraft. Here one Robert Blake, a young horror writer from Milwaukee, comes to Providence, moves into the very house where Lovecraft was actually living at the time, and meets a hideous doom. But jokiness aside, this is one of the great Lovecrafts, told in his best, restrained, later style.

Everything else in the issue is inevitably below the level of these two, to varying degrees. There's "Out of the Sun" by one Granville S. Hoss, about a scientist who creates solar conditions in a laboratory and generates the kind of life that lives on the surface of the sun, which proves to be a beautiful, nude lady. Of course they cannot meet or touch, since she thrives at temperatures that would incinerate him. This sort of unnatural romance inevitably does not end well.

The Fearn story melts in your brain as soon as you read it; I have to skim to remind myself what it was about. "Portrait of a Murderer" — something about hypnotism. The good guy kills the bad one at the end and is executed, but his ghost tells the story through a spirit medium. "The Cyclops of Xoatl" by Price and Kline is likewise complete hokum, set in Mexico, the countryside terrorized by a monster who turns out to be a mere human freak. The only notable thing here is that when the Yankee hero formulaically gets the girl in the end, she is a *Mexican* girl, which makes the story considerably freer of ethnic prejudice than most pulp fiction. Robert Bloch's "Mother of Serpents," about dictatorship and voodoo in Haiti is adequately creepy, if less enlightened, the author doubtless having done his homework from not-very-reliable sources, such as William Seabrook's *The Magic Island* (1929). Of course he was writing in a time when Haiti was, for most Americans, as remote as Mars and about as likely to be visited. "The Woman at Loon Point" by August Derleth and Mark Schorer is a completely routine werewolf story. Amelia Reynolds Long's very short "The Album" is about a sinister photo-album. If you see your picture in it, you disappear. Manly Wade Wellman's "The Theater Upstairs" has a predictable enough ending, but brings a cad to his just desserts eerily by means of a mysterious movie house which only shows films with dead actors and actresses in them. A lady was wronged, died, and now she looks out at him vengefully from the screen.... "It Walks by Night" by a very young Henry Kuttner (aged 21) is ghastly graveyard horror at its ghastliest, but very immature work. And there is a "Weird Story Reprint," by Honore de Balzac, "A Passion in the Desert," about a French soldier who develops a strange friendship with a panther.

Not all of this issue is worth reading, but we can see the uniqueness of *Weird Tales* here, a pulp magazine which was not afraid of literature. Otis Adelbert Kline and Balzac in the same issue. You'd never find that anywhere else in 1936! While *Weird Tales* was never consistently excellent, it differed from most other pulp magazines in that it *allowed* excellence. There was formula stuff, like the Kline and Price or the Derleth and Schorer in this issue. *WT's* entry-level standards were quite low, which allowed a lot of new writers into its pages, whether they were ready or not, but, most importantly, its quality *ceiling* was quite high. Such brilliance as Lovecraft or Howard at their best, or Clark Ashton Smith at his most bizarre and quirky, was actually possible here. Thus *Weird Tales* performed a unique function in its heyday, when most of its *best* material could not have been published in any other magazine.

ABOUT THE AUTHOR

Darrell Schweitzer is a critic, essayist, reviewer, interviewer, poet, and fiction writer. He has published over 300 short stories and three novels, plus book-length studies of Lord Dunsany and H.P. Lovecraft. He co-edited *Weird Tales* for 19 years, for which he shared a World Fantasy Award with the late George Scithers. This is his third collection of literary essays, the other two being *Windows of the Imagination* and *The Fantastic Horizon*. Many of his titles are available from Wildside Press. He lives and works in Philadelphia, and is married to novelist Marilyn "Mattie" Brahen.

ACKNOWLEDGMENTS

Embracing Yesterday's Tomorrows, or, Why We Still Read "Obsolete" Science Fiction was first published in *The New York Review of Science Fiction* #270, February 2011. Copyright © 2011 by Dragon Press.

Drilling a Core Sample: Thrilling Wonder Stories Summer 1945 was first published in *The New York Review of Science Fiction* #314, August 2014. Copyright © 2014 by Burrowing Wombat Press.

Robert Bloch and the Death of Science Fiction, 1951 was first published in *The New York Review of Science Fiction* #249, May 2009. Copyright © 2009 by Dragon Press.

Rusty's Spaceship Flies Again was first published in *The New York Review of Science Fiction* #296, April 2013. Copyright © 2013 by Burrowing Wombat Press.

Dying in an Ecstasy of Blood: The Half-Remembered Perversities of David H. Keller's "The Revolt of the Pedestrians" (1928) was first published in *The New York Review of Science Fiction* #284, April 2012. Copyright © 2012 by Dragon Press.

Randall Garrett's "The Queen Bee": The Most Sexist Science Fiction Story Ever Published? was first published in *The New York Review of Science Fiction* #254, October 2009. Copyright © 2009 by Dragon Press.

Hooray Bradbury! was first published in *Weird Tales* #345, June/July 2007. Copyright © 2007 by Wildside Press.

Why Stanley G. Weinbaum Still Matters was first published in the *Readercon 20* souvenir book. Copyright © 2009 by Darrell Schweitzer.

Excavating Ourselves: A Short History of Archeology-of-the-Present Books was first published in *The New York Review of Science Fiction* #291, November 2012. Copyright © 2012 by Burrowing Wombat Press.

Blobfest! was first published as "Time to Go to the Festival" in *Weird Tales* #349, March/April 2008. Copyright © 2008 by Wildside Press.

The Whole Wide Lovecraft: An H.P. Lovecraft Biopic? was first published in *Crypt of Cthulhu* Vol 19, No 1, Hallowmas 1999. Copyright © 1999 by Mythos Books.

John W. Campbell's Lovecraftian Tale was first published in *Weird Fiction Review* #3, Fall 2012. Copyright © 2012 by Centipede Press.

H.P. Lovecraft and the American Stonehenge was first published in *The New York Review of Science Fiction*, #325, September 2015. Copyright © 2015 by Burrowing Wombat Press.

Why Lovecraft is Funny was first published as "It's First Pronounced C'Jewlhu?" in *Weird Tales* #347, November/December 2007. Copyright © by Wildside Press.

William Beckford, Caliph of Fonthill Abbey was first published as the introduction to *The Vision* by William Beckford, Wildside Press, 2004. Copyright © 2004 by Darrell Schweitzer.

Some Ancestors of Vathek was first published in *Crypt of Cthulhu* Vol 4 No 5, Eastertide 1985. © 1985 by Cryptic Publications.

M.R. James and His Pleasing Terrors was first published in *Weird Tales* #353, Spring 2009, © 2009 by Wildside Press.

Peter Schlemihl and Other Classics That Nobody Reads was first published in in *The New York Review of Science Fiction* #315, November 2014. © 2014 by Burrowing Wombat Press.

Discovering James Hogg (Even if Lovecraft Didn't) was first published in in *The New York Review of Science Fiction* #251, July 2009. © 2009 by Dragon Press.

Halfway Between Lucian of Samosata and Larry Niven was first published in *The New York Review of Science Fiction* #323, July 2015. © 2015 by Burrowing Wombat Press.

The Lighter Side of Death: Robert Bloch as a Humorist was first published in *The Man Who Collected Psychos, Critical Essays on Robert Bloch* edited by Benjamin Szumskyj. Copyright © 2009 by Benjamin Szumskyj.

Reading the World's Oldest Novel: Some Further Thoughts about Genre was first published in *The New York Review of Science Fiction* #288, August 2012. © 2012 by Burrowing Wombat Press.

Texts, Authors, and the Enduring Mystery of Edgar Allan Poe was first published in *The New York Review of Science Fiction* #282, February 2010. © 2012 by Dragon Press.

People: It's What's For Dinner (All about Sawney Beane) was first published in *Weird Tales* #350, July/August 2008. © 2008 by Wildside Press.

The Complete Poetry and Translations of Clark Ashton Smith was first published in *The New York Review of Science Fiction* #304, March 2014. © 2014 by Burrowing Wombat Press.

All The Wonders We Seek by Felix Marti-Ibanez was first published in *The New York Review of Science Fiction* #238, June 2008. © 2008 by Dragon Press.

What Can Be Saved from the Wreckage: James Branch Cabell in the

21st Century by Michael Swanwick was first published in *The New York Review of Science Fiction* #236, April 2008. © 2008 by Dragon Press.

The Word of God by Thomas M. Disch was first published in *The New York Review of Science Fiction* #240, August 2008. © 2008 by Dragon Press.

On SF by Thomas M. Disch was first published in *The New York Review of Science Fiction* #267, November 2010. © 2010 by Dragon Press.

The Discovery of Sarban was first published in *Dead Reckonings* #10, Fall 2011. Copyright © 2011 by Hippocampus Press.

Atomic Mutant Hillbillies: The Hogben Chronicles by Henry Kuttner was first published in *The New York Review of Science Fiction* #317, January 2015. © 2015 by Burrowing Wombat Press.

Weird Tales Past: December 1936 first appeared on the *Weird Tales* website in 2013. © by 2013 by Darrell Schweitzer.

www.ingramcontent.com/pod-product-compliance
Lightning Source LLC
LaVergne TN
LVHW041615070426
835507LV00008B/263